4-26-02

Also by William H. Gass

FICTION

Omensetter's Luck
In the Heart of the Heart of the Country
Willie Masters' Lonesome Wife
The Tunnel
Cartesian Sonata

NONFICTION

Fiction and the Figures of Life
On Being Blue
The World Within the Word
The Habitations of the Word
Finding a Form
Reading Rilke

TESTS OF TIME

Tests of Time

William H. Gass

ALFRED A. KNOPF
NEW YORK
2002

THIS IS A BORZOI BOOK
PUBLISHED BY ALFRED A. KNOPF

Copyright © 2002 by William H. Gass
All rights reserved under International and Pan-American
Copyright Conventions. Published in the United States by
Alfred A. Knopf, a division of Random House, Inc., New
York, and simultaneously in Canada by Random House of
Canada Limited, Toronto. Distributed by Random House,
Inc., New York.

www.aaknopf.com

Knopf, Borzoi Books, and the colophon are registered
trademarks of Random House, Inc.

Owing to limitations of space, acknowledgments for
permission to reprint previously published material can be
found on page 321.

Library of Congress Cataloging-in-Publication Data
Gass, William H., 1924–
    Tests of time / by William H. Gass.
        p.   cm.
    ISBN 0-375-41257-3 (alk. paper)
    I. Title.
PS3557 A845 T47 2002
814'.54—dc21

2001050486

Manufactured in the United States of America
First Edition

IN MEMORY OF THE INTERNATIONAL WRITERS CENTER

1990–2000

AND FOR LORIN CUOCO,

WHO SERVED IT SO SUPERBLY AND SO SELFLESSLY

Contents

Acknowledgments ix

LITERARY MATTERS

The Nature of Narrative and Its Philosophical Implications 3
Anywhere but Kansas 28
Invisible Cities 37
Sidelonging 69
I've Got a Little List 78
The Test of Time 102

SOCIAL AND POLITICAL
CONTRETEMPS

The Writer and Politics: A Litany 129
Tribalism, Identity, and Ideology 172
The Shears of the Censor 179
Were There Anything in the World Worth Worship 196
How German Are We? 206

THE STUTTGART
SEMINAR LECTURES

Quotations from Chairman Flaubert 219
There Was an Old Woman Who 263
Transformations 295

Acknowledgments

Most of these essays appeared, though always in a somewhat different form, in the following books or periodicals: "Quotations from Chairman Flaubert," "There Was an Old Woman Who," and "Transformations" were in the third, fourth, and fifth *Proceedings of the Stuttgart Seminar in Cultural Studies* respectively; "The Writer and Politics: A Litany" was an introduction to the proceedings of the International Writers Center's conference, *The Writer and Politics,* published by Southern Illinois University Press; "Tribalism, Identity, and Ideology" was an address to the Modern Language Association convention in Toronto and published in *Profession '94,* the journal of the association; "The Shears of the Censor" came out in *Harper's Magazine,* "Were There Anything in the World Worth Worship" in *New Letters,* "How German Are We?" in *German Politics and Society,* and "Sidelonging" in the *Los Angeles Times Book Review;* "The Nature of Narrative and Its Philosophical Implications" was a paper presented to the Faculty Seminar at Washington University; "Anywhere but Kansas" appeared first in the *Iowa Review* and then in the *New York Times Book Review;* "Invisible Cities" appeared in *VIA,* the architectural journal of the University of Pennsylvania; "I've Got a Little List" was the Ben Bellitt Address at Bennington College and was published by *Salmagundi;* while "The Test of Time," chosen for *The Best American Essays 1998,* was the Woodrow Wilson Lecture in Washington, D.C., and appeared in the *Alaska Quarterly Review.* Each piece has suffered second thoughts, had cuts restored, tactlessness and injudiciousness rejoined, caution, like a scoutmaster's hat, once more thrown to the winds.

LITERARY MATTERS

Such is the short, irascible temper of the time that ethical, religious, and political issues cannot be absolutely shut out of even resolutely "literary" concerns. Italo Calvino's masterpiece Invisible Cities *has a moral as simple sounding and as soundly simple as Voltaire's "cultivate your garden." As so many authors have, Calvino suffered in his soul from the lies of Ideals. The cultural preference for narrative is not an innocent one either, nor is the drawing up of lists: whether of the ten best books in the last ten days or of those infesters of society who never would be missed. On mine are the many academic critics who have abandoned literature for a culture of* Empfindlichkeit. *It will surprise no one to learn that I much prefer my own bile and bad nature to theirs.*

The Nature of Narrative
and Its Philosophical Implications

ONE: TELLING STORIES AND
FASHIONING FICTIONS
*—Polemical Introduction During Which the Field Is Previewed
and a Distinction Is Endeavored*

Stories are things that get told. They can exist outside of any particular medium or any particular method of narration. Last week, Little Freddie saw a cartoon of "Jack and the Beanstalk" on television. He especially liked the giant, who frothed angrily at the mouth and whose nose, when he smelled the blood of that Englishman, took on the shape of a hound. The beans Jack got in exchange for the cow had smart-alecky faces on them, and Freddie enjoyed watching those faces register dismay when they were hurled into the garden by Jack's angry and emaciated mother.

In the tale Grandpa prefers (and will recite if he's asked), "hound" and "ground" do not rhyme. The way Grandpa tells it, the seeds sprout immediately and have thirty meters of twigs almost before the stalk leaves the . . . earth. The way I tell it, however, each scape grows so slowly that only generations later may a greatgreatgrandkid named Jack put a leg up on a limb. Aunt Cecile, who is a feminist, puts all the action underground, and has Jack climb down roots into the womb of the world. Perhaps the most popular account right now is by the rap group Faerie Boat, with its hypnotic bean counter's beat. At some point, we may decide that the telling has betrayed the tale and is no longer properly a version. Is it a version if we adopt the bean's point of view, for instance? if we set the story in Brooklyn and have the plant, like kudzu, consume the entire borough?

Every recital will be a version, but no version is the tale itself, which has by now taken its seat in the realm of Forms. I called upon the story of Jack and the beanstalk because the giant is clearly a henchman of the Demiurge. The way I tell it, the stalk pierces the clouds only after several centuries have elapsed, the giant is jolly and green and says please, and his hoard is composed of stocks and bonds.

Freddie asks Grandpa for the story because Grandpa gets on with it, which is what stories want, and what Freddie, who is a kid and impatient, also wants. The way I tell it, we watch the cow's milk dry up as slowly and in the same detail as a spill on the kitchen counter. The funny little man Jack meets on his way to sell the spavined creature has a beard I take an hour to describe. Stories fly like arrows toward their morals. Remember the Biblical story about Jonah?

> Now the word of the Lord came unto Jonah the son of Amittai, saying, "Arise, go to Nineveh, that great city, and cry against it; for their wickedness is come up before me." But Jonah rose up to flee unto Tarshish from the presence of the Lord, and went down to Joppa; and he found a ship going to Tarshish: so he paid the fare thereof, and went down into it, to go with them unto Tarshish from the presence of the Lord.

God doesn't care a sweet Smyrna fig for anything but results, so when Jonah runs away instead of doing the Lord's bidding, the Lord has him swallowed. What sort of fish? who knows? How does Jonah survive? who cares? But when Guy Davenport redoes the story, Jonah is said to have

> a fine black beard, round as a basket. Though his carpetbags were neatly strapped and his clothes showed that he was an

experienced traveler, there was a furtiveness in his eyes, as if there might be someone about whom he did not care to meet.

And Davenport tells us that Jonah's "body was inside the fish for three days, but his face looked from the fish's mouth, and he held on to its back teeth."

To begin with, stories break up the natural continuum of life into events. Next, stories arrange these segments in a temporal sequence, in order to suggest that whatever happens earlier is responsible for what happens later. The miraculous is naturalized—it's as easy as dreaming—the way the beans, the stalk, and the giant are given residence in the world, or as the fish is, with its finicky appetite. In stories, all events tend to be given the same weight or value: the cow's milk dries up, the family starves, Jack goes to town to sell the creature, and so on. In a story, it won't do to say: after the battle of Waterloo I tied my shoe.

This linear movement always has an aim—save Mom from starvation, extend Israel's territories into Assyria—and when the story has a happy ending, aim and outcome are the same: Jack nabs the gold to pay for his mom's food habit, Jehovah acquires the treasures and devotion of a great city where six-score thousand persons live, and much cattle besides.

In stories, there are agents and actions; there are patterns; there is direction; most of all, there is meaning. Even when the consequences are tragic, there is a point; there is a message, a moral, a teaching. And that is a consolation. It is consoling to believe that our lives have a shape, a purpose and direction; that the white hats and the black hats have appropriate heads beneath them, and are borne about by bodies with the right souls inside; that there are historical entities, called events, which we can understand, periods which have cohesion and personalities all their own, causes we can espouse or oppose, forces we can employ, and so on.

Stories have to have a certain size. An arrow, to boast of flight, must fly awhile. Jonah is about as brief as one dare be. When Valéry noted down an idea for a frightening story as "it is discovered that a cure for cancer is eating living human flesh: consequences," he knew he had only a germ, the seed of something which would probably grow past story into fiction; something we recognize as an idea for a Roger Corman movie. And when Tess Gallagher tells us Ray Carver took his copy of *The Best American Short Stories* to bed because he had a story in it, she has given us only an anecdotal sentence. Even here, the sort of anecdotal detail the sentence provides will depend upon the precise wording of its presentation, because, for example, taking a book to bed and taking a book into your bed don't point us in the same direction. How about: He took his book to bed and put it beneath his pillow, where, formerly, he kept a pistol? We are on our way at last.

But should we believe in the story's simple determinism, in its naive teleology, its easy judgments, its facile divisions of time, its Chutes and Ladders structure? especially when stories are morally devious. Their opening events are always an excuse, for the real aim of every story is a justification. Goldilocks is a teenytrasher who wrecks the peaceful house of the three bears; Jack is a dim-witted and ungrateful thief who not only steals from the giant, who never did him any harm, but also chops down the vine which got him to the gold; God makes a fool of Jonah to satisfy His own greed for adulation and dominion. It was all Eve's fault, don't forget; the story of the Little Red Hen does not encourage Christian giving; Noah's ark discriminates against gays; and Clint Eastwood is allowed to kill all the redlegs he can catch after we've seen that opening sequence in which his wife, kids, and cat are raped, scalped, stolen, and murdered by them. But how about the story of the boy who cried "Wolf! Wolf!"? Well, it teaches us not to lie continuously to the same people. I've yet to meet a moral that really was.

Stories invent a world which isn't there. Stories are abstract and indifferent to detail. A story asks for the complicity of its readers, who share its ups and downs and tacitly approve the wickedness it wishes to justify. Histories do mostly the same thing: write up the past in a way that will authorize some present misbehavior. Stories try to keep us naive and trusting. Yes, indeed, they console us. They console us by shielding us from the truth. That is one reason the nineteenth-century novel was such a delight to the bourgeois. It was story glorified by fiction. These novels (many of them great as works of art) made lives dedicated to power and money, greed and oppression, when clothed in Christian morality and other pious superstitions, sincere and meaningful. Nobodies were made to feel like somebodies. There are those who would argue that that was a good thing, though nobodies they remained. These novels diligently described life as a lot of ladders to be climbed. Occasions like confirmations and schooling, engagements and marriage, children and promotions, raises and retirements, were simply rungs on the way to honor, ownership, and salvation, like Jack shinnying up his phallus— quite a feat in itself.

Fictions, on the other hand, pull flashbacks and other tricks, fill their pages and the stories they pretend to tell with data: descriptions, expositions, conversations, digressions, monologues. There are characters with fictitious psychologies and fabricated pasts. There are chapters on the history of magic beans, explanations of why cows cease to yield, pauses which ask us to admire the beard we didn't know Jonah had. In his story he is an abstract instrument of God; in his fiction he is a false prophet.

It might be plausible to suppose, as Hilary Putnam does, that if we turn the crank on a certain character, he will project his world on the tabula rasa of our reading, as if the world were an inference and the inference were useful to us in our own; but the world of Céline's novels creates the character who presumably experiences them; there is no separation, and therefore there is no inference. The data of any fiction, without the style and structure of that fiction, cannot guarantee any kind of real consequences. As soon as a so-called truth is removed from a literary text, as it must be if it is to be of further use, it loses its predictive power. Only in Henry James, only Henry in his final manner, only in *The Golden Bowl,* only in this or that particular scene, can a set of consequences confidently come into view and be felt as inevitable; because, in fiction, such connections are established by the writing as a whole, and only by the writing as a whole; no amount of data diddling and systematizing will make its mechanical motions turn a wheel or plow a field. Or reasonably suggest a course of life.

Alliteration does more than candor can to justify God's ways to man.

We do tell ourselves stories in order to live. That is just another one of our problems, and one wonders will we ever grow up. But we do not tell ourselves fictions. Fictions are too complicated; often they are nearly as long as life itself. And the good ones are frequently just as puzzling, so we don't know what to believe finally about Madame Bovary any more than we know what to think of Father Mulrooney, who has been accused of molesting the pipe organ.

TWO: LINEAGE
—During Which a Genealogy of Narration Is Formally Begun

There is a good possibility that our fondness for narratives, as well as a great part of the structure of narratives themselves, derives from genealogy and the defining of kinship. Hesiod makes sense of the jumble of myths about the Greek gods by tracing their descent. Each beginning is a genesis, a begetting, and each such seedling later adopts precisely the shape of the tree of knowledge: the knowledge of whose kids are whose, and to whom they belong—boys as bearers of the name and guarantors of tribal continuance, girls for intermarriage and other forms of trade.

The family tree will eventually—it's hoped—descend like rain, each son establishing a new, though subordinate, beginning and each daughter connecting the family's fate with someone else's fortune. "I give you my daughter, you give me cows." The gods begin the same way their stories do—with the word.

This descent is therefore generational and linear, but the line, straight while contained within one life, and multiple—branching—as it expresses a family's spread, becomes cyclical the moment we allow our attention to shift from the father who has fathered to the son who will.

Myths of origin are the first genealogical narratives, and are laid out in a causal series. God is making man in His own image; the Demiurge is forming our world as a qualitative expression of quantitative law; dry lands are caused to emerge from the oceans as if they were models for swimsuit competitions; we make somehow, in our desperate imaginations, parents so we know where we came from, and we invent descents so we know what our history is: Gods, then heroes, then men—ages of gold are transmuted into those of bronze on their way to lead.

For Freud, illnesses are "fathered," often literally; everything important about a person originates within the family. The first disappointment becomes the model for all future disappointments; the first glimpse of something sensed to be sexual is tainted forever by the feelings it stirred; my stammer started, my vegetarianism has its roots, my preference for Republicans, as well as the day my heart first hardened—all are instigated in the family, tied to family figures, and are hence as tribal as the Sioux.

Time is thus the medium through which the first tales unfold, even if, as in Plato's *Timaeus,* Time itself (as the moving image of eternity) has to be created. Once . . . when? . . . upon a time.

Narrative is linear. It marches *in* moments from moment to moment. Although the telling of a tale may choose to begin at the ending and work back, as far as the story is concerned, there is a First Event, and this event is therefore privileged. The events which follow never follow at random, even though Goldilocks simply happens on the house of the three bears; Jack just bumps into the man who sells him his beans; Plato's shepherd, Gyges, rounding up his flock, fortuitously stumbles on the cleft where the strange corpse lies; Mary was merely resting by the window when the damage done by God's phallic light was announced.

The fact that Time can be envisioned only spatially, most often as an arrowed line, does not shake narration's faith in the string on which its episodes are strung.

If a story's strategy is based on seasonal cycles (plant propagation rather than the human kind), the time line is likely to be circular, time turning around on itself and its events repeating: the world is periodically consumed by fire, drowned by flood, or simply blown away in a wind, and everything then begins again.

Writers who enjoy mimicking this initial formula (out of chaos comes the tale), as Gabriel García Márquez does in *One Hundred Years of Solitude,* will make sure their tale ends with an incestuous sign of some sort—the pig's curly tail in García Márquez's case. (If sleeping with one of your ribs isn't incest, what is?)

Begetting is normal enough, and there's no story in it. The normal needs a nudge, a stable condition needs to be unsettled, a problem has to arise. Soothsayers have to arrive to inform the king that his kid will kill him. Something like that. Otherwise Cinderella will sit in the cinders, mop the floors, and carry out the slops forever, or at least as long as her life lasts. Zeus loves Hera, but oh-you-Leda, and his libido is stirred, and the story starts.

THREE: SEQUENCE
—or Zeno's Revenge

The big bang has bombed. God has admitted He could use a little light. The king in *Hamlet* will later echo His request. Gyges sees a strange ring on the dead man's finger. The Demiurge has done Time. The cow has gone dry. What happens next?

Time is ticking. The tale must fill that ticking with events, for events occur in time. Stories are strings of verbs. Once upon a time (no story has started yet), there was a king (not yet) who had a beautiful daughter (not yet) of marriageable age (still not yet) whom he loved very much (nope), so the king devised (here we are) a plan—an ordeal, really—for choosing (yup) a suitable husband from among her many suitors (whose suits are "the setup story"). Action is everything. Most movies understand this. Does anyone suppose the story of Jonah is *about* Jonah? Jones would do. God needs someone to scare the people of Nineveh into docility. It's the scaring that counts. Yes, verbs need nouns to be the agents of their doing and the object of their wrath, but only the way that strings need puppets. Aristotle insisted that tragedy concerns action. He also argued that anything is what it essentially does; so, for instance, to be a good man, I must lead the good life, which is one of self-realization.

But we expect a nice whole number like (1) to be followed by another nice wholesome number like (2), not by some freak like (1.1111111111111111111111111111111111111111111111111111). Sequences must be built up of elements (a) of appropriate "sizes" (temporal length), (b) of relatively equal importance (or value), and (c) of approximately similar "kinds." Goldilocks must spend roughly the same amount of text time ruining the Little Bear's life as she spends ruining the Big Bear's life. In stories, Jonah doesn't hear the voice of God, then lick his lips, smoke a cigarette, or even pack his suitcase; that would violate rule (b). Nor does he wet us with his stream of consciousness (acts and thoughts have different ontologies). Thoughts are rarely welcome in stories. Little Red Riding Hood doesn't wonder what big eyes Grandma has; she says: Those are big squinters you got there, Granny. "Saying" isn't thinking; we all know that.

The necklace makes a good model. In a story we can vary the size and value of succeeding events, but only if the variation is repeated as a pattern. XaXaXaX is okay. Not: lemon, orange, onion, screwdriver, sigh, stadium, flake of dandruff, agony of defeat. But: lemon orange, sigh groan, lemon orange, sigh groan.

Each action is its own entity. We need to know when we are in the frying pan and when in the fire. Actions are encouraged to repeat, without major modification, as when Goldilocks "eats the porridge," "exclaims, 'Hey, that's just right!,' " "breaks the chairs," "soils the bedding." Yet each is a firmly defined unit. In short: stories deny continua. They are atomists. Their worlds are made of blocks. Or film frames. Stories proceed in defiance of Zeno, who argued that plotwise you couldn't get from A to B or catch the tortoise or shoot an arrow in the air with any hope of its arriving anywhere. Between any two events (points), Zeno said, there might well be an infinite number of others (especially if the points have no size); but for story, there is nothing (which is a part of the story and needs to be told) between the voice of God and going pellmell to Tarshish. In fiction there are "breaks in the action," but fiction revels in its antagonism to story. It needs story, but often only to abuse it. Robert Musil's great novel, *The Man Without Qualities,* begins its eighteen-hundred-page journey in August of 1913 but never reaches its target date: the beginning of World War I, in August of 1914. Story is eager to reach its climax; fiction is all foreplay.

Because stories are made of modules, they can be analyzed in terms of "the recognition scene," "the ordeal," "the odyssey," or "the curse," "the return," "the revenge." And there are many more sophisticated modes of analysis which will include agents and objects as well. But art labors mightily to overcome such a Lego-like result. Hamlet's delay is not "a delay"; Lear's realization is not "another recognition." Immersed in a context, wedded to a single run of words (and unless an allusion to the folkloric is intended—the three witches, for example), fiction tries to undo the very formulas its narrative is made of.

FOUR: PATTERN
—or *Three Times Is the Charm*

Story impedes its own flow sometimes because it is in love with repetition: the "piling up" of verbal formulas, of "kinds" of acts, types of groupings, especially groupings of three. There are, not surprisingly, three Billy Goats Gruff, three bears, three wishes, three wise men from the East, thirty pieces of silver, three threats to the houses of the three little pigs, those three crows of the cock which embarrass Peter, *Macbeth*'s three weird sisters, and so on. (Not to omit the sonata's classic form.) Threes are sometimes structurally submerged. Jonah has three exchanges with God, for instance: at home, in the fish, at Nineveh. These repetitions produce both suspense and expectation—suspense since they halt the story's headlong bolt down the road, and expectation when we recognize the pattern and realize that the first two suitors must fail to answer their riddle at the cost of their lives.

When a pattern of repetition is added to the natural simplicity of the story's line, to its strong directionality, to its frequently important public meaning, the story's memorability is substantially increased, which was a vital consideration for early oral cultures. Moreover, stories, to add to the sense of inner inevitability they prize (of which more under "Causality"), and because each story aspires to be more than story—to be instructional, wise, moral, etcetera (a koan, a parable, a mantra, a rune)—stories are pleased when they can move in the direction of a chant, employ a refrain, suggest a secret. Hence stories work best when they are "time-honored," anonymous, or, even better, were uttered first by a prophet or a god, who, presumably, does not tell stories to put aside our fears or lull us to sleep, but has only important things to do. The message of the ur- or Platonic story is mysterious, moral, and cautionary precisely because it seems to have come from nowhere but the human psyche. Fictions are to be contemplated, pondered, enjoyed. Stories are to be heeded.

FIVE: CAUSALITY
—or It Has Already Happened

The bits which constitute the story have to be fastened together in some way; they cannot merely sit in a line like a bunch of birds. (Actually, the birds have a line to sit on.) (And are often the same redwings.) We know that "after this therefore because of this" is a fallacy, but stories don't, and the reason they don't is that the selection of "befores" is meant to be followed by certain "afters." Sometimes the story cites its causes in so many words: because Jonah ran away and shipped out in order to escape God's bidding, God sent first a storm and then a fish with a wide mouth, and when the fish had held Jonah prisoner for a time, Jonah bitterly repented, so God had the fish vomit Jonah forth onto the dry land.

Sometimes the causal principle is implicit. Gyges sees a ring on the corpse's finger. He slips it off (curiosity, greed); discovers, when his fellow shepherds sometimes talk about him as if he were not there, that he becomes invisible if the bezel of the ring is turned. He gets rich through theft, enjoys the queen (though, since he's invisible, how much did she enjoy *him*?), kills the king, and takes over (greed and more greed). The causal principle is the point of the story: namely, if human beings are freed from social restraint, they will demonstrate their true nature (greed greed and still more greed).

The causes which appear in stories are the same ones which Aristotle described: stories do not simply move blindly out from some catastrophe or First Cause as if enormous energies had been released, although they have such energies, and efficient causes are certainly present; but they are going toward a conclusion which will in no way surprise them. A tale without a final cause is a tired tale indeed. It is, in fact, a shaggy dog story.

Aristotle joined the concept of a linear causality to that of linear inference, regarding the middle term of the syllogism as the "cause" of the conclusion. This illicit mix of physical and logical necessity was exposed by Hume, but the union has always had such a great appeal to the intuitions of common sense that it refuses to go away. The seemingly straight-line movement of the mind in both logical argument and scholarly exposition fit the tow-barge picture of the causal chain too perfectly to be abandoned just because it was wrong, and the apparently parallel linearity of language notation (as well, eventually, as moving picture film) simply reinforced the connection like steel concealed in concrete.

Sometimes the tale unfolds as though its conclusion were implicit from the first page, exhibiting the powers of entelechy and the presence of the formal cause. (In an analytic proposition, the predicate is said to be included in the subject.) Often, however, the story is sophistically shuffled forward by pieces of machinery (stereotypes and other narrative clichés) or by acts of God or by mysterious magical interventions. Jack just meets a stranger upon the path to town and is swoggled into a trade, the stupid little stump, as his mom thinks: a whole dried-up cow for a few seeds. Ordinary life plants the gift and waits for it to grow, but magic makes the stalk higher than a tree, even though the material cause has to supply the growing stuff.

Because the causal order is represented in and on the line of time, it is regularly envisioned in the thinnest possible terms, and the domino effect describes the efficient cause, in this case, perfectly. But Aristotle thinks of the Final Cause as directing the First, so that when the Unmoved Mover is moved, it will be toward a far-off event which will not, for a very very long time, occur. (As the Final Cause, God does not yet exist.) Unless they are being made up on the spot, stories, when they begin, are already over. Once-upon-a-time knows that they all lived-happily-ever-after. It is written. It is just not yet recited.

The listener or the reader may not know what remains to be read or recited—not the first time through—but it won't be long before the last page is as expected as Grandma for Christmas.

The events of a story do not fall upon the ear like cards randomly upon the table. Rather, they speak of the power of Destiny. The gypsy reveals the tarots one by one with great ceremony. Chance seems to draw them from the deck in her fist, but actually they are slipping from Fate's sleeve. No magician sacrifices to Tyche.

When we are applying narrative notions to history, we refer to historical teleology very often as Divine Providence. If creation begins with the *logos* and lasts six days, decline—and consequently *human* history—begins with the expulsion from Paradise of Adam and Eve. Events leak slowly but steadily toward the last trump, when the dead will rise from their resting places to join the quick at the bar of judgment. Since a great many Greeks thought of history as cyclical, it does not have AN END; it has periods instead, punctuated by catastrophes, as Vico envisioned. I call this short-term teleology. I may be off to attend the Lyric Opera, but my ticket to Chicago will be round-trip. When I leave, it won't be my purpose to return; that does not become my purpose until I have completed my visit.

At the utopian end of history, for Marx and Hegel change becomes an inaudible vibration, so, like Judeo-Christian history, Idealist history is end-stopped. In sum:

(a) Texts themselves are predetermined; exist all at once; and, if they have been released by their godlike author to the world, are fixed (so to speak) forever. Books are bulks and occupy space like buildings.

(b) The reading of the text is determined a bit at a time as the lines unroll: the word "unroll" being read as it turns up. The reader, of course, may accidentally or willfully misread, skip ahead, repeat certain passages, and so forth, but the reader is then not "reading the text" but "reading *around and about in* the text." Paradoxically, the computer, often felt to free texts from linearity, scrolls more insistently than any book.

(c) The artistic organization of the text may require a representation of chaos, but that representation will be rigorously regulated. Artistic organization, esthetic fixity, may utilize a narrative form, but it just as often may not.

(d) A story must be made of and by narration, but fictions may merely employ narrative techniques without resorting to the composition of stories as such. Stories (plots), as I am defining them, have closure, and this closure is aimed at and determined by (a) and (b) and sometimes (c).

SIX: IDENTITY
—or The Encyclopedia of Masterplots

It would be silly to say that Kafka's *The Penal Colony* and Octave Mirbeau's *Le Jardin des supplices* are the same work simply because they have very similar plots. Actually, Kafka's piece, an outstanding work of literature, doesn't have a plot, whereas Mirbeau's bit of *épate* and painporn flummery has plenty. Plot is liftable, transferable, interchangeable, transformable, because plot is only fried by its details and can be removed from them, allowed to degrease on a piece of paper towel, before being served, brown and barely coated, on a warm plate. Plot is made up of a series of related functions.

(A—Indians) (B—attack) a (C—wagon train) and (D—kill,

rape, burn, and plunder). (E—Eastwood) (F—the trail boss) was (G—required to take the point) just before (B—the attack), and so was spared, but his (H₁—wife and family) were not. (E—He) (I—follows) the (A—war party) back to its (J—village), where, after (K₁,₂,₃—a series of adventures), (E—he) (L—rescues) (H₂—a girl they had taken captive) and (M₁—kills the chief) (N—in hand-to-hand combat). (A—The Indians) (O—pursue him and the girl). (K₁,₂,₃— After a series of adventures), during which he (P—falls in love with the girl), he (M₂—defeats the Indians) (Q—with the timely help of the U.S. Cavalry) and (R—rides into the sunset with the girl slung across his pommel).

(A—Hooligans) (B—break into) a (C—apartment) and (D—kill and rape) its occupants. (E—Bronson) (F—an architect) was in a (G—meeting with a client) just before the break-in, and so was spared, but his (H—wife and daughter) were not. (E—He) (I—frequents) (J—the neighborhood) where (A—the louts) hang out, and, (K₁,₂,₃—after a series of other vigilantisms), (E—he) (M—kills them one after the other) . . . etc.

Board games played with dice and spinners are made up of moves that are simply a series of additions and subtractions to a total, the sum reached represented by the movement of a counter across spaces (paths, trails) marked out on decorated pasteboard. They are therefore "all the same."

SEVEN: IMPERSONALITY
—or The Pointless Point of View

Fictions have points of view. That is, they are told from the position of one pronoun or another. These pronouns ("I," "you," "he," "she," "they") can have expanded or restricted fields of observation and reference. This analysis is well known. There must be more than half a dozen well-defined points of view. These regulate the scope and competence of the narrator's knowledge and authority. Stories are strange creatures, because normally they have no point of view, not even the godly omniscient one with which the nineteenth-century novel has made us so familiar. Because the story, as such, belongs to no medium and has no designated "teller," it acts as if it had no point of view in particular. Because it is a folktale or a myth, it has no author. Of course it happened, once upon a time, but so long ago no measure can measure the distance. It is past being past. Its form is as fixed as a commandment in stone, and no one can claim to have shaped, uttered, or indited it originally.

Here is one of the Grimms' tales, complete. Its impersonality, its lack of godhead or anything else, lies in the tone. It is not being told by anyone in particular to anyone in particular at any particular time or in any particular place or for any particular reason. It *is,* the way the universe is supposed to be. Take it or leave it.

The Goblins

Once there was a mother and the goblins had stolen her child out of the cradle. In its place they laid a changeling with thick head and staring eyes who did nothing but eat and drink. In her misery, the woman went to ask her neighbor for advice. The neighbor told her to take the changeling into the kitchen, set him on the hearth, light a fire, and boil water in two eggshells. This would make the changeling laugh, and when a changeling laughs, that's the end of him.

The woman did just what the neighbor told her, and as she was putting the eggshells full of water on the fire, the blockhead said:

> "Now am I as old
>   As the western woods
>   But never heard it told
>   that people cook water in eggshells,"

and he began to laugh and as he laughed there suddenly
came a lot of little goblins who brought the right child and
set it on the hearth and took their friend away with them.

The ur-story never heard itself told because *it* never has been.

EIGHT: MEANING
—or *The Riddle Unraveled*

Stories have morals if men do not. If X comes to a bad end, there
is a lesson in that; if X comes to a good end, there's another to be
had. It helps, if we are to believe the folktale, to be stupid and/or
innocent. Jack is a dimwit first, a thief later. Aladdin is a clever little cutpurse, but has impoverishment firmly on his side. Hansel
and Gretel, as well as Little Red Riding Hood, are cute little kids,
and Goldilocks doesn't really mean to trash the house of the three
bears. You are allowed to be clever, even sly, if you are a poor plain
person of the people (or a prince dressed like one), because the
smart-asses will have the wrong answers and lose their IQ'd
heads, whereas the simple boy will speak from the heart or get
whistled hints by a helpful bird.

Moral or not, stories have meaning. They are told for that reason. And they must be suspenseful or amusing along the way so
that the sharpness of their point will be felt. The Little Red Hen
doesn't do all that work for nothing.

Parables possess meaning, but only for the chosen. The Biblical parables are intended not to produce understanding but to
identify those capable of grasping them. To have no sense of parable is worse than having no sense of humor.

Although stories usually end by having their initial problem
solved or their imbalance righted, the meaning of the story
should not be marooned on the last square like Crusoe on his
island. It isn't just getting the gold, or fitting the slipper, or sailing
past the sirens that matters; it is that you have striven, and there-

fore succeeded; you have swum instead of sunk; you have gotten tough when things got rough; you have resisted this or that temptation.

Even when the story ends badly, the meaning assigned to it is *always* positive. I know of no exceptions to this. Oedipus ends up blind, homeless, on the road; but the city has been saved, and now Oedipus, like Tiresias, is a seer. Stories are reviewed by Doctor Pangloss, who imprimaturs only uplift. Even the cruel tales told of Slovenly Peter simply fit the punishment to the crime. If the rhyme says that

> Little Willie, in the best of sashes,
> fell in the fire and was burned to ashes.
> Now and then the room grows chilly,
> but no one likes to poke up Willie.

then in Willie's story it will be discovered that the little monster had it coming.

The end of another of the Grimms' tales is characteristic. Throughout the story our hero has been helped by a fox, but things have gone badly because the fox's advice has not always been followed. (There are three brothers, two of whom prove to be wicked, while the youngest, whom they take to be a simpleton, turns out to be by-gosh-good. In Grimm, more than one hero goes by the name Dummkopf.) At last, however, we reach the dénouement:

The king ordered all the people in his palace to be brought before him; so the youth, looking like a poor beggar in his rags, came too. The maiden, though, recognized him immediately and threw her arms around his neck. The wicked brothers were seized and put to death, while he was married to the beautiful maiden and made the king's heir.

But what became of the poor fox? A long time afterward the king's son once again was walking in the wood, when the fox met him and said: "Now you have everything you can wish for, but my misery goes on without an end, and yet you have it in your power to free me." And once more he begged him to shoot him and chop off his head and feet. So he did, and no sooner was it done than the fox turned into a man, and was none other than the brother of the beautiful princess, freed at last from the spell under which he had lain. And now there was nothing lacking to their happiness, so long as they all lived.

NINE: SIGNIFICANCE
—or The Answer Reriddled

The meaning of a story is not the same as its significance, for it is precisely the significance of its meaning that is in question. Of the three sisters, Cinderella is the meek and downtrodden one. She is put upon because her sisters are jealous of her beauty. So Cinderella must wear rags and sweep the hearth and wash the dishes and carry out the slops like a servant. The older, selfish, social-climbing, ugly sisters prepare for the prince's ball, and each hopes her breasts will draw the young man's eye. As things turn out, of course, through magical intervention, the modest maid is transported to the dance in style and wins the prince's heart during a gavotte, although she disappears at midnight's chime, leaving only her sexually symbolic slipper behind.

The prince goes about looking for the woman who will fit him; or, rather, the woman whose foot fits the slipper. The nasty sisters' feet are too large and won't go in no matter how hard they push and squeeze; however, to their surprise and discombobulation, Cinderella's foot is a perfect match. Which proves? that one must look beyond mere appearance, beyond clothes and money and humble station, to find good qualities which might be otherwise hidden.

The significance of the story is quite otherwise. Cinderella doesn't go to the ball wearing an old wig and a frowsy frock; she is dolled up to beat all, and it is because she is such a knockout that the prince hits the canvas. The glass slipper becomes a measurement of this otherwise hidden beauty. You can bet the prince puts her back into the fine clothes he'll have charged at Victoria's Secret. The finer figure is rewarded with power, glory, money, as well as a handsome animal for the pleasures of its bed. That is: beauty will out because that's what men want, and ugly does as ugly is.

Beauty overcomes her loathing for the Beast and eventually falls in love with him. Upon her kiss and the affection it represents, the prince is released from the spell which has imprisoned him in an ape suit or lion's skin—whatever. The meaning is, again: look beyond mere appearance, seek and value inner qualities. Right. Because the significance is: kiss the frog, bat, cat, and receive in the next day's mail a young handsome man of high social position full of the kind of gratitude which will make him putty in your hands. If you really loved the Beast, you'd be bereft when the prince appears. No, you are to love the Beast because the prince will be your reward.

Who's kidding whom?

TEN: JUSTIFICATION
—or Getting Even

Stories have an important social use, especially those which are frequently repeated and dinned into the ears of children. It isn't merely that they bear a moral like a medal on their chests; they justify certain attitudes and condone or encourage actions which are or will be undertaken. The meaning of a story is not simply meant; it is anointed. This haloed summing-up is then used to dupe its audience: virtue (that is, an agreeable passivity) will be rewarded with exactly the monetary, sexual, and social success denied those who incorrectly (greedily, actively, openly) pursue it.

The story of Adam and Eve has been used for centuries to

denigrate women and provide a reason for fearing them. That is its significance.

Revenge is a chief motif, and the aim of many a tale is its justification. Perhaps the greatest of the Grimm brothers' tales is "The Juniper Tree"—and a bloodier one it'll be hard to find. Once upon a time, at least two thousand years ago, a barren wife stood under the juniper tree in her front yard peeling an apple (uh-oh!). She cuts her finger, and blood dots the winter snow (why is she standing in the snow to peel her apple? don't ask). The seasons pass, nine months disappear in the space of a sentence, and the woman, not in the best of shape, surprises herself with a bouncing baby boy. Her happiness promptly kills her, and her husband buries her beneath the juniper tree, sobbing the while. But only for a while, because he soon marries again, and has a daughter, Ann Marie, by his new wife (a stepmother, so watch out!). One day the daughter asks for an apple for herself and for her brother too, but her mother makes her wait until her brother comes home from school. Told to select an apple from the apple chest, the boy leans in, only to have his head knocked off when his stepmother slams its heavy, sturdy lid down on him. (The devil got into her.)

What to do? His head tied back on with a scarf, the boy is propped up with an apple in his hand. Daughter (who is conveniently ignorant of all this) is told to ask for her apple from her brother, and to box his disobedient ears if he doesn't surrender it. Of course he won't, so she does, and his head falls off into a puddle of her future tears. Her stepmother, in her motherly way, says (in Lore Segal's luminous translation):

> "It can't be helped now; we will stew him in sour broth."
> And so the mother took the little boy and hacked him in pieces and put the pieces in the pot and stewed him in the sour broth. But Ann Marie stood by and cried and cried and the tears fell in the pot so that it didn't need any salt.

When Father comes home, he is told lies about his son's whereabouts and is served black stew for supper. Though Ann

Marie cries the whole time, Father so loves the stew that he eats it all, sucking the bones clean and throwing them under the table for the dogs. Ann Marie collects the remains, however, and buries them (beside the boy's mother) under the juniper tree. After certain dramatic scenic effects, a bird appears in the tree and sings this lovely song:

> "My mother she butchered me,
>   My father he ate me,
>   My sister, little Ann Marie,
>   She gathered up the bones of me
>   And tied them in a silken cloth
>   To lay under the juniper.
>   Tweet twee, what a pretty bird am I!"

The bird then flies to the goldsmith's (one), where it sings this verse so enchantingly that the goldsmith gives it a gold chain to sing the song again. It flies next to the shoemaker's (two) and comes away with a pair of red shoes. Finally, it sings for twenty of the miller's men (three's the charm), who lift the millstone with its hole onto the little bird's uncommonly strong neck as its reward for singing twice. Holding the chain and the shoes in its claws and with the millstone around its neck, the bird flies back to the juniper tree to sing some more.

Suffice it to say, Father has to come out to hear the bird, and receives the gold chain for his applause. Ann Marie must hear it, too, and gets the slippers for her attention. Finally, the stepmother, full of foreboding, comes out, and is flattened by the millstone into the shape of a patch of grease. Scenic effects follow (remember *The Wizard of Oz?*), and out of a few flames and a lot of smoke comes the restored boy: "and he took his father and Ann Marie by the hand and the three of them were so happy and went into the house and sat down at the table and ate their supper."

Clint can't match this, even if he blows the smoke from his gun barrel.

Some may say that the moral of the story is: murder will out. Well, murder will. Nevertheless, the real moral of the story is: don't remarry.

ELEVEN: REALITY HAS A HISTORY
—and History Tells a Story

We all love stories; it seems a harmless pleasure. Furthermore, narration is a fundamental technique for forming fictions, therefore stories are also an essential element. Stories are economical. They hit the high points. The king rose. The king ruled. The king was deposed. The king fell. Stories run on pattern and regularity, imitate causality (even if by magical agents), and comfort us because they mean something; they show lives and actions going somewhere, behavior punished and rewarded as seems proper. Stories are restorative. If they have unsettled beginnings, their endings come to a solid standstill. But is actual human history storied? Are our lives tales? Or is there simply sound and fury?

Not just stories but human society is full of narratives, which we set up and follow. There are even scripts: weddings, for instance, all our ceremonies, rituals, holidays, outings, including our habits too, the way and when and if we shine our shoes, the route to work, the menu of a meal (Chinese meals, as served in America, are, for me, intolerably disordered), the contents of a book, the schedules of teams, the hierarchy of classes in school, seniorities at work, the clock and calendar, appointment book, magazine subscription, morning walk, moves in chess, this and that, and nothing else: the deed that's signed, not the tie you were wearing when you signed it; the "I do" which does not admit of silent reservations; the cash transaction which is indifferent to the history of the bills.

Consequently, narrative forms have always enjoyed a privileged position, as if they were the best mirrors of reality; indeed, the notion of the mirror (though it inverts) is beguilingly isomorphic. But the mind never did march, only its linear logic did; human character neither was built in a day nor let out its contents like a tap to a vat. Correlation replaced necessity, probability certainty; entities were full of elements made of entities, yet entities were exclamations of relation. Death was a destination, not a consummation, and life, though full of purposes, had none, and though everything in life was a sign, life managed, itself, to be meaningless.

Story was a comfort, but if it was thought to be right for the realization of the world, except in the narrowest of cases, it was the comfort of a lie.

Fiction is story's polar opposite, though that does not mean they do not need one another, live in the same sphere, or have no common qualities. Both are cold most of the year.

Anywhere but Kansas

I was nearly ten when my parents gave me a chemistry set for Christmas. It came in a handsome wooden box, and contained a rack for test tubes, as well as niches where vials of powerful powders might be kept. There was a little packet of sensitive paper (litmus, I think), a knobbed glass rod, the obligatory manual, a metal loop for suspending a test tube over a flame, a conversion table (ounces into spoons), and suitably exciting poison labels. Dreams flew out of that box when its lid was lifted: dreams of bombs and poisons, of plots described in disappearing ink, of odors distressful to the weak. I set up a small lab in the basement, and there I performed my experiments. "Performed" is the right word. "Experiment" is not. For I didn't follow the booklet where it led, or listen to its lectures. I slopped about, blending yellow with white and obtaining brown, mixing crystals with powders and getting dust, combining liquids with solids and making mud.

Later, in high school, I would take chemistry the way I took spring tonics and swallowed headache pills. Although I broke beakers and popped little pieces of potassium into puddles of water to watch the water fly, I did occasionally manage to obey tutorial instructions as well, repeating experiments that others had long ago undertaken. My predecessors had asked their questions of Nature with genuine curiosity, and awaited, like eager suitors, her reply. My method displayed a different spirit, which was to fudge my procedures in order to obtain the result already written in the chemmy books. I was not being taught to experiment, or even to repeat experiments. I was being taught to cheat.

An experiment, I would learn much later, when I studied the philosophy of science in graduate school, had to arise from a real dissatisfaction with existing knowledge. There was a gap to be filled, a fracture to be repaired, an opening to be made. Nature's interrogator had to know how to ask the correct question, and to state it so clearly that the answer would be, in effect, an unambiguous "yes" or "no," and not a noddy wobble. Every experiment required a protected environment and an entirely objective frame of mind. The results should be quantifiable, and the process repeatable. Every successful repetition spoke favorably for the quality of the first occasion. Furthermore, experiments were never carried out against the rules, but were performed, like surgery, always well within them, otherwise they would not be recognized as experiments at all.

What is generally called "experimentation" in the arts more nearly resembles my ignorant and youthful self-indulgent mess-making. I was acting out a fantasy, not learning anything about chemistry, and while every smelly substance I concocted had to have been made according to chemistry's laws, I did not know those laws, nor could I have learned them from anything I was doing. And how many botches have been excused by calling them the results of the experimental spirit? We have to imagine an artist wondering what would happen if she were to do this, try that, perform a play in silence, omit the letter *e* in three pages of French prose, construct a world of clothes-hanger wire, color walls with cow manure. Having found out, though, then what?

A good experiment is as perfect and complete as the Parthenon, but in popular speech the word is derogatory, as if the experiment were going to be performed on the audience. Experiments, moreover, even if elegant and crucial, are admired for their results—the "yes" or "no" they receive—and (except for specialists) not for their procedures. We don't want to read interrogations; we want to read results.

Actually, the press admires them only when they cry "aye!" In the lab a "no" may not elicit cheers; it is nevertheless a bearer of important information.

Critics, patrons, academicians, characteristically insecure and immature beneath their arrogant demeanors, are devoted to rules and definitions of decorum. Scarcely has an innovative form, a daring method, a different point of view, established itself than its codification begins: it must be given a catchy name (and labeled "experimental" perhaps, at least "avant-garde," or something even trendier, such as "existential," "absurd," "metafictional," "minimal," "surreal," "postmod"); next, its superficial qualities are catalogued (it looks to the future in this respect, remains unchanged in that, returns to the past right here, but seems, at another point, content with the status quo); its cultural links are then explored and evaluated (does it reveal the sorry *Geist* of the *Zeit*? does it express malaise? is it symptomatic of some social sickness? is it toughly feminist? is it resolutely gay?); finally, it will be given a fresh critical vocabulary, a new jargon to fit this latemost fad like a cowboy boot pulled over a golfing shoe. Since, and sadly, by the relentless use of commandments and plenty of otiose rhetoric, the latest craze can be put in place as quickly as an ugly tract gets built, it is therefore repeatedly necessary for writers to shake the system by breaking its rules, ridiculing its lingo, and disdaining whatever is in intellectual fashion. To follow fashion is to play the pup.

Many fictions which appear to be "experimental" are actually demonstrations. When Galileo dropped his proofs from Pisa's tower, the proof was purely in the seeing. To demonstrate an equal fall for both a lead and a paper ball, he would have had to put Pisa's tower in a vacuum tube and monitor the competitive descent of his samples with instruments more precise than any he had at hand. But that was not the point: the point was the persuasion of the eye and the subversion of a misguided principle. If Doctor Johnson claims you can't write a satisfactory poem about a coal mine, the poet is, of course, called upon to write it. Disgracing one more rule will not dissuade everybody from the view that art is made by recipe, because the constitutionally constipated will begin drawing up additional regs at once; but it will encourage the intelligent suspicion that neither by breaking nor abiding is quality achieved.

So "subversive" is often a good name for certain types of fiction. Between my muck-about basement days and the discipline provided by my high school class, I enjoyed an interlude as a bomber. With sulfur from my then neglected set, a little potassium nitrate purchased from the pharmacist, and charcoal scraped from any charred board, I discovered that I could make gunpowder. By filling pill capsules (also obtained at the drugstore) with my gray mix and slamming the whole thing with a stone, I could make a very satisfactory bang. It provided me with an exhilarating sense of power. It wasn't long before I was coating wet string with my concoction in order to make a fuse. However, I was open to experiment: sometimes I wet the string and sometimes I made a paste and sometimes I soaked the string in the grainy mixture. Then a toilet-roll tube packed with paper and powder was set off with a sound so violent it shouted of my success.

"Make it new," Ezra Pound commanded, and "innovative" is a good name for some kinds of fiction; however, most newness is new in all the same old ways: falsely, as products are said to be new by virtue of minuscule and trivial additions; or vapidly, when the touted differences are pointless; or opportunistically, when alterations are made simply in order to profit from imaginary improvements; or differentially, when newness merely marks a moment, place, or person off from others and gives it its own identity, however dopey.

You may be the first to open a play with the word *merde;* or to write of America because you discovered it; or to detail the production of ball bearings; or to be brave enough to say straight out that, actually, the emperor's new clothes are tacky; or to be accounted a pioneer because no one had described, before your example, how it is to die of a bad disposition. Perhaps a poem on the taste of sperm will cause another sort of sensation. However, innovation that comes to something is nearly always formal. It is the expression of style at the level of narrative structure and fictional strategy. When we describe a writer's way of writing as individual and unique, we are referring to qualities it is often impossible and always unwise to imitate—Beckett is simply Beckett, Proust Proust—but original though their voices may be, they are not, just for that, innovative, because innovation implies the beginning of a new direction, whereas the style of late James (which I have the good taste to admire) has realized its completion, and signifies an end.

The style of *Finnegans Wake* was certainly new and inimitable, but it was the cyclical structure of the work which was innovative; it was the polyphony of the text, the principle of the portmanteau, the landscape of the dream, the extraordinary musicality of the prose, which provided that wealth of stimulating possibilities for other writers.

There is something to be said for just getting away from it all. Writers begin as readers of a driven and desperate kind. Over the hills and far away, Lady Castlemaine is meeting her beau beneath a blooming . . . what? . . . chestnut tree; Horatio Le Paige is pitching his last game, the bases are jammed, his arm is sore, the crowd is on his case, the catcher has called for an illegal pitch, which may be his only way out; Baron Pimple has caught Miss Tweeze without her duenna. Readers begin by wanting to be anywhere but here, anywhere but Kansas, and, when those readers begin writing, a good many of them will want to write anything except what they've been reading, not because some of what they read wasn't wonderful, for once upon an unhappy time these texts also took them anywhere but Kansas; but because such writing has become its own Kansas now, and represents dullness and repression and the damnably indifferent status quo. Anything, so long as it's not normal narrative . . . anything, instead of characters given sunken cheeks and a hard stare to set them apart, yes, better the Tin Man, better the Bert Lahr lion, but also anything other than the predictable plots and routine scenes, neat outcomes, and conventional values . . . anything but Oz. Transportive fictions make sure of that. Their originality may be secondary to their denial of everyday; their subversive qualities secondary to their profound desire to be anywhere else, anywhere that hasn't Aunt Em, anywhere not over that sentimental rainbow, anywhere so long as it's not to a sequel.

Many times metafictions, because they caressed themselves so publicly, behaved more like manifestos than stories. They were more "explanatory" than "experimental." Instead of showing that something could be done by doing it, they became tutorial, emphasizing technique; teaching the reader how to read; chastising him for his traditional bourgeois expectations; and directing his attention to art instead of nature, to the reality of the work instead of the reality of the world. That has always been a lesson more than hard to learn, for most people prefer to duck the difficult tedia of daily life, and ask that their experience of the wider world be filtered through layers of sensational detail and false feeling—hence neither living right nor reading well.

Exploding toilet-paper tubes had been such a noisy success, I moved on to lead pipe. Into a piece I had found which was about six inches long and half an inch in diameter, I packed plenty of powder, tamping it down with the wooden handle of a small screwdriver, and then closing up both ends with thin, minutely folded layers of cardboard. Set off by fuse alongside a neighbor's house, where I stuck one end in some soft ground like a flare, it exploded with a smoky roar that could be heard for blocks, and fragments of pipe flew everywhere, a large shard penetrating the wall of my friend's front room. I ran as if riding the wind. I believed I heard sirens—police after me? firemen to the house? my father rising toward the higher elevations of his rage? Ah, we do like to fancy our books are bombs, but bombs, we need to remember, in order to make a great show—to do their damage, prove a point, teach some slow wit a lesson—have to blow themselves to bits and pieces first.

When learning to play any instrument well, to wrestle, lift weights, dance, sing, write, it is wise to exercise. Try describing a hat in such a way the reader will realize its wearer has just had her dog run over. Practice putting your life into the present tense, where you presumably lived it. Do dialogue—let's say, between a hobo and a high-class hooker, then between an ambulance chaser and a guy who sells scorecards at the ballpark—let's say, about the meaning of money. Between pints, get the arch of the dart down pat. Shoot foul shots day in and rim out. Pick a sentence at random from a randomly selected book, next another from another volume also chosen by chance; then write a paragraph which will be a reasonable bridge between them. And it does get easier to do what you have done, sing what you've so often sung; it gets so easy, sometimes, that what was once a challenge passes over into thoughtless routine. So the bar must be raised a few notches, one's handicap increased, the stakes trebled. Tie both hands behind your back. Refuse the blindfold, refuse the final cigarette, refuse the proffered pizza. Do dialogue in dialect: a Welshman and a Scot arguing about an onion. Hardest of all: start over.

Of course, if you feel you have mastered at least some of your medium, you can improvise—take its risks and enjoy its pleasures. Now you trust yourself to go the right way, like a roach to the kitchen, as if by instinct: taking off from an idle word, a casual phrase, a small exchange between disillusioned lovers, a notion about narrative time you got while reading Bergson, an item in the morning paper; then letting the music lead, a surprising association rule, or a buried meaning rise raw and green and virile as a weed, until the rhythm of the sentence settles in, the idea begins to unfold like a flower, time finds itself without hands, a character begins to speak in an unfamiliar tongue, and the shape of the scene is in front of you—nothing to it—you modify the metaphor, vary the normal flow of feeling . . . yes, it is certainly lovely, the facility between give and go, the rapport you have with your material, ease of flow . . . yet one person's grateful pee is not another's—that's a law about all calls of nature—accordingly, the improviser must be careful to make his modulations, like those riffy moments in music, so splendid they shall seem contrived, and the best way to do that is to contrive them.

The explorer sees in front of him an unknown territory, an unmapped terrain, or he imagines there must be somewhere a new route to the Indies, another polar star, gorgons alive and well amid jungle-covered ruins, mountain views and river sources grander than the Nile's, lost tribes, treasure, or another, better way of life; because he is searching, not inventing; he is trying to find what is already there: regions of life as neglected as his own history, themes as far from general attention as a cavern at the bottom of the sea, structures as astounding as those that show up stained in tissue slices. Explorational fiction records an often painful and disappointing journey, possibly of discovery, possibly of empty sailing; yet never toward what may lie out of sight in the self (since that is what improvisation discloses) but toward what lies still unappreciated in the landscape of literature: implications unperceived, conclusions undrawn, directions everyone has failed to follow. The spirit of the explorer may indeed be to scalpel society and show its rotting organs, nor is every implication nice as toast with tea; however, the key to this kind of fiction is that the chest, which the existence of the key suggests, must be (or be believed to be) there in six feet of sand beneath the bolt-scarred tree. In that sense, exploration is the work of a realist, however fanciful that reality may seem to those encountering it for the first time.

Maybe we can pun our way to another genre, inasmuch as

labels seem to matter more than their jars. The prefix "ex-" apparently has to be there, since we already have the "explanatory," the "experimental" and "exploratory," as well as the sweat from "exercise." Nevertheless, we ought not to be tied tamely to the past. How about "innoversive fiction"? I like the "metamusical" myself. "Excremental" belongs to Joyce. "Minnovative" describes a movement whose small moment has come and gone. "Exploramental" makes me think of "floribunda," though I do fancy "postcynical" and could easily find a use for "metafutile." Remember when all we had to worry about was the Yellow Press, Blue Movies, and Black Humor?

I could see a plume of gray smoke when I looked back toward my imagined pursuers; my legs grew longer through every lope (I had experimented, I had made my exclamation point, and my lesson was now being taught), and I did not begin to gasp for breath and feel my blood beating hard in my head until I had run right out of my neighborhood and saw a strange little shop, and strange houses of one story, strange streets lined with shallow ditches, lots of transplanted Christmas trees, a strange black boat-tailed bird, strange absence of lamps, and felt I had found a country where every noun began with "strange" and "and" was its only connective. . . . My boom had blown me farther than the pieces of its pipe . . . to a strange—yes . . . to a strange strange lampless land.

Invisible Cities

Italo Calvino's *Invisible Cities* is one of the purer works of the imagination. It is prose elevated to poetry without the least sign of strain. Nevertheless, it has its subjects: memory, desire, the imagination that makes art, and the elusive nature of the mind. In addition, it is a profound study of the character of the city.

Invisible Cities is also a bookended book. It borrows the shape of its content from *The Travels of Marco Polo* and the material of its structure from Dante's *Inferno*. The first is a work which happenstance brought into being; the second, with its guided descent through a series of spooling circles, is one which art, cunning, and revenge composed. Both are works of travel, both mention marvels, both were written by soldiers—contemporaries—long absent from their native cities, both stand at the beginning and ending of an era.

Marco Polo, in the company of his uncle and his father, traders who had been to the East once before, reached the country of Kublai Khan, and his court in Peking, in 1275. Polo became a favorite of the khan, who loved to listen to his remarkable tales and employed him on business trips in central and western China. Polo is even said, by his own testimony, to have ruled the city of Yangchow for three years. In 1292, after seventeen years in China and a journey home which took an additional three, he returned to his native city. His arrival was poorly timed. Venice was momentarily at war with Genoa, and Polo, who offered his services to the navy, was captured and imprisoned for a year in the enemy's city. While thus confined, he dictated his book, a history of his travels, as well as a compilation of hearsay about the East, to one Rustichello, a fellow prisoner.

Why did he entrust the setting down of his book to another? May we suppose that Polo, who came from a well-to-do family, could write Latin, the language of the scholar, but never spoke it; that he spoke Chinese, and, of course, Italian, the popular speech of his people, but never wrote it? Perhaps he wished to reach a wider audience and chose a vernacular, as Dante did, but had at his disposal during the time of his confinement only a friend who wrote a French as full of Italian as an éclair with cream.

In any case, his history is a work shaped by the mouth and meant for the ear, just as *Invisible Cities* is, and it had to be assembled and arranged from recollections. It was doubtless spoken to "pass the time," to enlarge the prisoner's sequestered world and amuse his companions. Like the stories of *The Decameron,* of *The Canterbury Tales* and *A Thousand and One Nights,* the recital of these cities is meant to amuse; they are designed to educate; above all, they carry their auditors out of reach of death, out of sight of their confinement, and drive ennui away like a cur from a broom. It is little wonder, then, that Calvino's book begins with a section titled "Cities and Memory." Polo spoke of astonishing things indeed, and was possibly as truthful as he could be when he told of the existence of paper money, of asbestos, of coal, of spices of all kinds, and particularly when he described the amazing cities of the East. Chapter after chapter of his book simply depicts the character of this city, this province, or that. Surely his memory was spurred and directed by the questions of his listeners, just as the khan interrogates Polo in Calvino's account.

It was a time when cities behaved like nations and went to war with a frequency and ferocity which only the Peloponnesian War may have rivaled. Dante, traveling too, asks for aid—"Help me now, o memory that set down what I saw"—as he takes the steep and savage path to stand before the Gates of Hell: THROUGH ME THE WAY INTO THE SUFFERING CITY, THROUGH ME THE WAY TO THE ETERNAL PAIN. Florence for Dante. Venice for Polo. And Hell for us all—the invisible city.

The Travels of Marco Polo remained one of the principal sources of our knowledge of the East for centuries. The edition which should interest us most, perhaps, is the one in the Bibliothèque Nationale (Codex 2810). It dates from the fifteenth century and contains twenty-five colored illustrations—illustrations by an artist who had never been east of the Danube, of course. This pictorial edition was reprinted by Calvino's publisher, Einaudi, during the 1950s. My own Englished version dates from 1958. There can be little doubt that Calvino consulted the aforementioned Italian edition when he was composing *Invisible Cities* in 1971. It may, in fact, have inspired him (as the Visconti pack of tarot cards did when he wrote *The Castle of Crossed Destinies*), although the small doubt one is duty-bound to entertain is decisive. Still, the illustration one encounters when the book breaks open at one of its central sewings is of "the noble and magnificent city of Kin-sai," even if its pinnacles and flags, its tin, slate, and tile roofs, its dark dormers, the water which rushes through its streets, the bridges which loop over them, depict a kind of Venice, a Venice done in Tuscan tones, a Venice where the water streams between the buildings like windblown hair.

Marco Polo's cities were certainly invisible, as any remembered city, any sought-after city, any city rendered in words will be. Even at this moment, words are violating our vision; vision is vitiating our thought. The reduction of a concept to a single instance, the replacement of an individual by some generalizing name: this is an agon as old as philosophy itself. If we were watching a native dance in New Guinea, what we said in our surprise at the appearance of a mud man, if it went beyond directions like "Look!," would interfere fatally with our perception, just as our response to the mock attack of a camel driver disgruntled by the size of his tip, if it consisted of a moral lecture, might veil his amused but businesslike eyes; and what our reporter's pencil is inclined to write about the start of the dogsled race from Anchorage to Nome depends as much on presuppositions as the contest does on snow, for the truth here is simple and painful: the words which appear to reach out and envelop that clay creature, camel driver, or team of dogs have a greater inheritance from reality than do the mud men, camels, or sled dogs innocently enjoying custom or the laws of physics. The most ordinary words, as we are aware, are more general, more repeatable, more far-reaching in every area of implication, in their harness undeterminably stronger than our momentary perception of sixteen happy animals who perhaps believe they are out for an afternoon run. Think of the word *polis*—"city"—itself: a word which will be young still when every other city is a midden or in unsieved dust. It is the wretchedness of this truth (wretched because it is the dogs and their driver most of us admire; it is the mud man who frightens or amuses us, not a newspaper account; it is an ice-cream cone, not the words "ice cream," we want to put in our mouths), it is the injustice of any one word's overweening reality, which has made this truth so invisible.

What could Marco Polo's bedazzled readers do, as they followed his description of the noble and magnificent city of Kinsai, but think of Western towers and stone cornices and piered bridges, of Western water, when they visualized the city his words brought to life? All the cities he told about seemed exotic, magical, splendid beyond belief, cities of longing, but of their—the readers'—longing, and therefore clothed in the colors of the readers' lives. The difficulty is the same for us today when we read of the cities of desire depicted by Calvino's Polo for the khan: of Despina, for instance, the city which looks like a steamship when approached on camelback and we are weary of being swaysick on the sand; then like a camel when seen from the sea and we are anxious for the steadiness of the earth. We might imagine still another which sails its innumerable terraces into the sea like a ship. Both Kin-sai and Despina provide us with examples of the sorry impossibility of "seeing" through words, let alone "seeing" with them, although Calvino, Polo, we, and the Great Khan try.

Imprisoned by either walls or words, it is all the more important to try: to dream beyond the bricks; beyond the outer courtyard with its watchtowers, guards, guns; beyond the words which screen us from the world, beyond our own aims, fears, normally trivial aches and pains, which we nevertheless enlarge and objectify as bruises in hillsides, as knocks in walls, as cuts through mountains, as the leveling of plains. It is necessary to leave our cell and see the city—see the city in the cell, as the painter of legend perceives some stirring shape in spit or an errant puddle—to leave for a city whose walls rise around us everywhere the same, faceless as concrete and equally cold, or as difficult to dent as glass may be and as remorseless, as resistant to experience as plastic; such surfaces refuse the past, reject the scratches which calendared by days the ten years Gesualdo lay in rags, cast in a corner for climbing a vine to glimpse a bathing lady; these will not be found here, nor the small crack we may imagine is a river, nor the wallpaper whose patterns make a map, or patches of plaster damp like sweat in the pit of an arm; the mind cannot throw itself or any image against such pitiless sameness. Avoid such cities, such cells: all places where the light falls evenly as rain on day and night alike.

Cities can be cleansed even of themselves when they do not understand the true nature of their inhabitants, as was the case with one of Calvino's "Hidden Cities," Theodora, which cleared its skies of condors only to observe the increase of serpents, and whose victory over the spiders gave the flies free reign, while the extermination of the termites granted a kingdom to the woodworm. When, at last, the rats and roaches and gnats and flies, the fruit flies and mosquitos and every sort of vermin—all growing, flying, and creeping things—had been swept from the city, a city whose dream it seems to have been to be a hospital for the healthy, then

> *the other fauna* [came] *back to the light from the library's base-ments where the incunabula were kept; they were leaping from the capitals and drainpipes, perching at the sleeper's bedside. Sphinxes, griffons, chimeras, dragons, hircocervi, harpies, hydras, unicorns, basilisks* [resumed] *possession of their city.* *

In one of my imaginary cities, after a long period of misrule by birds, phonographs, and people, paintings left their frames and draped different landscapes over the baseball diamonds, Sabine ladies lolled about the shady streets, alert for adventure, and all the tinted animals roamed free. Their leader said simply: when the city reckoned its inhabitants, it neglected the antique pots, the rugs which had emigrated years before from Isfahan, the Chippendales, the Ensors, the Bonheurs, the stone idols, discontented lamps.

Marco Polo's actual prison companion, one Rustichello of Pisa, is, in Calvino's recasting, the Great Khan himself, confined to his kingdom, now grown so large it feels swollen and gangrenous, so distant in its borders that its edges can't be touched, vaporous and unreal except in the sober clear recitals of his friend and sometime ambassador the Venetian adventurer, who brings him news—news not of places, not of Westport or the Bronx, of college towns or ghettos, but of "Hidden Cities," "Cities of the Dead," "Continuous Cities," "Thin Cities," of "Cities and Signs": in short, of systems, meshes, interlocks, of webs. There is, for instance, the city of Zaira, which is not made of its bastions and arcades and steps but, like a burned-over forest, consists instead

> *of relationships between the measurements of its space and the events of its past: the height of a lamppost and the distance*

---

*All quotations from Calvino's *Invisible Cities* are from the translation of William Weaver (New York: Harvest Books, 1986).

from the ground of a hanged usurper's swaying feet; the line strung from the lamppost to the railing opposite and the festoons that decorate the course of the queen's nuptial procession; the height of that railing and the leap of the adulterer who climbed over it at dawn.

If the khan has been captured by his own conquests and is now no freer in the middle of his immensities than a rowboat on the ocean, or as we are, jetting along at 30,000 feet, Rustichello has been made a monarch by means of metaphor, because it is indeed to a king in this book that Polo speaks, to a different kind of fellow prisoner; and it is through the king's eyes that a design is discerned in the fierce smolder and aimless fire of his tales. A mind is made by the mind's eyes.

Scheherazade, staving off death with her stories, must borrow or invent, because she never leaves her husband's side; we may wonder, as we listen to Marco Polo tell the khan of the cities he has seen, whether he has ever really left his hometown or has simply turned round and round many times in one place, or unfolded from one bud an astonishing plenitude of petals, transforming a simple fountain by resemblance into a robust pot of blooming chives.

Fifty-five cities compose—invisibly, concurrently, continuously—Italo Calvino's epitomic city. Yes, it turns out to be the Venice we know so well, perhaps through a sober daily life there, or a few ecstatic visits, certainly from repeated readings and innumerable fantasies. Nevertheless, it is that same Venice which Marco Polo himself confesses he cannot imagine existing, even after Kublai Khan points out to him, with a negligent gesture which signifies some dearer purpose, the palaces whose marble steps lie immersed in water, the balconies which overhang the canals, the city's shimmering domes and silent campaniles. Venice is thus one miracle made of many, a contraction of the fabulous the way fingers form a fist, for it has preserved the evanescent marvels met with in Marco Polo's travels like fossils in its own stones and has flung over its fluid causeways such surprises as only lonely caravans encounter; yet it is also a Venice which has become plural, dispersed, ephemeral again, because it represents far more cities than those, real or imaginary, mentioned in Calvino's elegant and ruthlessly patterned text. It is not simply a symbol standing for Heidelberg, Frankfurt, Chicago, or New York, where one might actually have set foot; or those places which have perished like Babylon beneath the weight of years; or those that exist like misery before the onset of its cause, as improbable as birdsong whistled underwater—that is, those cities not yet found or even founded or fully realized—such as survive in fancy like Atlantis or my imagined city of Yclept (with its footfall-formed steps, its undimmable flowers, its playing fields in the shape of colorful cotton yarns, its not yet built barns for the storage of leftover letters like the letter *B*, where there will be gay blades in solemn scabbards, bees' knees spread out to dry on trays, bales of bated breath) or, for that matter, the way those ubiquitous utopias persist, like flocks of wishes with one wing, they are so incessantly and inadequately dreamt.

Venice cannot be said to serve simply as a sign, then, or an exemplification, for it has also become the city inside every city, the city beneath every city, the city that contains the cities that *are,* including the ones which barely subsist on the maps, their location indicated only by the dimmest of pink dots—specks which could, like a red mite, imperceptibly shift—as well as those cities which cannot be blotted out the way the ports of the Phoenicians were: I mean the camps of catastrophe, cities of sewers and open wounds and mass graves and the still-shitting dead, cities bombed into existence like Beirut or Sarajevo; cities like Cairo, scalded by their atmosphere, whose admired autumnal sunsets are caused by clouds of foetid gas; cities where growths of garbage define the parks, and every alley is intestinal; the cities we can only forget, it seems, by repeating them like a gunshot, by reproducing . . . reinvesting, rebuilding, reinhabiting . . . by reenacting their several and similar hells, not smoothly and professionally, but stupidly and clumsily, as if they were scenes in a high school play.

Calvino's cities spiral toward us as if unrolled by Polo before the eyes of his host. There are nine panels, each introduced to us by a brief snatch of conversation between the traveler and the king, and each concluded by the completion of that conversation, so that these passages, italicized in the text, form wholes of their own—nine of them as we descend, as Dante did, into the IN . . . into, as Sartre said, the Hell that is other people. The first group, as well as the last, contains ten accounts of fabulous cities, while each of the middle seven sets forth five. The image they form is that of a spool. If we add to the list of cities described the nine conversations which surround or variously intrude upon them, we arrive at a total of sixty-four sections, not accidentally the sum of the squares, eight on each edge, which make up the board for chess, a game beloved by the khan. It is also, of course, the grid of every great city. Each is built, like Calvino's book, upon an invisible graph. The chessboard is only incidentally a set of paths, for these paths are principally corridors of power, influence, force.

"Leaving there," the recital of the cities begins, begins with departure, a departure from an unnamed place, a city more invisible than any of the others; *"leaving there,"* the logarithm of the cities begins, because the way Polo's descriptions are unwound resembles a spiral, the spool of fate, the pattern sidles; *"leaving there and proceeding for three days toward the east,"* we reach the first of the memory cities, Diomira, a name which means "to look through with wonder." The words *"leaving there and proceeding"* inform readers that they have entered an account which has been going on who knows how long? *"Leaving there and proceeding for three days toward the east, you reach Diomira, a city with sixty silver domes, bronze statues of all the gods, streets paved with lead, a crystal theater, a golden cock that crows each morning on a tower."* As many domes as an hour has numbers. A city which is careful to

include all the ages: gold cock, silver domes, bronze statues, lead streets, a crystal theater. If you happen to arrive during the ninth month, *"when the days are growing shorter and the multicolored lamps are lighted all at once at the doors of the food stalls and from a terrace a woman's voice cries ooh!"* you will experience the kinds of connections the city always offers: those rational (as dusk comes on, so do the lamps) and random (a woman's voice cries ooh!). A cat has startled her; a caress has moved her; she has seen with appreciation the multicolored lights enliven the doorways. *"But the special quality of this city for the man who arrives there on a September evening . . . is that he feels envy"* for those who believe they are experiencing a kind of déjà vu, another evening like this one that's in front of us, twilit, lamps just now coloring the open stalls, ooh! . . . envy because they *"think they were happy that time."*

What can this envy mean? in our initial city, a city we associate with memory? Shouldn't we envy those who still believe that once, when young, they were happy, because they will have colored the past with sweet lights and made a lost ooh! seem romantic? The lead streets run back beyond the bronze gods, statued beneath those silver domes, to let us remember that, so long ago, the cock who greeted the dawn was golden, and golden was his crow. The man who, *leaving there,* arrives here knows otherwise.

The man who arrives in Diomira on a September evening is, of course, the khan, first of all, who is following Marco Polo's words as if on a camel; and then each of us, hearing the emperor hear his Venetian. The second city is a city of memory too. Isidora, or "gift of Isis," is built like Calvino's book is built; that is, of *"spiral staircases encrusted with spiral seashells, where perfect telescopes and violins are made, where the foreigner hesitating between two women always encounters a third, where cockfights degenerate into bloody brawls among the bettors."* The visitor arrives, weary of the wilderness where he has dreamt of a city he would like to enter. Yet the visitor cannot dream of a city he has not known, only of those he knew as a young man, and these are the cities he desires. So Isidora is a city he dreams too late, since *"he arrives at Isidora in his old age. In the square there is the wall where the old men sit and watch the young go by; he is seated in a row with them. Desires are already memories."*

The book of Marco Polo's actual travels told of marvels and mysteries. Its many sections were long on useful learning but rather short on moral lessons. Here, however, we have fables Aesop might have managed, not by imagining animals but by imagining cities. In Diomira we learn why we love the "good old days." In Isidora we are told that the future we desire is none other than our nostalgic longings. In Dorothea ("gift of God"), the town to which we come next, we discover that there are many paths through life, many cities in every city, many manners of description, because Dorothea can be understood (as *Invisible Cities* must be) in terms of its formal structure—four green canals divide the city into nine quarters, *"each with three hundred houses and seven hundred chimneys,"* each with its own monopoly, for instance, on *"bergamot, sturgeon roe, astrolabes, or amethysts,"* and each with its rigorous kinship laws—or, alternatively, through metonymy, by inferring the nature of the whole from a perception of its parts: women with fine teeth and a direct gaze, fluttering banners, turning wheels . . . in short, from particular details. Polo chooses both these methods when he has his "conversations" with the khan, because it will be some time before he learns to speak the khan's tongue.

From the foot of the Great Khan's throne, a majolica pavement extended. Marco Polo, mute informant, spread out on it the samples of the wares he had brought back from his journeys to the ends of the empire: a helmet, a seashell, a coconut, a fan. Arranging the objects in a certain order on the black and white tiles, and occasionally shifting them with studied moves, the ambassador tried to depict for the monarch's eyes the vicissi-

tudes of his travels, the condition of the empire, the preroga-
tives of the distant provincial seats.

From our own journeys (since each of us is Polo to another's khan), we may return with other wares, but that won't matter, for what will render them significant will be their placement on the pavement, the flights of influence they suggest, the orders they elicit from the eye, as I recently returned from a trip with the image of a painted board imprisoned on a roll of film in my valise: the painted board which served as a shutter, a metal drainpipe which fell down a yellow wall like a black stripe, a shaded lamp with a netted globe held out from that wall by a rod, a vase of dried flowers in a niche the shutter shielded when it was closed, while below this company sat an altogether Austrian stack of firewood, the log ends like stones in a country wall. I returned, not with these images alone, but with the wonder of their relationships.

What we frequently fail to understand is that a city is not an assemblage of buildings streaked by highways and streets; it is a subtle pattern of powers, like the board. Kublai Khan realizes that if he could understand the rules which direct and facilitate the movements of these objects, ignoring their specific shapes and unique natures, he would hold like a scepter in his hand the essentials of his empire and govern accordingly; so he replaces the objects Polo has been maneuvering about on the majolica pavement with pieces from his chess set, their ivory as slick as a kid's slide, and then he assigns to these, in a purely algebraic fashion, meanings appropriate to the moment: let x equal a seashell or a fan, perhaps; let the knight be, for now, an equestrian statue superbly stony in the square it stands on, for the pieces are as variable as a, b, and c; and let us permit the queen to be a lady looking down behind a fan from her balcony at a fountain, possibly at a topiaried tree into whose trunk she is quickly transmuted, into the pulp of its fruit, into a palmful of seeds.

The wise khan might imagine, then, a city made solely of movements, like some of the cities of desire which Marco Polo describes, a city composed entirely of staircases and paths, streets and thoroughfares and boulevards and alleys, elevators and playgrounds, sidewalks and tram lines and drawer slides and subways and bus stops and zippers and toilet chains and construction cranes. It is a city in which every block is a kind of smoky port.

In this scenario, young Frank Presto (or whomever we choose) is no longer the promising young lawyer, young husband and father, baseball fan, wearer of a pair of black and tan trousers, the young flutter in the king's eye he might be elsewhere—not in this city. In this city he is simply a commuter; he leans against doorjambs; he casters across his office from desk to window, from secretary to Xerox machine. His age is irrelevant. Age is an avenue of the demographic city. His promises rust in the wreckage that is the city of broken hopes. At this moment, Frank is only an element of circulation, a drop of blood in the body of the city whose skin we have just lifted like a shirt. And the khan plays game after game of city/chess like this, searching for secrets in the interlocking lines, in these moderate abstractions—in a white rook, black queen—through which he believes divergent avenues, or a city's radial center, might be seen.

For such a city, the khan could have calculated to a nit's pick the fall of bodies from high windows, the hubbub of behinds behind the copier, and, on their way from plate to mouth, the evasive loops of forks entangled in spaghetti. Trajectories, blinks, droplets of flu sneeze, the jitter of the pinball, brain scans, congregations of handshakes, goodbye waves, the flight of Time where the clock's hands hide its face: he might imagine all of these. Let's say he does. *At times he thought he was on the verge of discovering a coherent, harmonious system underlying the infinite deformities and discords, but no model could stand up to the comparison with the game of chess.* So the king presses on. He no longer interprets the pieces, lets them shadow forth a figure kneeling beside the fountain; he simply makes the proper moves, ponders the rules, admires the purity of each play's endless designs, the menace inherent in their innocent configurations.

There are, of course, "Thin Cities"—here, cities which grow like galls on the trunk of a river, which fill in a valley like morning mist, which lean against the irregular side of a mountain—and none of these "cities" can be said to be standing on a grid. But in the first place, the grid goes about with us like a compass on the bridge. Rays rush out of our eyes and reach for the horizon, and if we completely lose our place, as Dante did in that dark wood, if we become disoriented as though we had been spun around, then north will seem straight ahead, south will lie behind us like history, and west and east will empty out on either hand. The jumbled streets of old trading quarters, casbahs, and ghettos, those crowds of houses so dense that the streets become pushed inside: these tangles were always marks of a village or possibly a town, but never a city; and we visit them in cities the way we visit a museum, to contemplate the past, to read our real age, to see again in the barrio's local bustle its tight life, the small seed which has grown beyond all community like a pumpkin in a pea patch and is held together now, not by eyesight and kettle smell, but by invisible wires and inaudible messages, voices on errands, words relayed like lightning, letters which seem to leap up at once in many places like armed men from the dragon's teeth. And as the village grows into a city, the grid appears like the beard on a youth, and lengthens with it toward those weakening knees.

The game proceeds, yet a reckoning arrives. As Kublai Khan stares at a square just vacated by a fleeing king, he sees that these games of chess come literally to nothing (a weedy plant commands more harmony), and in that moment Khan and his game fall from Plato's orbit, because beneath the pieces the board is bare, the stones of all his cities' buildings dissolve in the lines which bound them, and these run pointlessly—invisibly—off into space. But Marco Polo counsels the king to part the pavement. On that slick ivory surface, on the fired clay, in that open square of wood which is at once a piece of playing field and a square of the city, what can one further see? the footprint of a pavement? perhaps a taut and angry fiber? the glaze of a dreaming eye? logs lazily adrift in a slow-moving river? a woman peering from an upstairs window? Every object is itself a cell which would contain us, yet every end has its outlet as well; and as we pass through a cave's yawn to the hollow of a hollow tree, from that hollow to an open door or window, we cross one threshold to achieve yet another, even more wondrous, wider world.

When the concept of the city, with its concrete streets and concrete towers, has been replaced by that of the game, with its architectural grid and gun range, its system of implicit threats, its irregular spheres of influence; and when that game, furthermore, has been, in its interest, exhausted; then the materials of the contest, its dinky tools, the ivory itself, its fingered skin, the shape of the cross on the king's crown, are entreated for results. A pillar becomes a tree, a tree a totem. The grid gives way, the board parts like the Red Sea, and the land it lay on reappears, as warm as a baby's blanket. We are not simply back with youthful—partly promising—Frank Presto again. We have crawled up his nose. We have entered his ear. We inhabit his lust. We are the bees who buzz in his brain.

Let me recapitulate our progress. It is a pattern to be found in all the arts. We begin our pursuit of the city by examining the particular, the things that cities are made of—squares, streets, buildings, bridges, people, parks—allowing the least leaf to be engraved upon our faces as though it has been long pressed there. We endeavor to give to the shallowest saucer great depth, but we do so through the intensity of our attention, by dwelling on the small bob of its basin, the thin rule of gold around its rim, the cup which will squat there when the tea is finally ready. We collect facts. We describe things as we believe they really are. Not only our streets, but our lanes, our halls and closets, are named in this realm of reference, this freeway of denotation. The procedure will give us one sort of city: a city of idle odors and random sounds, a city of character, of what is popularly called "place." Our city will have a personality, for we shall have rendered the gestures of its spirit, the way in which it resembles a young girl, a lecherous uncle, an old maid. Our city will be a richly human body made of countless bones. Many a corner will strike us like an elbow. Many a path will wear like a hole through our shoe. Many a brick will stiffen at our touch. The light will fall irregularly throughout the city, palely in this place, brightly in another, after the manner of our understanding.

Not content with this, we soon seek—in the playing fountain, the shaded courtyard, the kneeling man, the fan, in the look that leaps like a tree through the stone pavement—a pattern of powers, of influence and agitation; and like the Great Khan we withdraw toward the game, although it is still people we see moving about like pawns, and not yet pawns we see moving about like people. This method will give us still another sort of city, a city in which system is beginning to be born, in which terms are beginning to be replaced by relations, in which roles are beginning to define their representatives, and not the reverse.

As we see, the mathematically minded monarch scarcely creates one state of thought than he calculates another—pressing on, pushing his luck—so that soon he is reaching the particular only through the Idea, and what was earlier a bit of evidence for a generalization is now only an instance of one, just as an apple is an instance of the Idea "apple," the Idea "one." The signifier has swallowed the signified, although you may still observe it as a swell in the stomach, like a bulge beneath the bedclothes of a bereaved and sleeping body.

The khan comes at last to mathematics, to the ideal, to the city as a series of abstract interactions, to complete, unabashed *invisibility;* although we must recognize, as Calvino does, that there are invisibilities of at least two distinct kinds. The first is what is before us at the moment, in our mathematical mood, an unvarnished invisibility, an invisibility, in short, which does not hide itself, which comes clean, as it were, and which is, in that sense, not invisible at all. And then there is the second sort, which is like the proverbial needle, the purloined letter, or the figure in the carpet, palpable, present, but unnoticed, like a floating ghetto, an invisible visibility, hidden from us like a flaw in our character, embraced without realization or recognition. Better a visible invisibility, Aristotle is sometimes thought to have said.

But mathematics is only a game—don't we hear that often offered as an excuse for collective ignorance? Where is the city now, at this level of quiet unstreeted Idea? However, with Marco Polo as our guide, what help do we and the Great Khan receive? We return to the particular, it's true; we shall enter the door instead of merely passing through it—doors of every design desire us. We are about to bruise our eyes upon the hard ebony inserts of the game board; nevertheless, the game board is not that simple city square we began with, that regimental crisscrossing like the streets of Manhattan; it is but a small square of ruled wood, lined cloth, blind as a boarded window, yet full of look. What has really happened to us?

We have begun to listen to the sound of our own words, not merely to their meanings; we have begun to circle their shapes like a walk around a town; we have turned to the representatives of thought for sustenance, not to the thoughts themselves, or to the things those thoughts were presumably about; for just as trees are bark and leaves and light, and the forest is trees and leaflight too, so the city is made of millions of small forms and fine textures, of the very near and the quite far, and like the wilderness may have its own mountains, depending on place and point of view, tiredness and timing.

A city is a wall for words, misunderstood or simply imitated in spray paint; but it is a house for houses too, and so should have its doors and sudden windows, its stairs and stories, its halls and dining rooms and dens. We have explored our chosen city through the dreams of its streets and derelict alleys, its suspension bridges and bridle paths, the way Polo has in describing his cities to the king. Now we remain with the mute sign itself. The map of the city is the city. Billboards and building declarations are the city; every sort of symbol—the Arch, the Eiffel Tower, the Rialto or the Doges' Palace, the Canalettos—is the city the way the Capitol and our heroes Washington and Lincoln organize the aspirations of the nation. Our romance with the dome, that basin of the spirit, passionately continues, despite occasional detours for an adultery.

Shortly new words will begin to be heard in the sounds which old words make, as for instance in "swoon," which I understand, now that I speak it clearly and listen with a pure ear, is not the languid faint I formerly feared, but the casual and quiet glide path of a paper airplane.

> *The quantity of things that could be read in a little piece of smooth and empty wood overwhelmed Kublai; Polo was already talking about ebony forests, about rafts laden with logs that come down the rivers, of docks, of women at the windows.*

When we live in only one city, in only one kind of city, in an invisible city, we abstract—we cut apart—ourselves; and sometimes our cities are like abattoirs, fish markets, and butcher shops where our gesticulating corpses hang from hooks and our hearts crawl about like crabs in a basket.

I recall of Cairo the little shelters I saw on rooftops; people perched like pigeons on the cooling towers; the narrow warped boards which bridged the buildings, rocking even with a child's weight; the flapping lines of clothes strung between malfunctioning antennas to be wind-washed; the buckets in which water was kept; the small smokes from cooking fires, as acrid as an outcry, otherwise lost in the larger dusts from the desert and the exhaust haze from the cars. Not a city, surely, inside a city, but places for living, if you could call them such, which were not places ever intended for that: beneath the arches of the ancient aqueduct, on stairwells, within abandoned crates and cartons, derelict cars, in the barren concrete skeletons of unfinished buildings, in archeological excavations beside the pyramids—everywhere, spaces filled with people like water welling up from the ground.

In Manila I sat on a floor of broomed dirt, in a house surrounded by a sea of mud, and stared at the gray screen of an inoperable TV—for there was no electricity in the entire community—drinking tea from a cup so rough around the rim that one finger received a cut. Again in Manila, in vacant lots Marcos had had boarded up so the squatters would be hidden from the public and the highways, mothers, children lay on mattresses open to the sky—no fencing there to conceal them from the hotel windows—and received the frequent rains as if they were a blessing, twisting their clothes into ropes to wring the water out. As in Shanghai long ago, as in Hong Kong now, one can find river and seaways paved with boats, and upon the boats life, as indifferently abundant as mist, clinging to everything, moistening the sails and the polished railings.

Venice was, like Hong Kong, particularly a trading center, its buildings so fragile they seemed to be waiting to be taken down and sold, and such is Calvino's Esmeralda: a place of varying routes, of many noble and nefarious choices. It does indeed seem, with its paths and canals, its bridges and little alleyways and steps, its courtyards and churches, to be one vast area for movement and passage and travel. *"A map of Esmeralda should include, marked in different colored inks, all . . . routes, solid and liquid, evident and hidden."* The surveyor's task is made difficult by the swallows that follow and fly seditious flight plans. We have already visited this city, however, where, as you may recall, we found Frank Presto, somewhat besmitten, unrolling with difficulty, in the cramped and scarcely concealed corner behind his duplicating machine, a silk stocking it will not do to snag. How coolly Doris, for that is her present name, reclines within her secretarial dreams, for she is in motion, though reclining, like her city, and intends to rename herself Evita when the right time comes.

Phyllis, the city which follows Esmeralda in the text, is also like Venice, with surprises for the eye everywhere. But habit deadens our appreciation, and soon the city becomes imperceptible: *"the city fades before your eyes, the rose windows are expunged, the statues on the corbels, the domes,"* like torches, turn to smoke.

Not only are there cities which belong to the past, and are now invisible for that reason; but there are cities of the present whose existence is quite evident to any traveler with eyes alert and curious, but which are hidden to the inhabitants, who no longer need to experience their postboxes, their scented trees, in order to allow their dogs to piss against them on their twice-daily walks. A neighborhood may be missed entirely by a preoccupied visitor. I certainly do not notice now the soles of my feet, my weight, my restless or resentful ears, opposing opinions. Frank Presto has not observed the dust which has already gathered at the back of his new machine, much of which has been swept off by the milling movements of a sleeve. Great stretches of so many cities in our country are indistinguishable, and even when we peer at them (while searching for a fast-food joint, for instance), they are simply stretches, highways which have thrown out little asphalt lots along them like oozes of rust on a pipe. Amid so much tastelessness, it takes a pretty tasteless gesture to create a locale.

But when are cities invisible because they have no identity, and when is it because of our indifference, our bemused eye? We tolerate incongruities as we tolerate religions. Not far from one of the largest hotels in Anchorage a pleasant little hovel nestles. Behind it one may see a sign advertising car parts. It has a front yard—odd enough for the business district—where a snowman leans wearily west. Between the melting man and the frozen house, with its mandatory evergreen, stand the bony poles of a huge teepee. Our cities are like seas, and it is not uncommon to see one building seize and swallow another like a shark. Several cities come together in this corner of Anchorage, exposing their bones like elbows out of sleeves, nudging one another in the same space. Cities of custom and history and commerce and comfort come together like a crash in the street. But we are used to crashes in the street, just as we are used to collisions beyond the curbs.

All future cities are invisible as a matter of course, including the Chicago which my train has not yet entered; or they have no substance, like the suburb which will be appended to Des Moines, and not even seen then by the people who live in Moline. In addition, there are dreamtowns, Disneylands, various Parises of pleasure. Venice is easily each of these.

Yes, says the vapid traveloguer, Venice is a magical city, a city whose light is famous, whose doges were powerful, whose churches and plazas and monuments and palaces and museums are splendid, whose riches in paintings, tapestries, statuary, armor, glass, and other fine things are immeasurable. Oh, men were men then. It is a city that has captured the imagination of people of all times and places, provided they are actually, ostensibly, or invisibly German. Yet the canals of Venice stink of garbage; the city is old and dirty and sinking into its own swill. There is pigeon shit on the pigeon shit; there is the smell of mold and rot and sour wine everywhere; the plumbing is antiquated, although the city is nothing but plumbing; slime coats boat steps; the climate is conducive to fevers; rats are so prevalent they have made the city famous as a rest home and haven for cats. Venice has known power, wealth, greatness, shame. Now it is a poorly maintained museum and tourist trap. People carry pieces of Venice away in their valises: bits of cornice, slivers of Murano glass, plates of great and complex grace, as radial as some cities. It exists in the past even now, for there are no motorcars in the city;

but the present is present, nevertheless, in the noise of the vaporetti, in the din of the transistors, in the magazines from Milan and the pornographic paperbacks.

There is so much water in Venice that the city doubles itself constantly. The Ca' d'Oro glistens on the surface of the Grand Canal; orange rind clings to its mirrored filigree. Cities are sometimes called twins because they reflect each other across a river, like Minneapolis and St. Paul, and there are a number of twins among Calvino's creations. In Eudoxia, for instance, we can find a carpet which contains a complete map of the city, or perhaps the city is an image of the carpet, as the carpet may, in turn, map the sky. To illuminate the landing of a stairway, panels of stained glass foresee the development of the city. Which are the true forms and which the false? We can ask this question even when we believe we know which is the solid city and which the reflection.

Two boys of my invention are leaning over the railing of a bridge, staring down, hoping for the sight of a condom among the effluvia, or a useful box, a thrilling corpse. What floats by, scarcely noticed, is the image of the heartbreak of one lad, the eventual bankruptcy of the other.

In Calvino's Eusapia the populace has built catacombs which are a replica of the city, or have the dead built the city that stands aboveground like stones to mark their place? Ambiguities abound. Intentions are concealed. Is that canal my imaginary boys were staring at now flowing through the mirror in a Berlin palace? and is the innocent labyrinthal hedgerow which decorates the courtyard of the Hôtel Carnavalet really an incendiary plan for the restoration of the monarchy? Calvino's text gives birth to questions it does not raise. I wonder what the dead bury up there in Eusapia's broad day: grain? bulrushes perhaps? banks of cloud grass?

I live, myself, in a city of defeated expectations, a city of inept lies. One arrives at the train station in order to book a room for the night (there are no trains); lest I adapt myself to this new arrangement, another station will sell me chandeliers or office equipment. When will shopping centers become warehouses if warehouses are already galleries, ateliers, or rifle museums? Theaters quietly unseat themselves and perform their plays outdoors. One may dine rather well in a rehabilitated church (astonishing phrase!), at a table overlooking the no longer sanctified altar, where they keep the register of reservations, and return home to one's apartment in the recycled synagogue. So what if the window represents, in its painted glass, the eye of God?

Schools may be anything but schools: an old folks' home, an orphanage, an antiques bazaar, a detention center. Here, a grocery store sells art supplies; there, a gas station pumps meat and milk. Firehouses are especially vulnerable. This one is a raisin-cookie company. That one sells quilts. Abandoned power stations put on a beguiling puppy face and hope their shape will suggest something. One year a section of the city is a slum, the next year it is chic and saved. Soon, in such deceptive cities, mailboxes will swallow the mailman's hand, trees will help schoolchildren cross the street safely, the red light will mean run, and no one will speak for fear of being taken seriously. As for myself, I await the day when Holly Bush Lane is a row of brothels and the tall glass towers of insurance and finance contain nothing but waxed cartons of lemonade and drifts of surplus grain.

But the falsehoods began when the first earth was moved. The train station was built to resemble the Siena city hall or a castle in the Alps, itself a fake so fulsome it implicates the mountain. Banks were reassuring Greek temples at first, or colonial mansions, before they became gift shops, while a few now specialize in Chinese cuisine, each dish exquisite like the lakefront in some cities, the menu extensive, the meal a hodgepodge. Homes were built back then (though now "back thens" have overcome us like crime) to resemble ships, as was the governor's house in Macao, funnier than most jokes; some lie becalmed in fields still, or, like some buildings in Venice, marooned in an oil slick. There are cities in which railings have been known to overleap streets and run wildly in search of a porthole, a whiff of salt air, a flying fish. Usually ruins are remaindered, but occasionally one will become a piece of art, like a broken window, shattered marriage, derelict fuel pump, or pierced façade. Not every building remarries readily. Dirigible hangars have their own climate; clouds form; it even rains; it is not possible to play golf in them at every time of day.

Calvino allows each kind of city to appear, to fill a place on the board with one of its five manifestations (rook, castle, bishop, king, queen), to enjoy its springlike "break of day." However, every such epiphany, every "showing forth," goes ahead according to rules which have been rigorously formulated and pitilessly enforced (rules which I understand but choose not in this place to disclose). Having briefly shown itself, each city disappears the way an image on a scroll winds gently out of sight, possibly to return, but not on this trip.

There are timeless cities, not because they seem eternal, but because everything about them is the same age, like the nose, ears, chin of a face. Canberra, for instance, is a stage set which springs to life when you open your curtain, but it was not there while you slept. Like Clayton, Missouri, it has no history; it is not yet a city. The elderly hide themselves, their yellowing valentines and their laces. Yet such places, like Clayton, Missouri, will set aside a few blocks to be historical, to be designated Old Town and fronted by a gate. Then the modestly middle-aged houses of Old Town will be systematically demolished so that expensive banal duplexes can be built on their semi-historic graves.

Did we speak of the Devil? Here is Zora, a city as memorable as a jingle. It is a honeycomb in which we can place those things we want to remember. It is a city of labeled jars, of canisters which contain rice and recollections. Zora is not a city memorable in itself (in itself, it is self-effacing, almost invisible), but it is made of memory lanes like an old melody. We might imagine, for instance, an extensive cemetery, and then remember our friends and acquaintances, their names and most significant deeds, by carving them on tombstones carefully selected to signify the essential nature of their being. Of course, if they lack an essential nature, the tombstones may resemble nothing except one another. However that turns out, is not the organization of the spaces in the celebrated memory theater of Giulio Camillo the same? Isn't it what we mean when we say that something— the way you slipped that folded fifty in your bodice—is engraved on our memory? or the time, as kids, we jumped our bicycles over the steps in front of the cathedral in Cologne? Surely it's better than saying that your name has been writ on water. Yes, certainly, Venice is such a theater, where Marco Polo stored the cities of the East like spices brought back aboard ship, and where every bridge in every city sees its own feet and curving belly; and we have but to look round the rounded corner of the Gritti Palace to encounter Polo's memory of Olinda, the city which developed in concentric circles like a tree, the old walls and quarters expanding as it grew so that its bark could continue to encompass it, and whose newer sections, increasingly thin where they begin, press out from the inskirts of a city whose center has, by now, reached and resembled the horizon.

If we weary of the name Venice and of that *V* through which the gondoliers paddle, carol, and collect their fees, Florence can satisfactorily replace it, because *Invisible Cities,* as I've said, is a book about still another book, Dante's *Inferno,* composed as nearby to *The Travels of Marco Polo* as Georgetown is to the Capitol. The nine sections of Calvino's text resemble the nine circles of Hell through which Virgil escorts Dante, although Marco Polo carries the khan with him largely by turns of the wheel of the word. There is a definite, not to say plummetous, descent from the first part, which opens with "Cities and Memory," to the final one, which begins with "Cities of the Dead," after which we fall more precipitously toward those cities which are said to be "hidden."

In Calvino, though, we meet cities on our journey, not Dante's miserable men:

> Below that point we found a painted people,
> who moved about with lagging steps, in circles,
> weeping, with features tired and defeated.
> And they were dressed in cloaks with cowls so low
> they fell before their eyes, of that same cut
> that's used to make the clothes for Cluny's monks.
> Outside, these cloaks were gilded and they dazzled;
> but inside they were all of lead, so heavy
> that Frederick's capes were straw compared to them.
> A tiring mantle for eternity!
> (*Inferno,* canto XXIII, ll. 58–67. I am quoting from Allen
> Mandelbaum's splendid translation: Berkeley: University of
> California Press, 1980, p. 198.)

The dead, like those in Dante's Hell, often live more fully in that death than when they were alive. Now, finally, they have a look in their eyes. Nor do we know what rough candidate for the pit is this moment slouching toward Bethlehem to set off a bomb.

In Calvino, as in any actual urbanity, Augustine's City of God and City of Satan share the same streets and avenues, interpenetrate equally every relation. As I've argued, a single city is at once a cemetery, a slaughterhouse, a lying-in hospital, and a bordello. I have no doubt that the fountain which breathes its broken hopes in that forlorn Córdoba courtyard purls merrily in a cloister in Seville. Frank Presto will present his new secretary not only with a new pair of stockings but with a garter belt in black net to match them, even hold them up, but their love is shadowed by its own remote ruins now; the kneeling figure we observed earlier— who might have been fishing a fan from a fountain—that figure may simply be waiting for the shutters of the surrounding apartments to open to allow in the cool night air and his lecherous eyes.

The technique of this magical and fabulous fiction concerns the recognition of the Real, which is its insistent subject. Calvino has described himself as having a geographical neurosis, and we might imagine that here he has allowed that neurosis to rule, if not ruin, him; but Calvino remains the realistic writer he was at the start of his career: an author of social protest, of political engagement. He recognizes now (if this book can be entered as evidence) that being Real does not mean being committed to the imitation of the commonplace, the promises of parties and politicians, the trite, the ordinary, the mercilessly clichéd—and all imitation is commonplace; it is itself a cliché. On the contrary, Reality does not consist of things, their collections, or their shallow denominations. Chicago is not the trumpet of its towers, which herald it only as we approach. Reality is not a set of simple situations, nor is it one shade of anything, one blue color or brown shirt. It is not even a single system of relations—invisible as they all are. The experience of the city exceeds our experience of Proust. A great city's life lies in the details, in the details as they fulfill a whole. Consider what a little grass does to a set of steps, and then multiply . . . multiply. . . . Consider what a crack of light does to the dungeon, and multiply for freedom and for sky. Consider the multiplication not only of niceties but of vulgarities as well: signs, poles, wires, trash, broken glass, peeling paint, rotting boards. And multiply . . . multiply. . . . A hand like a hot towel held against the head, outcries of every kind, more numerous than beans, shit from a million bowels. This book, *Invisible Cities,* mistaken as an instance of the wild and woolly, is respectable in its traditional intentions: it would tell the truth; it would point a moral, suggest a way.

Calvino brings each of his cities before us through mime, and by dancing, as poor Polo must do at first, since he does not know the Great Khan's language. He renders each of them by means of essential relations—possibly dwellings or thickets of dwellings of odd kinds—not simply, then, of those parts which will somehow allow themselves to stand for their whole, either routinely, as a piece of pie must, or even more routinely, as a statistical sample lies its way into everybody's confidence; but, rather, more metaphorically, poetically, if you like, so that one detail resonates with the presence of the rest like the last *l* in the toll of the chapel bell.

Isn't that what happens to the elements of a successful city: they satisfy our needs, allow our lusts, remind us of our past, inhabit our future, encourage our reveries? Hölderlin's house stands, as it should, on a stream lined with dreams. The feel for the meaning and quality of a door or a gate does not stop there, opening both out and in at the same time the way a lamp in a window excites an exchange of light. What is a text but a community of words? A poem, to be sure, may stand on a white hill all alone like a country church, but a fiction is all jostle and solicitation like a crowded marketplace.

> *The man who knows by heart how Zora is made, if he is unable to sleep at night, can imagine he is walking along the streets and he remembers the order by which the copper clock follows the barber's striped awning, then the fountain with the nine jets, the astronomer's glass tower, the melon vendor's kiosk, the statue of the hermit and the lion, the Turkish bath, the café at the corner, the alley that leads to the harbor.*

For this sort of writing, in William Weaver's unmatchable translation, "exquisite" is an inadequate adjective. Can't we believe that on many a Trieste night, James Joyce lay awake walking the Dublin streets, rereading the signs, resting his cane in a comfortable and familiar crack?

We have seen cities clothed in colored tiles, courtyards composed of images and ancient scripts and antique statuary, streets lined with streams, lined with inclining tables and dissipated awnings. There are neighborhoods where, in the shelter of the trees, the houses contrive to dream the American dream. A single building can sometimes overpower an entire city and, like the

Arch in St. Louis, become more than an emblem, more than a feat to be admired: a conscience to be obeyed.

It would be a serious error to imagine that each city portrayed in Calvino's urban bestiary is a part of a larger, unexperienced megalopolis the way Westwood, Chevy Chase, Society Hill, or Shaker Heights are parts, even metaphorically. They are not hairs or fingernails or skin. They constitute entire cities in themselves. Like the body's circulation system or the interaction of the glands, they are just not *complete,* for the complete city is not only a city of signs like Las Vegas, each sign signifying still another, no real referent anywhere—but a city without either edge or center, one of Calvino's "Continuous Cities," like Los Angeles, while, in addition, it is a concentrated, pointed city, one that sits like a cap of snow on a hill's head and melts its sewage on the fields and roads below, as well as each of the fifty-five towns the text takes us through, including those that disappeared ahead of history and before we reached the title page; governmental cities too, capitals with a capital *C,* and those which will be paraded by our absent or our sleeping eye as the text turns silently inside itself, thinking like a drill bit does, bringing more aspects to inner view . . . continuously, invisibly.

Fifty-five is not a final figure. *"The catalogue of forms is endless: until every shape has found its city, new cities will continue to be born."* Yet cities come to an end when they lose their boundaries, when neighborhoods, districts, regions flow together with the sameness of a flooding river, masses of indistinctly different men covering the country. Then we encounter cities in the shape of Kyoto-Osaka, cities without shape, cities without limits or centers.

Not the last city, but the last one in Calvino's text, is Berenice, the unjust city, a meat grinder. Yet, out of reach and between the cogs and blades, another Berenice exists, a just city, one which deserves its name—"bringer of victory." Here, hidden, the just recognize one another by their manner of speech, by their temperate habits, their unflamboyant though tasty cuisine (which includes squash blossoms and beans). Here, however, within the very virtues of the just and their secret city, lies the sense of their superiority like the celebrated canker in the rose. To realize that your righteousness deprives you of the pleasures and privileges the unjust enjoy drives you to despise justice and resent your own virtue. By means of this grim dialectic another unjust city, hidden beneath the hidden, begins to grow, a cancer called "just cause." The evil make the good see themselves as better than it's a good idea they should.

> From my words you will have reached the conclusion that the real Berenice is a temporal succession of different cities, alternately just and unjust. But what I wanted to warn you about is something else: all the future Berenices are already present in this instant, wrapped one within the other, confined, crammed, inextricable.

In the unjust city—our cultureless world—the just—the cultured—recognize one another as citizens of the same secret city, but their very isolation and the protections of superiority they must adopt to survive encourage a bitter hubris, which costs them the esteem they had fancied was their fitting reward.

The ultimate moral of our story comes, as it ought, on the last page, when the disappointed Kublai Khan complains: *"It is all useless, if the last landing place can only be the infernal city, and it is there that, in ever-narrowing circles, the current is drawing us."* And Polo replies:

> The inferno of the living is not something that will be; if there is one, it is what is already here, the inferno where we live every day, that we form by being together. There are two ways to escape suffering it. The first is easy for many: accept the inferno and become such a part of it that you can no longer see it. The second is risky and demands constant vigilance and apprehen-

sion: seek and learn to recognize who and what, in the midst of the inferno, are not inferno, then make them endure, give them space.

This is not, perhaps, a startling conclusion, but neither is the news that one must cultivate one's garden. They are, however, important conclusions, simply shaped but complex in their context, and even considerably true.

And now if certain listeners, readers, travelers, should complain that they have seen the sacred city of Kin-sai before, not fifty-five towns in one town, only one in one; that they have seen the same woman lean from the same window more than once, and inferred that the flirt and the snoop were twins; that they have noticed how the same lesson lay unlearned in this city and in that, and concluded that the citizens were identical dumb students in a single slow school; that they have heard the words "gate," "square," "street," "tower," "vista," "courtyard," "steeple," "minaret" repeated like the rattle of a child's drum—noisily, pointlessly, in every wrong rhythm—heard the words and nothing more; then my, Marco Polo's, and the good khan's answer has to be, I think, that if you believe all crossings are alike because they are all called crossings, you shall shortly be at sea, for not all crossings even cross; and if you believe that, because different bricks must similarly repeat themselves to make a wall, no wall resembles any other, or conversely, that every brick wall hides the same house; if you think the beggar you gave money to on Monday is the banker who, on Tuesday, received your intimidated check, then you had better be happy to live in one thin city your lifeline long (for there will be no point in going to another), a city where everyone will have one dog, one car, one lingering cough, one husband and/or wife, the way we each have one mother; and I can only pity those who see no difference between Colette, who leaned down from her window in the Palais Royale that ripe May day and threw her fan into the fountain, and Cecile, who, in the maddening mug of one of St. Louis's insufferable summer evenings, hurled the straw hat with which she was trying to cool her honey-blond head at the back of a prowling tom, so that it fell in a slow swoon through the wet night air, only to be crushed in the gush of water coming from the hydrant in which we kids were playing . . . well, I can only pity and avoid them. For we—wet ourselves—watched the straw hat come apart like rushes drawn away into the current of a river, and while what might have been one of the world's eyes slowly began to lift its steel lid from the street, Polo, my playmate, said he heard in the hydrant the murmur of a distant falls, saw in its cooling spillage a great lake beyond, then docks, patient donkeys, a chimney'd house, a young woman watching from her window.

Sidelonging

When the Seine leaves Paris for the Channel, it makes several large loops while being forced by physics to skirt high ground. The first of these "bays" contains the hills of the Seine, low waves across a crescent-shaped region upon which the suburbs have intruded, but where large forests still remain, and also an area which shelters an airfield that was frequently bombed during World War II, so that craters can be seen on its many wooded walks. The Hauts-de-Seine half-moons a landscape that is historically layered, in touch with the city but almost country in character, neither entirely one thing nor the other, a condition which makes it attractive to Peter Handke's geographical novel, *My Year in the No-Man's-Bay,* where flora and fauna, climate and terrain, are traits like those ascribed normally to fictional creatures, and are the environments that the narrator walks through, either as himself or in the guise of friends who become his surrogate travelers.

In this bay, an area withdrawn from the whole, the narrator has marooned himself, and his journeys are confined to rambles that the onset of suburbanism has reduced and circumscribed. They take place over a terrain where any hill higher than a building becomes a mountain, but a mountain nevertheless so puny it fails to roughen the map: a no-man's-land where he—from January to December of 1993—will make his home and write this meditation on voyages once taken, or presently imagined, or repeatedly dreamed.

A nomad is one who carries his home along with him on his journeys, but there is another sort of wanderer depicted here: a writer who lives in fear of definition, of being fastened by a formula of words, of being pinned down at one stage of his development, always at risk of inadvertently acquiring roots, losing his detachment and therefore the distance he believes is essential to the practice of his art, a distance that is sometimes described as the space behind a mirror. He is searching for points of vantage from which to glance at, rather than scrutinize, the world, an angle from which he may take in the rest as if it were being seen out of the corner of his eye, because sidelong glances (a repeated motif) suggest that the observer does not wish to be included in the scene, is in the wings, offstage, not even a gent with flowers waiting for the diva in her dressing room.

The narrator's first name is Gregor, a name borrowed for this book from Kafka's *Metamorphosis,* and his last name is Keuschnig, the *K* coming from *The Castle,* with the additional suggestion of purity through the meaning of *keusch,* which includes more than a hint of virginity. There is an inviting but treacherous resemblance between Peter Handke's circumstances, as we know them from past news reports and books, and the novel-writing persona of the book he writes—not, of course, to him, a novel this time; rather, a meditation, a journal, a travelogue, an interrogation, an activity that becomes simply unaimed writing, unaimed in order that something fundamental may be struck. About time too, for this is a millennial novel. Characters from other books will show up briefly; periods from the author's career, scarcely disguised, will float like loosened leaves across the steady stream of this prose; difficulties wrestled with through several decades of public pronouncements will be confronted again, especially thoughts preconceived and jotted down in a journal written in the seventies during Handke's first "Paris period" (like the narrator's own earlier sojourn near the city) and published in English as *The Weight of the World.*

The feeling that almost everything I have seen or heard up to now loses its original form the moment it enters into me, that it can no longer be directly described in words or represented in images, but is instantly metamorphosed into something quite formless; as though the effort of my writing were needed to change the innumerable formless pupae inside me into something essentially different . . . and to fashion them into something radiantly new, in which, however, one senses the old, the original experience, as one senses the caterpillar in the butterfly! (Translated by Ralph Manheim. New York: Collier Books, Macmillan, 1990, p. 21)

In this later book, the anticipated metamorphosis is to happen to Gregor Keuschnig, a name that seems strange for a reader to write or to say, it occurs so rarely in these many rich pages, which we have to imagine in their original German (here transformed by Krishna Winston) dotted with *ich*s instead of *I*s: ich . . . ich . . . ich . . . ich . . . I walked, thought, felt, saw, remembered, imagined, feared, sought . . . ich . . . ich . . . ich . . . like footsteps on sodden ground.

For the second time the narrator retires to a Paris suburb, but on this occasion in order to encounter a self he feels may be emerging, to listen for the sound of his fundamental voice, to freshen his vision, to concentrate upon the earth and his relation to it, to sit still and see—out of the corner of his eye—the wealth of the world in the cheapened metal of a local coin. He is to be, as Handke again writes about himself in *The Weight of the World,*

the private detective, with no need to notice anything in particular, but authorized to notice everything, the starting of last cars, the tenants talking as if already asleep . . . [etc. . . .] the sound of tearing Scotch tape; dotlike sounds in the vines on the garden wall . . .   (p. 139)

At first his plan is to position himself by a single window and from that vantage point, improved by a bit of pruning, to perceive whatever odor, object, racket, passes in the street, stirs the leaves, moves in the gardens below him. Weary at last of his self-absorption, his wife departs, returning occasionally to bedevil him like a bad conscience, during one show of anger actually lifting him, like Antaeus, from the ground, just as a fellow author has previously done. Keuschnig is in fact felt to represent, even to embody, the culture of a small country, as Peter Handke is required to be Austrian by many of his countrymen. They urge him to return from the odd wide world to his humble village beginnings, and to drink as before from the town pump, quaff a dipper once more with the boys, visit in their pub, listen to and learn from their native voice; however, that kind of local connection will, Keuschnig believes, deprive him of the strength he feels when he is able to escape such narrow and parochial relations, when he stands instead on foreign ground, as an altered self, and from that vantage can rescue from the obscurity of their neglectful familiarity the simple sensuous qualities that would make up life if such qualities were allowed to be themselves—cellophane tape tearing, coins shifting in a trouser pocket—and, thus equipped with their realization, he could endeavor to answer the novel's first question, put more than once: "Who can say, after all, that the world has already been discovered?" Or possibly its second: "Is there anything or anyone with which one may appropriately identify?"

We ought to know best our place of birth, but home is where the hardened heart is. The cliché tells us we are fed through our roots; that we are consequently plants; and that our accomplishments crown us as trees are crowned by spreading limbs and shading leaves and plentiful fruits. Or if our soul aspires to more motion than a plant's, it should remember that the animal (which locomotes) has its tiny territory, its habitat, repetitive paths: familiar thicket, meadow, grove, or stream. Yet the human soul imagines places, times, scenes, feelings, thoughts that go far from its growth and hunting grounds, which it then marches toward and remains on ardent watch for, just as this novel, in the meditative tradition of fellow Austrians Musil and Bernhard, walks and looks and listens, ponders and broods on the so-called small, the so-called habitual things of this world: drizzle, birdcall, leaffall.

> The closer I came to the stones in the suburban house, often bumping them with my nose, and examined them, the more I had an entire planet within my grasp, embodied in this one thing, as once before, in childhood, the sight of a drop of rain in a yellow-brown-gray-white bit of dust on the path had made the world open up to me for the first time. *(My Year in the No-Man's-Bay,* translated by Krishna Winston. New York: Farrar, Straus and Giroux, 1998, p. 128)

If one is to see the world in a grain of sand, one must first see the sand.

> I sat with my suitcase in an outdoor café by the Gare de l'Est, the asphalt at my feet showing the innumerable over-lapping imprints of bottle caps from the hot times of year.
>
> *(No-Man's-Bay,* p. 113)

And understand how patinas are variously made, by additions sometimes, or by subtractions, while being similarly shaped:

> The trains whizzed through [a concrete cut] as if already out in the open countryside, and the air current they created always buffeted the luxuriant vegetation that hung down over the steep walls. . . .
>
> Time and again the vegetation was removed, and then, before new vegetation maybe took its place, a pattern of rough semicircles was revealed on the wall, often layered on top of each other, light patches scratched and etched in the concrete by all the bunches, fans, trailing streamers as they brushed back and forth. *(No-Man's-Bay,* p. 140)

Keuschnig's son precedes his mother in departure—tacitly agreeing with cliché—to search for his father, not at the sill of his father's sightseeing, but on the Slavic homegrounds where his father was himself once someone's son.

Solitude, in this book, is a happy circumstance. The narrator begins to breathe, breathe words. But when he does, his mind takes flight. Through the agency of a friend, an architect who has discovered a carpenter sawing away inside himself, he visits Japan and builds with another's hands symbolic huts; using the limbs of a singer, he hikes in the Scottish Highlands, just as, with a painter, now a filmmaker, he trudges over Catalonia; in the company of a willful former beauty and still-longed-for lover, he explores coastal Turkey, and by means of his local priest, he does a round of visits in his native village. His son, as I've said, is in Yugoslavia, where his father's thoughts nose after him. Finally a nameless reader—bluntly named Reader—who is following, like a demented or faithful fan, the narrator's authorial footsteps on a former trip through Germany, has his own feet observed as they stand in the tracks of that trail, marked and matched by the omniscient eye of the writer who first made them.

One ought to read this book, I think, the way one reads *Walden*, because, although the region in which it is set is not entirely unoccupied or wholly woodsy, it is, like *Walden*, the record of a single eye, a solitary soul, and a lonely mind. What its remarkably evenly toned though complex prose creates is a consciousness, a consciousness which will take in people occasionally, but much as it takes in a backyard bush; a consciousness which can sit in one place, its body's back comfortably against a stump, to do nothing there but observe (and assemble sentences), because it has become a lichen on the stump and can consequently appreciate the way a turtle crosses a stillness, a muskrat sizes things up, a lizard passes weakly out of its slow life, or how the demonic energy in a sudden swarm of bees electrifies the sky, or why the softness of some doves disarms, or how the shadows of a few fish, like those from fire, fool the fisherman, or the reason the silhouette of the eagle signals the future path of its prey, or why the ripple of a watersnake is the double of itself, why twilight bursts with bats.

Or why the sudden appearance of glorious mushrooms—king boletes—in the ruts of repeated cyclists resembles the rise of something supremely fine, something worth sharing, from any-one's earth, from the rot and dreary conclusion of a hidden life.

The reader should hang over this text like a lover postponing the pleasure of full lips. The reader should be prepared to enter and reside in the province of a mind made powerful by solitude, a mind inventively and energetically cleared for development, dramatization, and intensification, as Handke describes it, free of preconception; a mind which has held its torn-up roots in front of its eyes and watched the earth there dry to a dust that any force-ful bit of breath may blow away: all in order to realize an epic unlike other epics, those histories which are always lamely over before they've begun, and instead to render "the epic tale of tomorrow."

Tomorrow? It is gradually disclosed to us that this book was written during a single year, 1993 (Handke tells us by posting dates on the last page). Yet it is set in 1999—a year said to be one of civil war throughout the world, especially in Germany, and therefore a good year to retire to some no-man's-bay where one may freely sail and safely land. But the war, since it is a civil one, is a struggle against traditional ties by those customarily tied. It is fought by parrots, pairs of shoes, purses. Against their cages, their mates, their money. By the accoutrements of rituals that rise up against the ceremony. By rain allowed to wet only asphalt.

Disconnection can scarcely be carried further. Friends need to be freed of friendship in order to become friends again. While the narrator is forming an attachment to a small boy he has by chance watched toddle around, and while he is happy about feeling fatherly for the first time, his own son is in Yugoslavia dumping Dad like a rucksack off his back. That woman friend in Turkey, who went about hunting for talismans that would tell her of her fate (but, when removed from the site of their discovery, lost their charm the way colored pebbles or seashells do when, dry, they find they've been poured, in the glare of kitchen light, into a dull heap upon a kitchen table)—she had to learn to see the things of the world without their signs and her imputed portents. Artists had to leave their art, as one leaves someone beloved, with regret and anger in order to return and begin again. This author himself ultimately must. The Reader, deprived of books by the quixotic act of tilting at a line of cars so that authorities quite predictably led him away to the pokey, ponders what reading really means. And they all head back to the bay from whence they were, on their *Wanderjahr,* sent.

Having escaped from their cage into chaos (and it is only custom that describes chaos as frantic and noisy), objects, qualities, actions, relations even, find themselves free from one another, just as human beings may be, and can allow themselves at last to choose and be chosen instead of being born and bound. For this narrator and this novel, a true place or a true country of connection—a no-man's-land—occurs only through the interceding of a meditating mind, a mind bent over to inspect and to respond, to let things have their silent say. In short, place is a page.

American Readers—so-called real ones—gave this book few and mostly tepid reviews. They said it was self-absorbed, went nowhere, and was tedious. That is how the teapot looks sitting on a table covered with shallow saucers and dinky cups: fat, overbearing, full of an ambition the saucers would share if any of the dainty teacups were to wet them.

Toward its close—although like all great books *My Year* has no ending ("The omega, the last letter of the ancient alphabet, has the form of a jump rope")—the narrator addresses his tools, the implements he has used to record or, rather, to transform his year.

So many pencils have I used up in this one year that the drawer is already having trouble closing from all the stubs stuffed into it, and from each I have taken leave, on another sheet of paper, in writing: "Thank you, Spanish pencil! Thank you, Yugoslavian pencil! Thank you, white pencil from the honeymoon hotel in Nara, Japan! Thank you, twenty-second black Cumberland pencil! Thank you, pencil from Freilassing in Germany, even if that is perhaps not a beautiful place! Thank you, pencil from the bookstore in the bay, even if your lead kept breaking during sharpening!"

(No-Man's-Bay, p. 429)

This reader wants to thank them too.

I've Got a Little List

As some day it may happen that a victim must be found,
I've got a little list—I've got a little list
Of society offenders who might well be underground,
And who never would be missed—who never would be
    missed!

The Lord High Executioner's list has been compiled "on the off-chance," in case, because you never can tell. Students of rhetorical forms, of which the List ought to head the list, call this kind of compilation a "maybe, maybe." It belongs with the sort of wishes you would make if you had three, or the number of women you might hope to seduce if you were rich, handsome, famous, young, unafraid, and the women were still alive and lonely. Or, if you were Captain Bligh, the books you would choose to be marooned with, or if you were Mr. Saturday Night, the jokes you would tell as a stand-up comic, the roles you would play if you were Sir Oliver Richardson, the renowned thespian. Since most of these "maybes" are "never, nevers," it should be clear that some lists are actually counterfactual, like daydreams, and require the subjunctive.

However, the Lord High Executioner is dealing in possibilities which are quite real, if by real we mean "staged." "There's the pestilential nuisances who write for autographs." (The subject-verb agreement of this entry is terrible and taxes poetic license to the limit; however, the list of poetic licenses is rather a long one.)

Ko-Ko's collection is also of the kind popularly called "a shit list," or variously "a hit list," "the list of Adrian Messenger," "the ten most wanted," and so on. Schindler's list is not a shit list, but its contrary, a shinola list. Otherwise, the form is the same. Ko-Ko's hit list has another quality. *The Mikado* ran for more than six hundred nights following its opening at the Savoy on March 14, 1885, and has been performed many thousands of times since. It amuses directors to revise Titipu's roll of candidates by replacing out-of-date targets with the names and characteristics of victims more suitable to changing times and places (a little local reference is always good for a laugh). (Nixon was a popular substitution until bumped by Ross Perot.) In sum, there is nothing sacred about the entries, only the list's directing principle is immortal (and the tune, of course); which is rather a good thing, for otherwise we might be reluctant to put on *The Mikado* today, because the song's second stanza begins:

> And that nigger serenader, and the others of his race,
> And the piano-organist—I've got him on the list!

We shall probably want to choose motorcyclists for summary removal from the world instead. I'm sure they'd not be missed. Or persons who chew gum and paint their toes. Or talk-show hosts and all their fans. But what about "the lady from the provinces, who dresses like a guy"? We could all happily do without the Politically Correct. By scratching the lady from the provinces off the list, thus not giving offense to transvestites, and putting an officer of the language police in her place, we can remain PC and get rid of PC at the same time: "There's the censor from the feminists, her scissors held on high, who doesn't think she castrates but would rather like to try." I think I'll keep "that singular anomaly, the lady novelist," although lady novelists are no longer singular but as plural as pokeweed, and maintain a literary lobby larger than the Plaza's Palm Court.

In its relative indifference to the nature of its members, this list of the "unmissed" resembles the yearly competitions for the Worst Dressed or what I would like to see in the Michelin guides: Destinations Worth a Detour to Avoid, daggered from one to three like the rosettes, and certainly changeable, since the number of warning icons Atlantic City may deserve will doubtless change from time to time.

Normally lists are the purposeful coming together of names like starlings to their evening trees. They tend to confer equality on their members, also like starlings in their evening trees. The list of the ten wonders of the world does not imply that the wonder given as #1 (at the front or the top) is #1. The thousand and three ladies on Don Giovanni's were each equally enjoyed, the list presumes, all equally loved. The first comestible that comes to mind, when the stomach turns its thoughts to gluttony and gluttony's groceries, generally heads the shopping list, which has normally no other order than chance associations: you just shook the last grain of salt from the shaker, the ad in the paper says that pork butts are on sale, you've had to resort to Kleenex in lieu of toilet paper.

Nowadays, despite our egalitarian and plural society (or perhaps because of it), we are obsessed by hierarchies in the form of lists. There are popular software programs known as "list servers," which manage electronic mailing lists and document their distribution over the Internet. They can make a list from a mouthful of mush. Nick Hornby's popcult novel *High Fidelity* describes characters whose lives are ordered by their love of lists, always superficially evaluative and always the same length: the top five Elvis Costello songs, the top five *Cheers* episodes, and, like the Lord High Executioner's list, the first five rock bands that will have to be eliminated come the Musical Revolution. The book's principal protagonist goes further: he has a list of girlfriends who caused him the greatest grief when they dumped him.

These orders, unlike one's laundry list, are imaginary. The choices set down are like the interpretations of ink blots, revelatory only of their maker. But if the comforts of mere enumeration are shallow and illusory, so are most comforts. The top six . . . (why be a slave to the five and dime?) . . . the top six illusory comforts are: a Sports Car, a Winning Team, Confession, a Savings Account, a Marriage License, a White-Collar Job, a Ranch House in the Suburbs.

Book lists are often neutrally ordered by the alphabet. Lists of things to do could suggest, by their arrangement, a succession of actions—first this, then that; find nail, shoe horse, win war—but they don't have to, and they usually don't: mow lawn, have snooze, buy beer.

The list detaches objects from their place in the world and enumerates them elsewhere. You could list the contents of your pocketbook for a Sunday-supplement article on what ladies carry in their purses. Every year, a few months after Christmas, a sprightly and amusing piece of this kind will appear in the daily paper. The jailer will make such an inventory, slipping small change, charge cards, and other incriminating items into a plastic sack along with his smirk. The seven objects most usually found are: Roll of Tums, Out-of-Date Address Book, Business Card of a Manufacturer of Glass Brick, Key to Lover's Apartment, Note to Lover from Lover's Mum Substantiating Lover's Unhappiness with Lover's Spouse, Unpaid Parking Ticket, Canadian Dime.

Sometimes a book dealer will shelve his books according to the first letter of their subject, and, within that, by author's name. This gives the ordering a hierarchy. Then the catalogue's alphabetical structure and the structure of a corresponding state of affairs in the shop will be the same. Such lists function like road maps, where cities and towns with their coordinates are enumerated on the flaps.

The organizing principles of lists, then, are

a. as encountered or found (the contents of the pocketbook), or as remembered (a guest list), or as needed (to reorder when supplies run out); or

b. as arranged by an already ordered external system, often so that the items on the list can be easily found (alphabetically or numerically, for instance), a systematizing which sometimes becomes hierarchical; or

c. as dictated by the order of the things themselves (library list and library shelves), certain inventories, or the table of contents of a book; or

d. as rated in terms of some principle of value or importance.

Occasionally two or more of these organizations will be applied at the same time. As my need for an item arises, I may put it on my list in the order in which I shop at the supermarket: produce first, for instance, lettuce before onions, meat before crackers, cat food before bleach, soap before shoelaces. Notice that this is not the same as book by subject, then alphabetically by author, because one arrangement does not logically have to precede the other.

Lists are juxtapositions, and exhibit many of the qualities of collage. The names which appear on them lack their normal syntactical companions. Most lists are terse, minimal, bald; they are reminders, commands, aspirations. We do not trouble to write: one medium head of nice fresh red Boston lettuce, two large slicing tomatoes if ripe, a small bottle of Dr. Bland's salad dressing but only if it's in that cute chef-shaped bottle, and so on. We do not describe our New Year's resolutions or any other things to do in detail: remember to move that Norfolk Island pine out of the sunroom, it needs a northern exposure; or this year try not to swear so fucking much, especially in front of the provost.

Clearly, we face complications. When I write "bleach," I usually understand myself to mean a certain brand, and when I beg myself to moderate my passions, a terse word or two on the list (drink less, don't paw) may stand for a thousand dreamlike meditations. Are these subjectivities mutely on the list as well? *How do I love thee? Let me count the ways* . . . but while the poet is publicly boasting about the depth and breadth and height of her soul's reach, of the purity of her feelings, and declaiming about a passion she used to spend on saints, perhaps the *Kama Sutra* best describes her more intimate and private impulses.

Certain words rarely appear on lists ("screw you," for instance), and here is a list of a few of them: (a) "always," (b) "if," (c) "negation," (d) "halfheartedly," (e) "Lithuaneousness," (f) "partially clothed," (g) "tintinnabulation." Adjectives of a descriptive kind frequently show up on lists, however: "yellow cheese," "large eggs," "skim milk."

The punctuation most closely associated with lists is the colon, because everything that follows the colon is supposed to form a list. The colon is often an abbreviation for "namely" or "for instance," but only when there is more than one instance involved. There are thirteen ways of looking at a blackbird, namely . . .

Lists tend to suggest or supply alternatives, and these are not necessarily of things mutually exclusive: how to get spots out or ways to get to Chicago. They supply possibilities: the people who might be interested in hearing you sing, the different kinds of games you could play in a stadium, the uses of a chartreuse ceramic ashtray in the shape of a seashell.

Lists suppress the verb and tend to constantly remind us of their subject, for lists have subjects: the list *of* fruits to buy at the market, the ruck contained *in* the pocketbook, the junk *for* sale in the churchyard Friday morning, the perfumes *on* the counter, the titles of books *about* leprosy, the queens of England *before* Victoria.

Yet the verb lurks like a cur just out of reach of our kick. Most often it takes the form of a command: Buy! Remember! Invite! Do! Write! Thank! Imprison! Proposition! However, since the command itself is never set down, the list feigns passivity and politeness.

When we write the word "Kleenex" on an envelope flap, we haven't achieved a list yet, though we may have begun to make one. Two needs—"Kleenex," "cauliflower"—merely make a mis-fitting pair, while "Kleenex," "cauliflower," and "catnip" record an incoherent plurality. However, alliteration calls attention to the numerousness of the trio, and I think that with four we can say we have a list. Now things can be added to it, whereas before, while we could write "cauliflower" beside "Kleenex," we couldn't add "cauliflower" to a list, since we didn't have one yet. Niceties of this sort give great pleasure to the logician. As they should.

Having a list, we can properly speak of things being "on" or "off" it. "Kleenex" was not on a list until "catnip" came along. Getting off a list is no easier, certainly, than getting on one, especially if, like a train, the list is moving. Ko-Ko is perfectly willing to let us substitute appropriate victims in place of

> What d'ye call him—Thing'em-bob, and likewise . . .
> What's-his-name, and also You-know-who—
> The task of filling up the blanks I'd rather leave to you

but that's only while the list is a rough draft. People who live in trailer parks would certainly not be missed. They are on God's list, clearly, for He is always trying to upend them or knock them over with one of His Big Winds. Anyone who ever touched a gun in fun or fury could be bangedy-banged, for all I care, but others might want to be more merciful. Some of us, this very moment, unbeknownst, are being dropped from an invitation list. But when we have executed (to use the appropriate word) the command which is implicit in most lists (Do! Buy! Invite! remember that list?), plopping the bright green bag of frozen peas on top of the spuds, and crossing out parsley too and Cheez Whiz, because they are already in our basket, we might think (having failed to consult our local logician) that the spuds and peas and parsley are no longer on the list; or, as in Ko-Ko's case, having cut off the Judicial Humorist's head, that he's there no more because he's here no more; but no, even though there is a cross across his name now, and a cross above his grave too, he's still on the list, which, without changing a line, moves its members and their status in time from "To Be Executed" to "Execute!" to "Executed." In a similar way, the grocery list becomes the register slip. So the prosecutor can ask you if you had rat poison on your shopping list the day before your wife's fatal illness, and you are not allowed to reply: "No sir, because I crossed that item off after I bought some."

Normally, an act or object finagles its way onto a list simply by being written down in the neighborhood of the group or, better yet, finds a place in the column or the queue. It is bad manners to break into the queue or try to take over the capital of the column. Nevertheless, as we know, it happens. To the list "apples," "oranges," "lemons," "limes," "lighter fluid," where am I sensibly going to add "grapes"? Surely not after "fluid," where "AAA batteries" goes. So I squeeze it in above "limes."

There are certain lists one wants desperately to be on—the Social Register, the high school honor roll, foursomes waiting to tee off at Pebble Beach—and these lists guard their precincts: the names of their members aren't written on napkins or the backs of envelopes. Getting on these lists is frequently expensive (bribe-style balls have to be thrown, costly caterers called in) or requires a lot of networking, ass kissing, or plain hard honest work (to make the dean's list, for instance). However, for every desirable one there is another it is essential to avoid, like the roll call way up yonder.

Thus lists have requirements for membership (or getting on), like being thought to be the right sort, and requirements for continuing to be included (or staying on), like paying your dues, and conditions which must be met if you want to be dropped (or removed), like embracing the Jewish faith. I've warned that some lists are impossible to escape. If you were ever Mabel Dodge's fourth husband, you will always and forever be, though divorce or death overtakes you.

Could we draw up a complete list of lists? No . . . not even of the genre, let alone the species. There are all the shopping lists, just to begin with—groceries, sundries, hardware, drugs—and the Christmas cards you sent—that lot—set over against the few you received, as well as invitations for dinners, birthdays, and receptions, a column of things to do before the party—those disgusting plastic cups to purchase, three dozen paper plates the color of beef blood, candles (do we need four?), tapers (steal them from the church), oh yes, and napkins small enough to ensure that at least half a finger will be smeared with sauce. Meanwhile there are appointments to keep, don't forget, calls to return, and the other notes necessary to jog that part of the mind which plays the role of Memory—pick up dry cleaning. More? Sure: addresses for next year's cards or the exhibition opening, the lists which fetch us catalogues, newsletters, charitable solicitations and other scams, through the mail. And those lists drawn up by scholars, cranks, and other anal-retentives so you won't have to remember: chronologies of presidents and kings, lists like the principal battles of the Civil War, or your curriculum vitae: your several spouses (but not why), your jobs, clubs-associations-committees, public works, honors, and other lies; and, closely connected, almanacs, desk-wall-pocket calendars, as well as rates and schedules for bus-train-boat-plane, or tides or phases of the moon, or comets and meteoric showers, or simple tables of contents: parts, sections, chapters, verse; best/worst most/least lists of every imaginable act and entity: voice throwers, horse winnings, rain amounts in August, penile dimensions, multiple births, canons of excellence; next, catalogues of books or objets d'art, discographies, antiques, and inventories of household goods for insurance purposes, of the store's stock, of your wallet upon overnight confinement in the pokey (remember? I spoke of it before); notebook-type lists like a madam's clients, their preferences and prices; and then compendia of all kinds: dictionaries, encyclopedias, atlases, telephone and cookbooks, video and Mobil guides, indexes, nearby bed-and-breakfasts; wine lists and honor rolls, restaurant and computer menus, stock and other exchanges, want ads, wish and waiting lists, shits and shinolas (as I said); all sorts of methods and procedures, how-tos by the hundreds, for instance, Roberta Coughlin's book *The Gardener's Companion,* which contains more than three hundred and fifty lists of practical and cultural information, of houseplants which will still live hung in baskets, of Shakespeare's flowers, "daisies pied and violets blue and lady-smocks all silver white and cuckoo-buds of yellow hue"—but let's get on: vulgar noises that amuse children, ways to placate spouses who are irate because you've sent their delicates through the high/hot cycle, how to remove love hickeys in a hurry, persuade some young gentleman to change a tire, make bail, buy a good bagel, find a bathroom in a strange town; what's more, cook kale—or, to take a different tack, there are rule books and commandments: don't litter, foul the pathway, commit adultery, pee in the pool; profits and losses too, expenditures and sales, pages of obits, places of worship, programs of cinemas, recaps of TV serials, exhibits at museums, and rosters of teams and volunteers, which isn't the half—the fourth—the eighth of it . . . of them, I should say . . . of lists.

The libretto of *The Mikado* begins with a cast of characters, and when Gertrude Stein wrote her little play called "A List," she carefully lined her characters up in a column along the margin of the action—the action consisting mainly of a list of the phrase "a list."

Marius. A list.
Mabel. A list.
Martha. A list.
Martha. There is a great variety in the settlement of claims.
    We claim and you claim and I claim the same.
Martha. A list.
Maryas. And a list.
Mabel. I have also had great pleasure from a capital letter.
Martha. And forget her.
Maryas. And respect him.

Marius. And neglect them.

Mabel. And they collect them as lilies of the valley in this
     country.

Martha. A list.

("A List." *A Stein Reader,* edited by Ulla Dydo. Evanston, Ill.: North-
western University Press, 1984, p. 401)

My moving van is parked outside. I need to make a list of the
liftable contents of this domicile. My list will transform the relationship the house's furniture has to walls and floors from one of
feet and inches, shoes and fingers, to a temporally neutral column of names (like Martha, Maryas, Mabel, and Marius). If I
pretend to be Homer praising the heroes who came to make war
on Troy, I am likely to arrange my song so that it shows who vol-
unteered first, who second, and so on, giving a temporal meaning
to the series which it might not ordinarily have. If I am making an
action into a list, I shall have to divide it the way the flight of
Zeno's arrow was divided, the way a camera would record it,
because a camera is a list maker, the film nothing but a series of
shots in the order of their snapping. My list might then suggest
how I shall encounter dwellings on a stroll, or how I shall remember having passed them in Calvino's lovely prose.

> The man who knows by heart how [the city of] Zora is
> made, if he is unable to sleep at night, can imagine he is
> walking along the streets and he remembers the order by
> which the copper clock follows the barber's striped awn-
> ing, then the fountain with the nine jets, the astronomer's
> glass tower, the melon vendor's kiosk, the statue of the her-
> mit and the lion, the Turkish bath, the café at the corner, the
> alley that leads to the harbor. (*Invisible Cities,* translated by William
> Weaver. New York: Harcourt Brace Jovanovich, 1974, p. 15)

I have wandered into the literary part of town before I intended
to, but the list is often just such a little tour, as it is at the opening

of Juan Goytisolo's extraordinary novel, a novel made of lists, *The Virtues of the Solitary Bird*, where the infamous apparition, the monster pictured by Felician Rops as the Sower of Discord, materializes and makes its slow clogshod way through the grounds and lobby of an otherwise unnamed hotel-hospital-spa (but only, as apparitions must, subjunctively):

> . . . had it entered like everyone else through the arch of the carriage gate, crossed the little courtyard with nineteenth-century bathtubs ingeniously planted with perennials, proceeded toward the staircase and its gas lamps of outworn majesty, opened the door giving access to our ravaged and destroyed kingdom, paid sixty-five francs to the blonde cashier who gave out tickets, little individual bars of soap, shampoo, and other beauty products and aids to bodily cleanliness . . . (*The Virtues of the Solitary Bird*, translated by Helen Lane. London: Serpent's Tail, 1991, p. 11)

Had it entered . . . But did it? What do apparitions do?

There are philosophers who believe that our experienced reality forms a temporal list. It is a series of impressions, or complexes of impressions, which can only be recorded: this, this, this.

To sum up so far (to make a little list): when we are confronted with a list, we have to ask what the purpose of the list is, for a list is a purposeful collection. Then we have to wonder whether the list is spatially or temporally ordered or is neutral and loose in that regard. Next, we need to know whether whatever order the list has is mirrored in the things the list is a list of. Does it possess an isomorphic formality with elements outside itself? Beyond that, we have to find out where the weight of importance lies: is it in the things listed? is it in the words listed? or do both matter, and if so, to what degree? In short, is it a List of Ts or an L of Things? Finally, we must determine whether there are any other principles ordering the list apart from space-time ones, and if so, what these are. Lists of dates are obviously chronological; dictionaries are alphabetical; but when John Donne writes of death that it is a "slave to fate, chance, kings, and desperate men," sound and meter as well as meaning, structured in terms of high/low pairs, are determining the line (fate high, chance low, kings high, desperate men as low as you can get).

In addition to internal order, external relations, and aim, lists have entrance requirements (how do you get on?) and expulsion principles (getting left off, crossed off, or checked off). Lists are either open-ended (the state capitals you have visited), incomplete (birds of North America), variable (contents of a closet), or closed (books you read last year); they are finite (Aunt Millie—a beachboy—for Christmas) or infinite (even numbers, also odd), definite (three small Granny Smith apples) or vague (something for dinner). Finally, a list creates a site, something like the logician's universe of discourse, a place where everything on the list can coexist, a common space.

Jorge Luis Borges refers to a "certain Chinese encyclopedia" which says that

> animals are divided into (a) those that belong to the emperor; (b) embalmed ones; (c) those that are trained; (d) suckling pigs; (e) mermaids; (f) fabulous ones; (g) stray dogs; (h) those that are included in this classification; (i) those that tremble as if they were mad; (j) innumerable ones; (k) those drawn with a very fine camel's-hair brush; (l) et cetera; (m) those that have just broken the flower vase; (n) those that at a distance resemble flies. (*Selected Non-Fictions,* by Jorge Luis Borges, edited by Eliot Weinberger. New York: Viking Press, 1999, p. 231)

Michel Foucault, who makes some interesting comments on this list at the beginning of his book *The Order of Things,* says we cannot imagine the kind of place where these animals could be brought together and sorted out. There is no peaceable kingdom for them. The site is impossible to conceive.

It is certainly true that this list deliberately contains heteronomous groups of more than one sort. In the first place, its classes are not exclusive. Animals belonging to the emperor (a) might be trained (c) or embalmed (b). Redundancy is likely, as if my grocery list asked for bread as well as anything on sale. Suckling pigs and stray dogs are grouped with painted or fabulous ones in such a way as to deny the overriding importance of another distinction: that between real and imaginary, for instance, or alive and dead, as if my market list included not only milk but the nectar of the gods and three dipperfuls from the Fountain of Youth. Borges' list is so messy we cannot define its entrance requirements. It also includes categories which attack the logical structure of every list. Suppose my grocery list included "and so on" or "another of the same"? (j) "innumerable" suggests animals which in fact can't be listed, while (h) those "included in this classification" allows many to get in twice. Creatures that have (m) "just broken the flower vase" get on the list, but then must be taken off again because, as time passes, they will no longer have "just" broken it. A variation of this category might be six already eaten eggs, or one-half of a watermelon the moment before a fly lights on it. (k) animals "drawn with a very fine camel's-hair brush" expresses a quirk or whim—the bristles of the camel's-hair brush cannot be coarse—as if I would buy tomato soup only in a dented can. Finally, (n) those animals "that at a distance resemble flies" introduces dangerous subjective and relativistic elements. Elephants, seen from far enough away, will look like flies, while flies won't look like flies through a powerful microscope.

Yet this list has a site after all, I think, and has been cunningly put together by Borges to create one. Every entry discloses something about our principles of classification by violating several of them. And if its items violated all possible principles, we could say the list was "exhaustive." However, there are no negations on Borges' list—"animals not the totemic emblem of a football team," for instance—or, after all, any entry for "man."

Some lists list. Other lists list examples of what they wish to list. Suppose that on the surface of my shopping list there is a spot of cooking oil, a smear of jam, some bacon grease. This set of "fingerprints" is not a real list, but an inadvertent demonstration of what might be named on the real list. Foucault points out that on Borges' list only the names can be brought together, never their referents; but he fails to observe that in fact these categories belong together because by not belonging together they reveal another set of things (illogicalities) which do.

Listing is a fundamental literary strategy. It occurs constantly, and only occasionally draws attention to itself. It can be so brief as almost not to be there. "Alex went to the bank, to the casino, and to the dogs, in one day." It can be so prominent it proclaims itself as some fictional reality's single ordering device. Here is Juan Goytisolo's apparitional figure again, still slogging through the subjunctive:

> . . . then had the clogs cautiously placed themselves on the lower steps broadening the field of vision of the figure and, at the same time, that of the overawed spectators, a big loose tunic over its filiform extremities, pouches or petticoats with dozens of dolls, a floating lilac-and-rose-colored cape in which its face was enveloped as in a flag . . . its movements were viciously languid, perhaps beneath the veil or the tangled locks . . . it was now taking in the lounge, the seats to one side covered with worn red oilcloth, Second Empire gas lamps, wall paintings of Near Eastern landscapes, green hills, horsemen, silhouettes with burnooses and haiques, a spiky minaret of a mosque, a half moon white as snow, a scene full of atmosphere, nostalgically familiar to our spirited lovers for a day, composed . . . by a great artist, a discreet regular of those baths devoted the bliss and cleanliness of the body, before, long before we, even the most intrepid veterans among us, had become initiates of

the rites and ceremonies of the temple, had sought the tenderness lying in wait in the pupils of the tiger, that luminous and brutal ecstatic escape from the suffocating squalor of our lives, paradise, a flaming and fleeting paradise like all the edens of the world . . .

(Virtues of the Solitary Bird, p. 12)

The garb of a ghost merges with a list of things in the allegedly real world only to slip into another of things in a painted one, and these lists lead to a list of the painted world's qualities, and then to one which characterizes its artist as a frequent visitor to the spa, before concluding (in my selection) with a list of the pleasures of escape to be had if one accepts the embrace of the hotel, its grounds, and its steamy springs.

The list is a natural form for poems like François Villon's *Legacy,* but the lines of many of his ballads are hung like clothes from the pole of the list's purpose:

> I know flies in the milk,
> I know men by their clothes,
> I know good from bad weather,
> I know fruit by its color,
> I know trees by their sap,
> I know when all is the same,
> I know who's busy or idle,
> I know all, save myself.

(from "Ballad of Small Talk," translated by Anthony Bonner)

His ballads concerning the lords and ladies of bygone times are lists almost by nature, so that it hardly matters who composes them. Certainly, the fall of the high and mighty is a medieval formula. Here is John Skelton playing at it.

> Why, what cam of Alexander the greate?
> Or els of stronge Sampson, who can tell?
> Were not wormes ordeyned theyr flesh to frete?

And of Salomon, that was of wyt the well?
Absolon profferyd his hearte for to sell,
Yet for al his bewte wormys ete him also;
And I but late in honour dyd excel,
Et, ecce, nunc in pulvere dormio!
(from "On the Death of the Noble Prince, Kynge Edward the Fourth")

The memory of ladies lost is not confined to Villon or to such long-ago times. William Carlos Williams carries on the tradition:

There was Margaret of the big breasts
and daring eyes who carried
her head, where her small brain rattled,
as the mind might wish,
at the best, to be carried. There was
Lucille, gold hair and blue eyes, very
straight, who
to the amazement of many, married a
saloon keeper and lost her modesty.
There was loving Alma, who wrote a steady
hand, whose mouth never wished for
relief. And the cold Nancy, with small
, firm breasts
       You remember?
            a high
forehead, she who never smiled more
than was sufficient but whose broad
mouth was icy with pleasure startling
the back and knees!
(from *Paterson*. New York: New Directions, 1963, section III, p. 192)

Strolling, remembering women, bequeathing properties, determining fates, bemoaning greatness fallen once again to dust: such pastimes are so listlike the form needs no prompting to appear; but every description also creates a list, for even when the features of a face coexist (or when many impressions occur simultaneously), they cannot do so during their recital, when the nose or eyes can be placed, with the freedom of Picasso, before the chin or after an ear or in front of a topknot of disciplined hair. The qualities I might want to credit an apple—its tart juice, its crisp white flesh, its slick red skin, its tough stiff stem, and so on—proceed differently across the page than they simultaneously are in life. I can compose, then, quite a different object by arranging these properties according to some experiential order (where shape, stem, color, and skin would come first), or in terms of desire (then its flood of juice and quash of tart pulp between the teeth might lead the imagination), or by stressing symbolic factors instead (Eve, tree, worm), or by concentrating on the way the language moves, fancying a phrase like "voluminous juice," in my mouth more than the apple's taste, which can sometimes be insipid.

The list is the fundamental rhetorical form for creating a sense of abundance, overflow, excess. We find it so used in writers with an appetite for life from Rabelais and Cervantes, or from Burton and Browne, to Barth and Elkin. Why be merely thirsty when you can brag, like Grangousier (in Jacques LeClercq's version): "I wet, I dampen, I moisten, I humect my gullet. I drink—and all for fear of dying of aridity!" Our list, in this case, is not so much one of alternative actions but of possible words—a sequence of synonyms—the wealth of words suggesting an abundance of satisfactions. Desire is never dampened by its dampening, but only grows greater, and its object is not consumed by its consumption but is multiplied, and pleasure is not lessened by its repetition but enriched and revered. None of this is true in life, another reason why the page is to be preferred.

Our aforementioned Greatgullet loved to slake his thirst so much he sought after salted meats to increase his need.

Thus he was ordinarily well provided with hams from Mainz in Westphalia and Bayonne in Gascony; with oxtongues and chitterlings in season; with salted beef and mustard; with sausages galore—not from Bologna, for he feared the Italian poisoner as a curer of bacon, but from Bigorre, Longaulnay, Brenne, and Rouergue, all places nearer home.

Bologna may not have gotten on the list of sources for Grangousier's meats, but it did get on the list of words. "I love Anne, not Phyllis, Margaret not Marion, Kate not Jane, and am indifferent to Mary, Rose, and Carolyn." The list of the beloved is three loves long; the list of names is nine.

Like the scholastics whom they are kidding, Montaigne, Burton, and Browne are fond of citation. You doubt that a child can take eleven months to come to term? Rabelais produces authorities beyond count, including Hippocrates, Pliny, Plautus, Marcus Varro, Aristotle, Aulus Gellius, Servius, Justinian, and "a thousand other fools whose number has been increased by the lawyers."

Thomas Hobbes, who thinks so little of the scholastics he'll not bother to make fun of them, nevertheless uses the list with great effect, both as a weapon of his rhetoric and in argument. Here is one of the great lists in our language, one of admirable wealth and energy, and one of overwhelming persuasive power.

> And for that part of Religion, which consisteth in opinions concerning the nature of Powers Invisible, there is almost nothing that has a name, that has not been esteemed amongst the Gentiles, in one place or another, a God, or Divell; or by their Poets feigned to be inanimated, inhabited, or possessed by some Spirit or other.
>
> The unformed matter of the World, was a God, by the name of *Chaos*.
>
> The Heaven, the Ocean, the Planets, the Fire, the Earth, the Winds, were so many Gods.
>
> Men, Women, a Bird, a Crocodile, a Calf, a Dogge, a Snake, an Onion, a Leeke, Deified. Besides, that they filled almost all places, with spirits called *Daemons*: the plains, with *Pan,* and *Panises,* or Satyres; the Woods, with Fawnes, and Nymphs; the Sea, with Tritons, and other Nymphs;

every River, and Fountayn, with a Ghost of his name, and with Nymphs; every house, with its *Lares,* or Familiars; every man, with his *Genius;* Hell, with Ghosts, and spirituall Officers, as *Charon, Cerebus,* and the *Furies;* and in the night time, all places with *Larvae, Lemures,* Ghosts of men deceased, and a whole kingdome of Fayries, and Bugbears. They have also ascribed Divinity, and built Temples to meer Accidents, and Qualities; such as are Time, Night, Day, Peace, Concord, Love, Contention, Vertue, Honour, Health, Rust, Fever, and the like; which when they prayed for, or against, they prayed to, as if there were Ghosts of those names hanging over their heads, and letting fall, or withholding that Good, or Evill, for, or against which they prayed. They invoked also their own Wit, by the name of *Muses;* their own Ignorance, by the name of *Fortune;* their own Lust, by the name of *Cupid;* their own Rage, by the name *Furies;* their own privy members by the name of *Priapus;* and attributed their pollutions, to *Incubi,* and *Succubae:* insomuch as there was nothing, which a Poet could introduce as a person in his Poem, which they did not make either a *God,* or a *Divel.*

(*Leviathan,* part I, chapter 12)

Among the more admirable kinds of lists is the menu, and among the many memorable moments in Robert Coover's novel *Pinocchio in Venice* is the meal which Professor Pinocchio nibbles at on the first evening of his arrival in Venice. He has been led to the Gambera Rosso by his hotel proprietor, who, though protesting that he is a bit off his feed, nevertheless manages to devour a nice long list of goodies, and by the hotel's porter, whose appetite has been whetted by work and a liberal tip. This roll call is interrupted by commentary, as long ones often need to be.

[The porter] proceeded to devour monumental quantities of tortellini and cannelloni, penne all'arrabbiata, rich and tangy, spaghetti with salt pork and peppers, heaps of thick chewy gnocchi made from cornmeal, tender pasticcio layered with baked radicchio from Treviso, pickled spleen and cooked tendons (or nervetti, as they call them here, "little nerves," slick and translucent as hospital tubing), bowls of risi e bisi and sliced stuffed esophagus (the professor skipped this one), fennel rolled in cured beef, and breaded meatballs with eggplant alla parmigiana. His doctor unfortunately having put him on a strict regimen . . . he was denied the pleasures of the fish course, but he was able, in all good conscience, to round off his evening's repast with a dish of calf's liver alla veneziana, wild hare in wine sauce with a homely garnishing of baby cocks, beef brains, pheasants, and veal marrow, a small suckling lamb smothered in kiwi fruit, sage, and toasted almonds, and a kind of fricassee of partridges, rabbits, frogs, lizards, and dried paradise grapes, said to be another famous specialty of the house and particularly recommended for persons on stringent diets.

(Pinocchio in Venice. New York: Simon and Schuster, 1991, p. 34)

If we put all these rich words in our mouth, we shall dine well indeed, and conclude by exclaiming, as the porter does, "I'm as full as an egg."

No list of lists can pretend to be complete that hasn't one of Whitman's on it; however, just as the poet's frequent commands are pointless and unnecessary—"Flow on, river! flow with the flood-tide, and ebb with the ebb-tide!"—and followed by exclamation points as if something wondrous were being urged, his lists aren't always like the incantatory opening of "Out of the Cradle Endlessly Rocking," but are often only stubbornly grandiose. "A Song for Occupations" has a list that begins

House-building, measuring, sawing the boards,
    Blacksmithing, glass-blowing, nail-making, coopering,
    tin-roofing, shingle-dressing,

> Ship-joining, dock-building, fish-curing, flagging of
> sidewalks by flaggers . . .

and continues with a diligence that never flags:

> The cotton-bale, the stevedore's hook, the saw and buck of
> the sawyer, the mould of the moulder, the working-
> knife of the butcher, the ice-saw, and all the work with
> ice . . .

line after—altogether—thirty very long lines, each lamer than the
one before:

> The men and the work of the men on ferries, railroads,
> coasters, fish-boats, canals . . .

until it concludes (the list but not the poem) with unintended
humor (in addition to its leaden echo):

> I do not affirm that what you see beyond is futile, I do not
> advise you to stop,
> I do not say leadings you thought great are not great,
> But I say that none lead to greater than these lead to.
>> ("A Song for Occupations," Library of America, *Poetry and Prose*,
>> pp. 360–62)

As for rodomontade, what else is the braggart but a list maker
(unless he does dances in the end zone, his fine opinion of himself nothing beyond muscle), just as slanging matches are a measure of strength and endurance: you this, you that, each more
awful than the other, until invention flags, the name-calling
becomes mechanical, vocal exhaustion ensues, and it's over. In
The Sot-Weed Factor, when the whores go at it, two hundred
twenty-nine nasty names are traded—English answered by
French in increasingly hoarse howls.

When it comes to bluster, no one can blow wind better than
Carlyle, whose work moves through its lists like a train through a

tunnel—in the dark, surrounded by cinders, smoke, boiler steam, and whistle hoot. Apostrophes, too, are one of his specialties, and he continues to love colons, exclamation points, and compound nouns, and to knight his nouns with capital letters in the German manner.

> Frightful to all men is Death; from of old named King of Terrors. Our little compact home of an Existence, where we dwelt complaining, yet as in a home, is passing, in dark agonies, into an Unknown of Separation, Foreignness, unconditioned Possibility. The Heathen Emperor asks of his soul: Into what places art thou now departing? The Catholic King must answer: To the Judgment-bar of the Most High God! Yes, it is a summing-up of Life; a final settling, and giving-in the "account of the deeds done in the body": they are done now; and lie there unalterable, and do bear their fruits, long as Eternity shall last.
>
> (*The French Revolution,* bk. I, chap. 4)

Is it stretching our example to claim this is a list? As most things are in Carlyle, the structure of the list is obscure, yet there with a vengeance. It is a list of Death's names or properties.

> King of Terrors
> Unknown of Separation
> > Foreignness
> > Unconditioned Possibility
> the Judgment-bar
> a summing-up of Life
> a final settling
> the "account of the deeds done in the body"
> (as long as) Eternity (shall last)

But only on the right list, where all things, when they pass away, pass to—the *Book of the Dead;* since to leave the list is to leave life, and not because life is one damn thing after another, as has been claimed, but because day after day arrives like another item to be catalogued: Saturday, September 9, I rose in a damp dawn to hear the paper delivered, dropped my poor head one more plop upon a callous pillow, listened to the cat lick her fur, followed the ambulance down a distant street, wondered what lunch would be like, if it would do me any good to smile at the morning mirror; and—because once these moments have been named, they can be rearranged, find their freedom from factuality in rhythm, sound, placement, subtleties of association, fresh conceptual systems—then I can wonder what lunch will be like, listen to fur being licked, plop my poor head upon an indifferent pillow, rise at dewy dawn to crack a smile at my morning's mirror, and leave the ambulance absolutely off, to die away in an unrecorded distance, the way I, too, would leave life if I didn't have my list.

Ko-Ko's claim to the contrary notwithstanding, it really doesn't matter whom you put upon the list—on the list they're *never* missed.

The Test of Time

What must a work do to prepare to pass the Test of Time? Is it a written test, this test? and does it appear at a certain period in a work's life the way final exams do, or tenure reviews, or professional boards?

In perhaps an odd way, the answer to these questions is "yes."

Is it related to "the survival of the fittest" and the idea that the last one standing is the winner?

Sure, somewhat.

Is the test graded, and if so, by whom?

There can be no doubt that some works are felt to have stood the Test of Time better than others. The Test of Time is not simply pass/fail. One of the severest examiners is Time itself.

Is it therefore possible to receive a C-minus on the Test of Time?

Well, the equivalent.

Or is the test more like an ordeal which cars and trucks and airplanes are put through, to see if they are safe and well made?

Certainly—that too—for a work must sustain a lot of hard knocks, neglect, and rejection before it can say it has passed.

Is the Test of Time an exam which must be periodically repeated, like those for a driver's license?

More than that. The test is continuous.

Is there a theological component, like damnation, redemption, and salvation?

Alas, yes.

What happens to works which fail to pass the Test of Time?

Nobody cares.

Is the Test of Time something the State administers, or a professional board, or a training school, or is it a private kind of thing like a questionnaire in a magazine which will tell you, say, if you are sufficiently outgoing?

The State and its cultural agents administer part of it, but professions contribute, and schools share. It is also very much a private, nearly internal test, which works employ in the process of their creation.

So works which pass the Test of Time are never again ignored, misunderstood, or neglected?

No. Works which fail find oblivion. Those which pass stay around to be ignored, misunderstood, exploited, and neglected.

But they bring their authors honor, their creators praise?

Those responsible are all dead.

So what is the personal gain from making immortal works if the maker isn't immediately rewarded?

None whatever.

Is the Test of Time a rescuing argument?

Frequently.

When is it most commonly employed? In a rescue?

Yes.

Is the Test of Time, then, a good test, with a reasonable record of success?

The Test of Time is not a test at all. It is an announcement of temporary victory: "I am still alive." The dead do not report. As such, it is only old news.

So what happens, finally, to works which have withstood the Test of Time?

They become timeless.

2

We also frequently say "Time will tell" when actually it is we who read the expression on the clock, because Time's voice is simple and singular like the rattle of an alarm or the rouse of a rooster. And generally it means that we intend to postpone judgment; that we shall have to wait to find out if a marriage will be happy or a business successful, or whether some evaluation or prediction will be verified. Will the wine improve? Time will tell.

My last example was somewhat misleading. In time, Time may collect its toll, but taste will tell.

There is no more popular appeal, when considering the merit of works of art, than the one to Time, and when I say "popular" I mean across the board and up and down the scale. It is assumed that there is no better reason for granting greatness to an artist than the fact that his or her works, after several centuries, are still being seen and admired, heard or performed, or read and written of. The quality of being constantly contemporary—or of stubbornly surviving the vicissitudes of history, taste, and the whimsicalities of fashion—is the single quality most commonly found among major works of art, when all their other characteristics—medium, subject, attitude, length, complexity, profundity, range of feeling—differ considerably.

Conversely, there is no sign of future failure that's more reliable than the popularity of the moment, and by "popularity" I mean across the board in the noisy markets of popular culture, as well as up and down the scale from the cribs of country music and the pillows of sentimental romance through midcult's porncorn bloodletting or foreign-film idolatry to the most recent academic trend and intellectual fawning, with its high-fashion fields of influence and its pompous lockjaw jargons.

The Test of Time is a stretch of Time conceived as a gauntlet to be run. And any long stretch will do, as if Time battered its principals equally through every section. We don't say: the period from 1750 to 1912 was particularly benign, and almost everything written then survived until they hit the bit between 1913 and 1938, which we now regard as a quarter century of catastrophe, a typhoon of a time when most works of art were lost without remainder.

Another way of envisioning the test is spatial. Our creative acts fill the creative sky like stars. There are dim ones and bright ones. The constellation Rhetoric which contains Cicero and Quintilian is more distant from our system than the brilliant nova of the Greeks. Vico shines but not as brightly as Plotinus.

We must remember too (so we can discount them), that there are works which so adorn their era and wrinkle their age that you can't study the period without studying their role in it, although outside their beloved period they languish as immediately as a wildflower taken from its meadow.

Since we live in a society concerned mainly with money and amusement, it might be appropriate to examine an early use of the Test of Time: when it was employed to defend utilitarianism from the charge that the Principle of Utility was an instrument of the philistine—one of those rare cases in which the defendant defends himself, since utilitarianism and philistinism are identical twins. Jeremy Bentham asserted that pushpin was as good as poetry as far as the hedonistic calculus was concerned, if pushpin did indeed give as much pleasure to as many people as poetry did. We might replace pushpin with some mechanical amusements like arcade or video games. How would we determine the differing amounts, since a subjective inventory is impractical? Just as the level of pain for a person might be measured by the degree to which the entire organism is affected by it and mobilizes to respond, so we might estimate the expected pleasure of a particular activity indirectly by assessing the amounts of time, energy, interest, and money that are spent to achieve it—like packing a picnic lunch and driving six kids and two dogs to the beach—as well as considering the actual pleasure received through the frequency of the activity's repetition. Six kids and two dogs? that thin stony beach? never again.

On this basis, video games would appear to be far more important than poetry if we consider society as a whole. Mass culture is what it is because the masses prefer it. And they prefer it because it is easy to obtain (it does not require training or an advanced education or even an IQ). It amuses; it consoles; it allows people to vent their feelings in a relatively innocuous manner; it permits easy identification and promotes illusions of control; it establishes communities of common experience and provides the middle class and middle-class intellectuals with something they can talk about as if they had taste, brains, and breeding. Although the middle class would like to disavow any membership in the masses, the middle class is now far too large to be anything else. Besides, its taste is in no way more refined than that of the lower, only better packaged and more hypocritical. A taste for Bach partitas is not middle-class. Academics, whom one might expect would be willing to support at least some examples of cultural quality, keep a hamper of towels handy to throw in the ring if any blows are actually struck. As Harold Bloom remarks in *The Western Canon* (New York: Harcourt Brace, 1994, p. 520): "The morality of scholarship, as currently practiced, is to encourage everyone to replace difficult pleasures by pleasures universally accessible precisely because they are easier." And why not? Why play the wild bird in a world full of feeders? Whereupon, the tough-minded Benthamite might rest his case.

And shrug when accused of cultural leveling.

John Stuart Mill had a softer head (and poorer logic). Shakespeare might lose out to Mighty Morph in the short run (he, in effect, said), but if we consider the long haul, well, these lowlife entertainments disappear like morning mist, other amusements replace them, whereas great poetry, theater, fiction, art, endures, and in so doing piles up pleasure points. In the long run, Proust will outplease pushpin, pinball, pachinko, and indoor soccer. To the Greatest Happiness for the Greatest Number (to which Mill had to tack on the stipulation that each person was to count as one, and no one for more than one) must be added the phrase "In the Long Run," with the long run no twenty-six-mile marathon but, rather, a race millennial in length. How long? The suspicion is: for as long as it takes to restore the canon to its eminence.

To the quantitative sum of pleasure and pain we could insist upon adding a judgment of quality as well, which might require the employment of competent observers: those able to experience the pleasures of video games and Bach chorales equally, and be in a position, then, to judge the qualitative superiority of one pleasure over another. So modified, the principle of utility is: the Greatest Happiness of the Highest Kind for the Greatest Number capable of experiencing the Highest Kind, otherwise watch football, drink beer, and eat ice cream, you happy slobs.

Although there may be a few persons capable of enjoying honky-tonk and high mass, pork rinds and puff pastry, celli concerti and retch rock, and therefore be in a position to pronounce upon the quality of each of these endeavors as well as the cultural level of other pleasures, it should be clear that a life of idiocy and a life of civility are rarely joined, and that we have probably stretched our standard beyond its useful limit; for how do we know when the pleasures of the Bobbsey Twins have been thoroughly felt, so that if they appear to be losing out on the qualitative side to Samuel Beckett's tramps, it may be because only the most devoted fans of each have enjoyed their favors fully, and no one can manage to be equally crazy about both.

There are at least two other problems. It may be true that *Hamlet* will outlast *NYPD Blue* and therefore amass more pleasure credits, however this will require *Hamlet* to survive on its merits in order, eventually, to please so many more; it won't be its pleasure-giving qualities at any moment which keep it alive but, rather, its aliveness which makes its pleasure-giving possible; moreover, the proper contest is not between the latest bad play about AIDS and a distant boom from the canon, since The Nonce is meant to be consumed and discarded in order to make way for more Nonce of the same ninnified kind. Why recite Rilke or stage Racine one more time when rap will release one's venom better than most snakes, and when the visual jokes and verbal snickers which make up sleazy sitcoms will restore deserved dignity to big boobs and deep cleavage where Matisse and his odalisques flatly fail. Any popular pastime is soon replaced by another of the same sort, so that the competition we are contemplating should be between similar kinds of empty amusement or consoling kitsch in one corner, and the pot of paint lately flung in the public's face in the other—between crap as a class and the classy as a class—and this contest is no contest; it is a mismatch of monumental proportions: the balance continues to favor whatever is compliant, cheap, and easy.

Occasionally those who confuse an egalitarianism which is politically desirable with a cultural equality which is cowardly, damaging, and reprehensible remind us of the good old days when the masses (how many?) flocked to the pit of the Globe and laughed their lungs out (at what?) at the bad puns and tomfoolery of Shakespeare's clowns, or of the crowds who filled the Athenian theater to be cautioned by Sophocles, or of the thousands who read Dickens devotedly and wept at the death of little Nell, or of the many comrades who filled Communist arenas to hear their Russian poets rant and brought flowers to heap at their feet as if they were prima donnas. In short, some poetry has beaten pushpin in the past, and we ought to take a peek at why instead of whining about popular taste. Cultural levelers hope the upshot of such an examination will support their view that "higher" culture no longer appeals to the people because it has forgotten the people (who are its roots, its audience, its aim), becoming elitist, hopelessly avant-garde, and out of touch with real life and real life's real problems.

However, the evidence is that whenever people have a choice (under Communism citizens had none), they will select schlock with a greed and certainty of conviction which leaves no doubt where their preferences lie; that furthermore they have always done so: in churches they kneel in hundreds at the gaudiest shrines; they troop in thousands to the loudest and least talented rock 'n' rollers and their spectacles; they take pasteboard passions and paper mysteries onto planes; they purchase period furniture and prechewed food; they crowd into movies which glorify stupidity; their idols are personalities, their dreams sentimental, their realities dubious gossip.

And why not? what has hoity-toity culture ever done for them? If they go to the cinema to watch Abel Ganz's *Napoleon* instead of flocking to the flicks to snicker at Steve Martin, they will still be robbed on the way home; their hearts will remain in the same chest; their eyes will stay fixed on the main chance; it will take aspirin to hide their aches and pains; and not a single simple-minded belief will be changed. Levelers can find some comfort in the fact that the cultivated (society dames, academics, intellectuals, professional people), although they may not murder their spouses or rob banks as regularly as the poor and ignorant, manage to envy, conspire, cheat, abuse positions of power, begrudge or resent the success of others, lie and otherwise control events, embezzle, defraud, betray, with an eagerness equal to any, and in numbers sufficient to suggest that no major moral differences between the classes exist.

The Russian novel, English poetry, German music, Italian and Spanish painting, French food, American movies, Italian opera, the English stage, Flemish tapestries, French wine, Viennese operettas, Czech toys, Chicago architecture, Parisian style, Dutch diligence, have enabled their nations and cities to act with piety, circumspection, and respect for others—haven't they? to be sensitive to needs and fears far from their own—haven't they? to avoid aggression, aggrandizement, and exploitation, in order to act always to produce the greatest happiness for the greatest number—everyone counting, but no one counting for more than one. Thank heaven for these higher cultures, which have brought peace and security, certainly prosperity and comfort, to the world.

A derisive noise is appropriate here. As the moral educators of mankind, masterpieces have been one big floppola.

That is why the Test of Time has to be invoked, because the Test of Time puts people at some distance from their selfish selves, allows them to correct more immediate mistakes, permits missing manuscripts to be found, contexts of interest to be enlarged, local prejudices to be overcome. The visionary and the vulgar, the discriminating and the sentimental, the precise and the vague, are so frequently, and against all rational expectation, found together in the same bed that the finer qualities present are compromised and besmirched in the eyes of those otherwise fit to see them. The crude laugh out loud or easily weep at the scandalous scene set before them, the way Dickens' readers giggled and gasped at the doings portrayed in his lively but sentimental cartoons. However, Dickens' language, his rhetoric, which rises sometimes to Shakespeare's level (as well as so much else which rises with it), is ignored by those bent on melodrama, while it is discounted by the snobbishly fastidious who see it as servicing only soap opera and special pleading. The Test of Time sieves inhuman failings like silt through a prospector's pan, leaving a residue which is clearly either gold or gravel.

So conceived and supported, the Test of Time is nevertheless made ineffective by the intractable naiveté of its assumptions. For isn't it naive to suppose that history will allow only the best to survive? is it that considerate? does history spare cultural icons when it does not hesitate to defeat virtue, or when it permits the truth to be trampled under the feet of ignorant fanatics? does it cry out "Halt!" when a fine building is about to be destroyed? does it reroute bombs? does it encourage care and stewardship for the Fine while forgetting the False? Haven't we been told that the human race made progress when it replaced the great Greek gods with a bewhiskered tyrannical granddad whose mean spirit is as big as his beard?

In what world do we live if we think only the good guys win and virtue is always rewarded? In a free market, the vulgar, we have learned, will grab all the meat and potatoes and elbow the refined, empty-handed, out the door. People are wicked because wickedness gives them an advantage. When the Romans overran Greece, they took bare-assed marble boys and busty girlies home to decorate their villas, and melted bronzes down to make pitiless the points of their spears. Pagans, Christians, Moslems took turns burning the books of Alexandria's library. Invaders loot, sack, pillage, rape, and burn. Whoever they are. Whatever it is. They steal to sell. They steal to display, to vaunt, to collect. Indian mounds are leveled like harvested fields, and gold and slaves are sent back to the capital. Those who rise up against criminal divinities stupidly burn down the temples of the super-stitious (which may be glorious and beautiful) instead of the superstitions of the superstitious (which are ignorant, ugly, and obscene).

Of course, we should not blame "history." History is not an agent who goes about trampling traditions into dust, ending lives, stifling others, despoiling the land, and poisoning the sea. History is humanity on its rampage. Considering the frequency of natural calamities, our treatment of warfare as a seasonal sport, and the insatiable squirrelliness of human greed, it should be an occasion for surprise when anything excellent survives.

3

How indeed does it? In the same way that Elvis Presley does. So far. It has fans. The devoted gather, often slowly at first, each fan feeling alone with her enthusiasm and despised for it—odd-eyed because El Greco or Modigliani or Picasso pleases; odd-eared because Schoenberg or Burl Ives or Bartók is thrilling; conceptually queer because Celan makes instant sense, or Hopkins thrives, or Musil musiks the mind. Or because WOW, man.

When the work which is worshipped has been roundly reviled, it becomes even more precious. It shows society up. It verifies the fan's feeling of being isolated and unappreciated, in a foreign land, surrounded by indifference or hostility. The "new" architecture is attacked because it is felt to be opposed to present preferences; the "new" music undermines an entire tradition; the "new" painting accuses reality of appearance; the "new" writing is incomprehensible, obscene, blasphemous, politically incorrect; thus each art finds its "new" adherents among those similarly disaffected.

"Fan" is a shortened form of "fanatic," and it is true that the fan's faith is often half-sighted if not entirely blind, often fueled as much by the dislike its object provokes in others as by the love its object inspires in him; so that the fan often falls for a message which isn't there, is moved by emotions which aren't expressed, by strategies which haven't been employed.

Fans form clubs or find other ways in which to share their enthusiasms. The fan's love does not resemble romantic passion in every way, because it is rarely possessive; it is more like chauvinism in the sense that the fan's feelings make him the member of a defining cult or tribe. He's prepared to love anybody Irish, anyone French. A fan is prepared to devote far more time to the pursuit and glorification of his idol than most people are, even those who find the composer's music or the author's works intriguing or uncommonly fine. Eventually, fans will found a holy shrine. These shrines, in their turn, will employ professional "keepers of the flame"; they'll put out bulletins and publish magazines; they'll manufacture relics, peddle icons, sponsor gatherings; and before you can say "Mickey Mouse" or "Bobbie Burns" there'll be a group in place whose livelihood, not just their enthusiasm or donated time, will depend upon the continued idolization of the idol—and by the enlistment of greater and greater numbers. Economic interests are generally more reliable and enduring than love. Social status hangs upon money like a fob from a watch, and power from both. The keepers of the flame, like the clergy, will have many more reasons than adoration to carry out their duties. Not infrequently the fan's devotion is no more than displaced patriotism, as when a poet is loved because he is Welsh or Scots, and the natives are gleeful that someone of their race with genius has been found. In any case, any adoration, which isn't drama, spectacle, and public relations—which is simply rich understanding and deep appreciation—can come last.

In short, the work of art, the performer, the beneficial idea, have become "the treasures of" an institution—the Mona Lisa in the Louvre. It is the institution and its interests which carry their symbol before them like a flag, a chalice, a trophy, across the treacherous bournes of Time. If you think it is hard to find true virtue hidden somewhere in this story, you are right. The institutions, in their turn, become tools for large ones: if a young nation, a new movement, needs heroes and poets, some Longfellow will be chosen and brought to the schools like a captive in chains, or some hero like Nathan Hale will be installed in the national story like a bishop in the church; this painted pop-up history will then be taught to helpless kiddies to confirm the prejudices of their parents so that the myth of a magically united and superior society can be passed on to its prospective citizens in order that they may each equally enjoy the pleasures of chauvinistic self-satisfaction, while, at the same time, conserving their oh-so-common cultural values, preserving the legitimacy of the status quo, and guaranteeing, consequently, the continued power of the State and its teams of pickpockets.

If there is someone sane you wish to drive mad, merely institutionalize him; if there is some Good you wish to besmirch, some Truth you wish to undermine, organize it; if there is some noble and glorious career you wish to destroy, parade its accomplishments past a committee.

The canon—Shakespeare, Dante, Chaucer, Cervantes, and so

on—blessed by Harold Bloom—are alas not there because greatness is both steed and shield to carry them on through the indifference of history, past its nervous overseers and their obedient
serfs. Leaders—political, religious, economic—care nothing for
merit; they value only use. And they succeed because the led are
no differently inclined. The poor may not be poor because they
are poor of mind and heart (as some suggest), but their minds and
hearts are certainly not a bit better for it. Their sort of simple life
is simpleminded; a life close to the soil is lived near the grave; the
workman's pride in the work of his hands was long ago mecha-
nized; the rhythms of Have and Want and Get never change.
Those who are "out" are not better for being there, otherwise why
would they seek a change?

But they—those who fancy they are not making out very well
like other folks are supposed to be making out in the wonderful
world of those other folks—will be quick to see in what direction
the canon fires, and will have the rhetoric I have just rehearsed as
handy as spit in their mouths. They will memorize the ways they
have been cheated; they will have care-baskets of truth on their
side; they can point to a campaign of discrimination, injury,
neglect; they can quite rightly complain of unfairness and bigotry
and misuse. They will advance their own art, their own neglected
texts, their own critical methods, their own mythologies in opposition to the cultural icons in place. Nothing could be more natural, nothing more righteous than their indignation. It will seem
that they alone love literature, let it act importantly, help it to
shape their communities; and to a degree—lacking money,
power, and other forms of glue—they will be right; but make no
mistake: like the Puritans, they'll love liberty only when facing
their enemies, who don't want them to have it. It will turn out,
moreover, that the struggle against their common adversary will
not permit internal divisions. For a time, freedom of thought and
action will have to be sacrificed to the goals of the group, and so
on—how often have we heard it? Not bold new behavior, not

innovative notions, but conformity and compaction are the consequences.

Since minorities have no armies and few fields to fight on, their members bicker like faculties over the most minor matters, bitterly opposing this or ardently espousing that, as if a schedule change would alter the course of the Gulf Stream, a staff appointment in the history of igloo design revolutionize the building code. But these quibbles screen the truth from outsider eyes. Disciplines have been derailed, departments destroyed, careers ruined, so that "right thinking" might prevail. Tweedledum and Tweedledee are fighting with nothing over nothing because they haven't guns yet. Then it will be life and death.

Groups squabble about literature because they have other than literary uses for the literary. The schools, which are busy finding ways to get the answers to the Test of Time smuggled to their chosen favorites, as coaches slip the answers to their players so they may pass the latest examination, will now and then speak of Art and claim a disinterested purity. And there are an unorganized few (the unhappy few whom I should like to represent, "the immense minority," as Juan Ramón Jiménez so significantly puts it) who sincerely love the arts. There are those for whom reading, for example, can be an act of love, and lead to a revelation, not of truth, moral or otherwise, but of lucidity, order, rightness of relation, the experience of a world fully felt and furnished and worked out in the head, the head where the heart is also to be found, and all the other vital organs.

I have the good luck not to live in an English department, so I have not had to observe directly or suffer intimately the sophistical poses of pluralism and the opportunistic fads of fashion which the courtiers of our culture have paraded on its runways, but my feeling is "it has been ever thus." Philosophy departments, where my presence has been more frequent, have, during my brief sojourn in their narrow halls, practiced the prejudices of Idealism, Pragmatism, Positivism, Existentialism, and Phenomenology, and served the interests of special groups (a practice they once despised) by offering biomedical or business ethics, game theory, philosophical psychology, and feminist studies.

Inside the Academy, at the Symphony, within Museum walls, each warring faction will boast that God is on their side, and claim transcendence for their values and opinions. This is done by trying to ensure that only their ideas, and works correctly expressing them, get put before the public in the future, and by reanalyzing the past for as far back as the catalogue has cards (a deliberately out-of-date metaphor) in order to show, as I previously characterized their internecine struggles, that "it has been ever thus," whatever it is they say it is now.

Outside, in the vendors' streets, there are nothing but temporary tents. The lasting, the universal, are despised (except by those who are still peddling the classics to old fogies). But who really wants reruns of already winded warhorses? Well, only those arrogant and rapacious revivalists who set *Rigoletto* in the Bronx and who want Dido and Aeneas to sing about their love while costumed as colonials. Their pitiful originalities would have once brought them to the gibbet or the stake.

The ideal cultural product comes powerfully packaged, creates a mighty stir, can be devoured with both delight and a sense of life-shaking revelation, provides an easy topic for talk, is guaranteed to be without real salt or any actual fat—contains no substance of any substantial kind—so that after you have eaten it, for days you will shit only air.

So are all these works, which appear to have persisted, the way postmen once did, through dark nights and bad weather (the past's periodic eclipses of reason, and other ages of ice), here now only through evil machination or by odd accident? The poet may duck, escape his time, as Quevedo writes:

> Retired to the peace of this desert,
> with a collection of books that are few but wise,

The Test of Time

I live in conversation with the departed
and listen to the dead with my eyes.

(Quoted by Octavio Paz in *The Other Voice.*
New York: Harcourt Brace, 1991, p. 111)

but the work cannot choose its companions or by itself steer a favorable course. Yet, oddly, something like that happens. Minds find minds. The intelligent heart beats in more than one head, and a wise book contains a consciousness which has at last made something wonderful of the world.

For when I follow Thoreau's prose, I am in no ordinary footsteps. *Walden* has been read and reread; it is hallowed; it is an American classic; it sells because generations of students at all sorts of grade levels are asked to answer questions about it; and it is still seen to support this group, that cause, have relevance. How full of these tourists the woods are, how trampled the paths, how bored or nervous or put upon the picnickers feel, forced to spread their blankets over these placid pages.

Have they felt a sentence start like a rabbit from beneath their eye? Or watched a meadow made small by the sky, or studied a simple street, or felt the wind flutter a row of wash like flags hung from a window? And been taught by such a sentence what it is to be alive? Rilke wondered:

> Are we, perhaps, *here* just to utter: house,
> bridge, fountain, gate, jug, fruit tree, window—
> at most: column, tower . . . but to *utter* them, remember,
> to speak in a way which the named never dreamed they
> could *be.*

Gertrude Stein wondered more than once what went into a masterpiece: what set some works aside to be treasured while others were abandoned without a thought, as we leave seats after a performance; what there was about a text we'd read which provoked us to repeat its pages; what made us want to remain by its side, rereading and remembering, even line by line; what led us to defend its integrity, as though our honor were at stake, and to lead it safely through the perils that lie in wait for excellence in a world where only mediocrity seems prized. She concluded that masterpieces were addressed, not to the self whose accomplishments might appear on some dossier, the self whose passport is examined at the border, the self whose concerns are those of the Self (I and My and Me and Mine); but to the human mind, a faculty which is everywhere the same and whose business is with universals. Masterpieces teach that human differences are superficial; that intelligence counts, not approved conclusions; that richly received and precisely appreciated sensations matter, not titillation or dolled-up data; that foreplay, not payoff, is to be preferred; that imagination and conceptual solutions, not ad hoc problem solving, are what such esteemed works have in common. And we, who read and write and bear witness and wail with grief, who make music and massacres, who paint in oils and swim in blood—we are one: everywhere as awful, and as possibly noble, as our natures push us or permit us to be.

Say a sort of "amen" to that. But the trouble with transcendence is that the transcendent must rise, and to make that possible it must lighten its load, dump detail as worse than unwanted, toss aside everything that thickens life and leads us to lick it like gravy. Overboard go all gross things, as if the crude and hollow and impermanent weren't recurrent. Transcendence is not what masterworks teach me: they teach me immersion. They teach me that the trivial is as important as the important when looked at importantly. They tell me that evil is lasting and complex and significant and profoundly alluring, and that it requires our appreciative and steadfast gaze more than grace and goodness do, who receive it like starlets—only too often ready to giggle in reply.

And we, who must be transcendent too, if universals are to take any notice of us, lose ourselves in the course of this diet: our little habits, simple pleasures, traits which set us aside as a certain someone—perhaps a lovely leg we shave and sand and wax as if it held up period furniture, or a voice we exercise as we would a show horse, or the way we cheat at Parcheesi or treat the sweet tooth we suffer and adore with weekend sundaes, or try to defeat the line a strategic elastic has left on our body by undressing in the dark and relying on the skin's resilience to erase the statement by morning.

Even ideas (and certainly their abstractness recommends them), when they are thought, are drenched in the particularities of time and place and mood and purpose, because minds, it turns out, are as particular as toenails, and are always like a working part of a tired foot too, companion to the other toes; so that your belief in God and my belief in the divinity of the dance aren't just notions we've put mustaches on to differentiate them, but are as peculiar to us as our visage is, our fingerprint, our taste in clothes, our loyalty, our laugh.

As Ernst Cassirer said of the aim of Kant's critical philosophy: "To step into the infinite it suffices to penetrate the finite in all its aspects."

We are in cahoots with art. We want everything to survive, even flies. And there they are, on that slope of Rilke's lines: the gate, the house, the fruit tree, window—awaiting our look to be realized, not as house or tree or window but as a smeared gray pane, a pane as gray as the walk is where it proceeds through that skimpy sick grass there past a leafless tree up to the weathered front door, ajar as if to welcome our entry, but actually left open by the whole of Yesterday when that Time went, with its features and its friends, never to return. When we entered, if we took note of the weathered top of the kitchen table when we entered, and how a dim gray light puddled in some of its scars and leaked the length of its cracks; if we saw, when we entered, how the blue pitcher stood amid crumbs of bread like a bird that's just been fed, and how a dish towel hung for an hour over the ladderback of a kitchen chair, drying its sweat-shaped patches of damp before being taken up to be dampened again; had we found the paint or prose or pipe for them; had we rhymed a skillet's sear with a knife's scratch, then we'd have them still, still as Walden's water was when Thoreau skiffed at night across it and cast a line:

> Sometimes, after staying in a village parlor till the family had all retired, I have returned to the woods, and, partly with a view to the next day's dinner, spent the hours of midnight fishing from a boat by moonlight, serenaded by owls and foxes, and hearing, from time to time, the creaking note of some unknown bird close at hand. These experiences were very memorable and valuable to me,—anchored in forty feet of water, and twenty or thirty rods from the shore, sur-rounded sometimes by thousands of small perch and shin-ers, dimpling the surface with their tails in the moonlight, and communicating by a long flaxen line with mysterious nocturnal fishes which had their dwelling forty feet below, or sometimes dragging sixty feet of line about the pond as I drifted in the gentle night breeze, now and then feeling a slight vibration along it, indicative of some life prowling about its extremity, of dull uncertain blundering purpose there, and slow to make up its mind. (*Walden,* chapter 9, "The Ponds")

We cannot say with certainty what will live, and survival, by itself, is no guarantee of quality; but I think we can say something about what is deserving. Thoreau's two unsimple sentences put me out on that pond, in prose as clear as its water is. Now I can mourn its present turbid state, and fashion a fine romance from my memory of a time when kids could stay out late to fish, and feel the distant friendship of the stars like the lights of Atlantis in the water. But the magical stillness in the prose, its easy motion, depends upon its calm and measured breathing, its quiet but ever-present music, its unhurried and appreciative perceptions, like a slow swallow of wine.

All those numbers would paralyze most paragraphs. However,

here, as I move my mind along the line, holding its hush in my ear, of course I do not see the dimpling surface of the lake—the lake is miles from me, the time is out of reach, the categories of existence clash—but my consciousness *conceives* the seeing, *conceives* the thirty rods of distance to the shore, *conceives* the twitch a nibble makes, how the pole's handle tickles the angler's palm, and consequently understands the decision slowly forming down there from the nudge of the fish's nose.

There's no moment too trivial, too sad, too vulgar, too rinky-dink to be unworthy of such recollection, for even a wasted bit of life is priceless when composed properly or hymned aright, even that poor plate of peaches slowly spoiling while its portrait is being painted—not, however, the peaches themselves, which must rot to realize their nature, and not a sore tooth's twinge, and not a battle's loss or love's loss, or the cutest darling dimple, or a bite of pie the peaches could have been better put to use in; no, rather, their rendering—that's priceless: the Cézanne which gives to the mountain more than it merits, the juice which runs from alongside that aching tooth when the topmost peach is bitten, but only when a sentence performs the biting, and the juice is wiped off by the word "sleeve," and the smile of satisfaction can be read as it spreads across the face of the page.

When Hopkins wondered "how to keep," whether there was "any any,"

> none such, nowhere known some, bow or brooch or braid
>   or brace, lace, latch or catch or key to keep
> Back beauty, keep it, beauty, beauty, beauty, . . . from
>   vanishing away

he knew, of course, the answer; which was yes, "there is one," there is a place where

> the thing we freely forfeit is kept with fonder a care,
> Fonder a care kept than we could have kept it, kept
> Far with fonder a care

but he said it was "yonder," in effect, up in the air, as "high as that," when all the while he knew where it was: it was there under his forming fingers; it was in his writing, where the real god, the god he could not avow—dared not worship—worked, wrote, writing his rhetorical regrets, putting his question so perfectly the proof was in the putting.

Hopkins, in one mood, writes,

> Nothing is so beautiful as Spring—
> When weeds, in wheels, shoot long and lovely and lush,

while in a wintertime time, when his faith nears icy cinder, he complains,

> No worst, there is none. Pitched past pitch of grief,
> More pangs will, schooled at forepangs, wilder wring,

but there's no contradiction here; it's not that one of them is right, that he should buck up and be brave or leave off sentimentalizing about one more season. And the fact that for a moment, in his heart, his faith is renewed or shaken, while in mine, his reader, belief being absent, faith has no place to stand or snow in which to shiver—that difference makes no difference; it is as irrelevant as yesterday's air, because opinions, principles, philosophies, systems of belief, are also a part of the passing world, beauties themselves, some of them, rich in invention, as full of our longing as legs in long pants; and our longings are real, if what they long for isn't; they also need their celebration, since each of them is like a baited line sunk into a Deep beyond our seeing—searching—waiting for the nose of something there to twitch it, waiting for a nibble.

Celebrate sorrow—why not? celebrate pain, invent a Iago, bring on the awfuls, Bosch's brush awaits to do its best by the worsts. Christ hangs from the cross like an ill-hung suit, yet the meaning of His suffering is our redemption. My heresy is: redemption is on the canvas, in the image and its pigments, in the skill and attitudes that brought paint to this pass.

4

How best to ace the Test of Time? in a world where everything good happens later than you'd have liked, and everything bad breaks out before you expected it? Good times do pass, and bad ones, dear heart, for all your poetizing, are bad; the good is quick as a bird, the bad is slow as ooze, and, dearie, for all your whistling Dixie, evils are not nice. If Hopkins is down in the dumps, he is miserable down there, and no fine lines will redeem the dumps, or save him from his doubts, or relieve him of the truth: God's not going to pluck him out of the earth where he will surely lie and surely rot; not as if he were a parsnip pulled clear and shaken clean. Anyway, rinsed of the grave, he'd only be headed for the soup.

Thoreau went boating as a boy, and dropped his line, and never did it happen in prose of any kind, including his own: the line's great curve behind him as he trolled was drawn in cold pond water, crystalline. Now Walden is threatened by developers every year, and the water has been soiled by decades of rancid runoff. What has been saved, then, what has been preserved, what has withstood time? . . . and the sawyer's saws? The Binsey poplars were suddenly felled, as if in front of Hopkins' saddened eye, blunt stumps lining the bank where he passed as faithfully as the river, their short life shortened by someone who could cut, and could cancel his care before it came up into consciousness . . . who could ax one and watch it fall and then another.

> My aspens dear, whose airy cages quelled,
> Quelled or quenched in leaves the leaping sun,
> All felled, felled, are all felled.

"Wake and feel the fell of dark, not day." This is how; this is why. The paragraphs of *Walden* form in words what never happened. I agree: events encouraged those words, events surprised them into existence; but Thoreau made his memory, created water that never was . . . oh yes, they tossed the brands they burned to lure the fish up out of nighttime as if the sun had risen, they tossed the brands like fireworks and listened to them return to enter the water with a kiss; but they did so by swinging their arms then, and not in so many, not in any, words: "And when we had done, far in the night, threw the burning brands high into the air like skyrockets, which, coming down into the pond, were quenched with a loud hissing, and we were suddenly groping in total darkness." Thoreau was not Thoreau then, just a boy, playing a flute to charm the perch, catching pouts with threaded worms, and not a word, I'm sure, disturbed the serenity of that life.

So had it not happened—and where is that Walden now?—it would have happened anyway, but not in Time, who allows the ax to swing like a second hand, but in the prose or in the poem where, down in the dumps, a pun appears to point out to us that life, that misery, does not pun and does not rhyme and has no rhythm, sprung or otherwise, so inadequate is it; and why not let life pass, then, get along; life, thank god, happens only once, and its pains are merely painful, hurtfully plain, while in the poem pain is wrung from the poet as if he were wet wash, but since he's been pitched past pitch of grief, the ringing has a pealing sound: the pangs of pain, the procession of those p's.

Didn't the poplars cage—quell—the sunlight themselves, so how can they complain? and weren't those burning brands quenched as well? One light went while rising; the other fell. Time holds occasions open like opportunities, but the poet's poem never was in time like the trees or his grief or Walden's water was mid night. They, those things, the terrible sonnets, every one, were composed, brought by Hopkins into being, not when he was down in the dumps, not while he was Hopkins, but when he was a Poet, truly on top of the world, the muse his mother; and the poems supplant their cause, are sturdier than trees, and will strip the teeth of any saw that tries to down them.

Because when the poplars went, they went without the poet's passion for them as present as their leaves. And we, as readers, are not brought to Walden Pond in some poetic time machine. We experience Walden as it passed through Thoreau's head, his whole heart there for us to pass through too, his wide bright eyes the better to see with, the patient putting together of his prose to appreciate. Of the pond, the trees, the pain, the poet may retain—through the indelibilities of his medium—moments which, in reality, went as swiftly as a whistle away; but he will also give them what was never there in the first place: much afterthought, correction, suggestion, verbal movement, emotion, meaning, music. The result is the combination of occasion, con-sciousness, and artful composition which we now—oh so fortu-nately—have. Thus the night was not as it was described, neither the fishing nor the pain; events, actions, objects, didn't repeat; the feelings were never felt, the wringing and the quelling, they were as baked as biscuits; and the thoughts were never thought that way—what thoughts there were are as long gone as the row of trees—they were composed; in sum, the pond we know, the trees, the pain, the poet's passion for each actual thing, the philosopher's concerns, mourning the fallen trees, they never were anywhere but in Hopkins' words:

> When we hew or delve:
> After-comers cannot guess the beauty been.
> Ten or twelve, only ten or twelve
> Strokes of havoc unselve
> The sweet especial scene,
> Rural scene, a rural scene,
> Sweet especial rural scene.

That is half our answer. It was lovely to be on Walden Pond at midnight, fluting the fish, but lovelier and more lasting in the ver-bal than in the fishing lines. It is painful to lose faith even for a moment or see a row of crudely hewn trunks where your favorite rustic scene once was, but mutilation's sorrow is inspiring in the reading, although we realize the poem does not soften the blows felt by the trees.

Here is the other half. Don't take the test. Poetry makes nothing happen, because it refuses to be a happenstance. Poems are not events. They are realities remarkably invested with value. They are a woman, a man, a mind made of words, and have no body, and hence no needs.

So be advised. For works of art, the rule reads: never enter Time, and you will never be required to exit.

SOCIAL AND POLITICAL
CONTRETEMPS

The following group of essays was called forth by circumstances—in particular the social and political plight of the writer in our contemporary world. They may be overly fulminacious in consequence, and cause the reader to find the repetition of my animosities wearisome even if shared. I can only hope that the occasions and contexts differ sufficiently to give them a fresh edge. It is a caution scarcely necessary, but these essays should not be read pell-mell. In daily life we usually enjoy a week between sermons, although news of evil and the incessant activities of sinners arrives at every morning's breakfast table with our coffee and our fruit.

The Writer and Politics:
A Litany

Socrates was accused and tried and convicted of corrupting the youth. His enemies said he believed in gods other than the gods of the State. It would become a convenient charge, a familiar crime. And Socrates hadn't written a word, though he would inspire some. Plato got even by banishing most poets from his ideal republic (a gesture whose import was so theoretical it failed to unkilter a single rhyme); for, after all, if the poets had not actually invented all the gods, they had certainly assigned them their places in the Olympian hierarchy and written their roles in the sordid tales which were to be their myths. How should one punish such offenses: to have invented gods who do not exist, or written lies about those who do? We are all prepared to applaud eloquence when it is employed in the service of truth, but when it is turned the other way, should we continue to admire it anyway—although now as the display of splendid technique and an instance of inspired rodomontade?

Sir Thomas Malory was a parliamentarian before he became a crook. He was charged with robbing churches, with extortion, with rape, and jailed nine times by our least numerous count. During his idle days of imprisonment he penned what became the *Book of King Arthur and His Noble Knights of the Round Table*. Evil to the end, he cribbed its people, its plots, and their unfolding from previous romances. Ditto a lot of that for O. Henry. François Villon was pardoned, fled town until he felt his crimes had been forgotten, or otherwise escaped incarceration for brawling, burglary, petty theft, and fatally wounding a priest, finally disappearing altogether, probably a good idea. Benvenuto Cellini waited until the arrival of old age, another kind of prison, before writing his autobiography; but he was quarrelsome in his youth and murdered at least two men before fame eased him into innocence. Giovanni Casanova, Chevalier de Seingalt, likewise led a life of interesting dubiety—gambling, whoring, spying, duping, playing with black magic—until the heretical presuppositions of his illicit spells clapped him in prison. His dramatic escape parallels the earlier feats of Cellini, and gave him even more to brag about.

The Charterhouse of Parma, one of the great political novels, nevertheless turns on nothing more political than love. Here the prison romance is carried to new heights, namely to the top of the three-hundred-foot Farnese Tower, where, in its more elevated cell, Stendhal's Italian tenor–like hero, Fabrizio del Dongo, has been unjustly clapped, almost as Cellini was in Castel Sant'Angelo, or like the novel's more explicit model, Alessandro Farnese, who escaped from such a tower by means of a rope (as we like to measure things today) the length of a football field. But lo! from his perch Fabrizio can glimpse the governor's beautiful daughter, who lives in an adjoining turret, and naturally he falls in love and refuses his opportunity for freedom because it would mean losing sight of her. What woman could resist such sappy devotion! But then! she orders him to flee on her account, and thus Fabrizio begins his famous descent in pages through which one holds one's breath.

The notorious Marquis de Sade, who made libertinism a profession, passed twenty-seven years of his life in the lockup, where he wrote most of the trash which made his name a Name. Brought up by his uncle, a profligate abbé, he was only months into his arranged marriage when he was arrested for actions at an orgy. Released, he began to misspend his wife's dowry, much of it on a little house he had built for his debaucheries, the rest on a famous whore he had now taken as his mistress. He subsequently elopes with his wife's sister; is condemned to death for poisoning and sodomy; is shot at by the father of a servant girl, whose aim is unfortunately untrained; is hunted by the police; and is imprisoned in the Bastille, where he incites the people to revolt by scattering notes from the window of his cell and addressing them through a funnel he has devised to magnify his voice. We can get an idea of what he said by reading his "Address to the French Nation: Yet Another Effort, Frenchmen, If You Would Become Republicans." The unlucky marquis is transferred to an insane asylum only days before the Bastille is stormed and its prisoners released. For de Sade, every sexual act was political, and buggery was simply a way of marking your ballot.

Marco Polo was made a prisoner of war by the Genovese, and it was in jail that he told his eventually famous tale to a fellow detainee who no doubt listened in Venetian but wrote down what he heard in a sort of French. Like so many flies, Polo's merchant friends are alleged to have gathered around his deathbed to beg him to erase those made-up miracles like gunpowder and paper money from his pages and take back his enticing lies. Ages after, doubters took back their incredulous states of mind like IOUs that remained unclaimed. Ben Jonson contributed to the maintenance of artistic standards by killing an actor in a duel. Sharing similar values, the court let him off. Chaucer was a French prisoner of war before embarking on an extensive and successful public career: controller of customs, justice of the peace, clerk of the king's works, royal forester, member of Parliament. Frightened by hellfire and other unpleasant fates he felt awaited him, he cravenly disavowed his secular works. Similarly a soldier, Charles d'Orléans, was captured by the English at Agincourt. The Duke of Burgundy ransomed him after twenty-five years on the promise that Charles would marry the duke's niece. Hobson's choice.

Miguel de Cervantes was captured by Turkish pirates and dungeoned in Algeria. Perhaps this rehearsal prepared him for his later incarceration for fraud. In any case, he began *Don Quixote* surrounded by thick walls and dim light. Sir Walter Raleigh suffered the disfavor of the court on three occasions. During his second stay in the Tower of London he completed the first volume of his *History of the World,* while during the third he lost his head. What he had written was never an issue. Thomas Wyatt also went often to visit that perilous Tower, though each time he was put in, a very well placed lady got him out. John Bunyan was arrested for unlicensed preaching. During his first stint in jail he invented that great title *Grace Abounding to the Chief of Sinners,* and then he even went on to write the book. During his second prison sentence, he began *Pilgrim's Progress.* George Chapman mocked the Scots and was jugged by James I, who was one of the Scots mocked. John Wilmot, the second Earl of Rochester, was convicted of abduction, though he later made an honest woman of the heiress he had kidnapped, both marrying her and giving her three more children than he gave his mistress. Rochester misspent his life in a series of almost classical debaucheries. His cowardly repentance and religious conversion at the end did not save him from Hell, where we can be confident that, between moments of beautiful lamentation, he is still burning.

Galileo experienced house arrest and was also, in different circumstances, compelled to recant, although he had attributed his work to a nom de plume. Boethius was arrested and executed in Pavia. Between these two events he wrote *De consolatione philosophiae.* One hopes his prescription worked for him. Descartes deemed it wise to delay publication and to move about a lot. Spinoza was hounded for heresy, and a contract, it's said, was put out on his life. It is doubtless small comfort to Salman Rushdie to have such distant and distinguished company. Francis Bacon prosecuted his patron, Essex, for treason, and was found guilty himself of bribery and consequently expelled from court.

Vianini was burned at the stake. Only philosophers remember this. At the hands of the Inquisition Giordano Bruno suffered the same painful fate. Nothing was ever done to Louisa May Alcott. Aretino specialized in scurrilous libels, and he was thoroughly thrashed a few times by his enemies, but he was able to stink up his pages with happy impunity because he kept friends in high papal places and aided many a scoundrel with his wealth. In short, he played politics and sang the conniver's tunes. For his skills, the gods let his liver fail, and he died, they say, when a blood vessel burst in his throat while he was laughing at a bawdy joke. In sum, he had a good life, although he hardly led one.

Petronius did not have such luck. Falsely accused of treason, though guilty only of elegance and good taste, he was forced to open his own veins. Henry Howard, the Earl of Surrey, was also groundlessly accused of the same high crime, and despite a distinguished career of service in the military, he was executed on Tower Hill. However, George Villiers, the Duke of Buckingham, was a legitimately schemeful sort. An accomplished court intriguer, he shifted his weight like someone on a skateboard, and earned Dryden's description of him as a "chemist, fiddler, statesman, and buffoon." Thomas Hobbes and Edmund Waller were Royalists or Roundheads as the occasion required, proving once more that a cleverly managed lack of loyalty is like money in the bank. Edmund Burke, paymaster and member of Parliament, spent most of his life opposing not only revolutions but their causes. Although he was in and out of office, as politicians often are, and an accomplished maker of enemies, his eloquence was never interrupted but grew admirably—albeit futilely—grander as more and more rebellions broke out despite his warnings and advice.

The Romans were hard on their heroes. Cicero was not particularly brave, but his words were, and it was for them that Mark Antony had Cicero's head and hand nailed to the rostrum of the Forum. Mark Antony still has his admirers, proving that nothing is unimaginable. Sir Charles Sedley was a retired rake who sat in Parliament and wrote love lyrics. His head remained firmly on. August Kotzebue, on the other hand, was always in hot water. Arrested as a German spy by Czar Paul I and sent to Siberia, he was pardoned the next year and made director of the German theater in St. Petersburg. A little while later, having turned his coat inside out, he returned to Germany as an agent of another czar, this time Alexander I. His duties included editing a reactionary weekly in Mannheim, but—for such are the risks of extremism and notoriety—he was murdered by a member of a radical student movement. Among his other misfortunes, Kotzebue was married three times. Sarah Orne Jewett and Willa Cather were spared such indignities. However, Luís Vaz de Camoëns ill-naturedly wounded a court official in a common street fight and was imprisoned without any apparent stimulation of his muse, who showed up later to assist the composition of canto after canto of *Os Lusíadas*.

Christopher Marlowe was certainly a lowlife, probably a spy as well, and was murdered in a barroom brawl. Francisco Gómez de Quevedo y Villegas (may his name lengthen like Pinocchio's nose) was repelled by the corruption he encountered at the court of Philip III, and began to scourge the courtiers with satirical verses. However, having killed a negligent opponent in a duel, he ran away to Italy. There he found employment as an agent for the Duke of Orsona, whose own political machinations backfired, bouncing Quevedo back to Spain. His satires got him in trouble again, and he was shut up in a monastery for nearly four years. Roger L'Estrange became Quevedo's English translator. Both a Royalist and a Protestant, he was trusted by neither side in the Civil War. Nor did he trust them. All hands were correct. Although he published innumerable libelous pamphlets himself, he was an ardent opponent of the press's freedom. L'Estrange was one of our first professional men of letters and so sold his pen to whoever would pay (Dr. Johnson claimed); consequently, most of what he wrote is wholly forgettable. His enemies so little esteemed L'Estrange, they thought his jailing nearly beneath their notice, though he had sat in Parliament and was eighty-two when the authorities troubled themselves to put him away. So much for good character! for an honest career! let us lift a glass to blind prejudice! another to deceit! each to be preferred to piety or fidelity or a foolish reluctance to cheat. Despite his numerous failings, Sir Roger's translation is a miracle.

Baldassare Castiglione managed to represent several dukes with distinction himself and served as the papal nuncio to Charles V, all the while composing the courtier's handbook. *Il libro del cortegiano* is full of advice lost on most of the louts on our present list. An exception, of course, is Sir Philip Sidney, who kept his character clean by dying young, offering his canteen to a common soldier though sorely wounded himself, and publishing all his works posthumously. Thomas Shadwell made the lucky mistake of angering Dryden by trying to place his Whig on the great poet's Tory. Dryden rewarded him with immortality as the target of his satire *Mac Flecknoe*. Ah, and then there is the case of Camus, and the contrary case of Carlyle, and the difficult case of Céline.

Alcofribas Nasier's first satire, *Pantagruel,* was called obscene by the authorities at the Sorbonne, as was his second, *Gargantua,* and even his third, although, possibly out of weariness, they didn't badger the author about the fourth. The spurious *Fifth Book of Pantagruel* was probably faked by François Rabelais in an attempt to cash in on Nasier's success. *Madame Bovary* put Flaubert in the dock and gave him his fame, as well as initiating the dyspepsia which probably killed him. Congreve was rewarded with employment as a commissioner for licensing hackney coaches, and then rewarded with the office of commissioner of wines, before becoming secretary to the island of Jamaica.

Cavalcanti, a friend of Dante's and a Guelph to boot, was exiled to Sarzana, where he died of malaria. Céline was decorated for bravery, don't forget. Sébastien-Roch Nicolas Chamfort ghostwrote for some moderate French revolutionaries. Moderation is not a revolutionary's strong suit, and during the Terror the times turned against him. He botched his suicide and died eventually of the botch. Most of his points of view were sharp and exemplary: natural ills produce in their student a contempt for death, he said, while social ills promote a contempt for life. Wordsworth, whose opinions were warm toast beside those of Chamfort, could manage only an appointment as a tax collector. *Leaves of Grass* got Whitman fired from a similar position, although Edwin Arlington Robinson held on to his sinecure at the New York Customs House until his long poems became book club selections.

> Edna St. Vincent Millay
> went to Paris and tried to be gay,
> but play as she might
> the rhythms weren't right,
> and a Pulitzer whisked her away.
> Wrote some poems and directed a play
> in the state she decided to stay.
> To come to no harm
> she retired to a farm,
> but with seeds in her hair
> was no happier there,
> mid the romance of new-mown hay,
> till she saw beauty bare
> at the foot of a stair,
> where Edna St. Vincent Mil lay.

Religion, which did so many writers in by both bullying their bodies and browbeating their brains, served François de Chateaubriand well, giving him a soft seat next to royalty and a lot of cushy diplomatic jobs. Initially exiled to England, he returned as the French ambassador, with a lady under each tender arm like loaves of French bread. No one has ever written more wonderfully about the self. How can things like this happen, we have to ask. The handsome and noble Pico della Mirandola dutifully but dangerously compiled nine hundred theses which he proposed to defend in a public speech he would make in Rome. The pope, however, thought otherwise, and Pico took a vacation in Paris. André Chénier was guillotined on Robespierre's order. Georges Feydeau was left undisturbed, while Johann Christian Hölderlin, William Collins, August Strindberg, Torquato Tasso, John Clare, Christopher Smart, Friedrich Nietzsche, Robert Walser, and William Cowper went mad without any political encouragement. More wives went nuts than their writer-spouses, which makes sense. Aphra Behn, like Beaumarchais, was a spy for the crown, but she received so little reward for her services she was compelled to spend some time in debtor's prison, starting to write only when released. Lord Chesterton played politics like whist. William Wycherley and Thomas Dekker were also done in by debt. Daniel Defoe was a bankrupt too, but it was his political pamphlet "The Shortest Way with Dissenters" which brought him to the pillory and put him in prison. The troubadour Blondel de Nesle, by singing a song they had jointly composed, located Richard Coeur de Lion in an Austrian keep, the first step in the king's eventual escape.

Peter Porcupine spent most of his life fighting libel suits, then was convicted of sedition and sent to prison, though this did not interrupt the production of his inflammatory pamphlets. Céline, don't forget, healed the sick, while Colette bared her breast on the stage and kissed another woman on the lips. Despite support from Wittgenstein's charitable foundation, Georg Trakl was whisked into the Austrian army and shortly committed suicide. Dostoevsky associated with the wrong socialists, a group which the czar ordered rounded up and condemned, although they were, as planned, reprieved at the last moment and posted to

Siberia. Instead of being struck by a bullet, Dostoevsky was stricken with epilepsy.

Madame de Staël pushed Benjamin Constant into politics, a game which got him exiled to Germany, where he wrote *Adolphe,* his famous novel. Tides turn, and in time he became a French deputy. Terence began life as a slave, which is political enough. Thackeray, for political reasons, resigned from the staff of *Punch.* Big deal. Although Pushkin had no definite political point of view, he was banished to the Black Sea because of his youthful verses, and hounded by the censor thereafter. His needless death in a stupid duel was gossiped into a government plot; consequently Pushkin became political in his afterlife. Byron's flamboyant career was also transformed into legend, even though it was legend enough the way it was lived. His self-imposed exile increased the number of his wonderful letters, and his death, from a fever in far-off Greece, promoted his causes at the expense of his verse.

The first Earl of Clarendon had another kind of character. A monarchist, he found himself finally forced to live in France after a series of failures as lord chancellor, including an abortive war against the Dutch. Corneille had his ups and downs, but he managed to serve in Rouen's Parliament for twenty-one years while establishing classical French tragedy in the rest of the country. Both brothers Grimm were exiled because of their opposition to a coup d'état by the elector of Hannover. Fray Luis de León's translation of the Song of Songs into Spanish was denounced by the Inquisition, and he was imprisoned. Four years later his *traduction* was forgiven. Franz Grillparzer's melancholy disposition was not improved by Metternich's censors, who hounded him. Knut Hamsun was a quisling before Quisling came along, and remained one even after his treason had been given another's name. While emperor, Marcus Aurelius persecuted Christians and waged war along most of his borders. He nevertheless retained his status as a stoic saint. No one needs to be told once again about Disraeli. Or of John Dos Passos, who began as a liberal and ended il-. If tuberculosis is a politically produced disease, as I suppose, depending as it does on malnutrition and indifference, then it should be noted that writers as various as John Keats, D. H. Lawrence, Katherine Mansfield, Jules Laforgue, Laurence Sterne, Robert Louis Stevenson, Thomas Wolfe, Anton Chekhov, Francis Thompson, Gustavo Bécquer, and Henry David Thoreau died of it. Perhaps we should redeem this paragraph by mentioning Benedetto Croce, who stayed a staunch opponent of Fascism and served in the post–W.W.II Italian government.

Gabriele D'Annunzio, a decorated Italian patriot, had the balls to bed the Duse and to seize Fiume in order to prevent its accession by Yugoslavia. However, his balls betrayed his brains; he was made prince of Monte Nevoso by Mussolini and decorated, not for bravery this time, but for his Fascist fanaticism. By the victory in Florence of the Black Guelphs, Dante (one of the Whites) was driven into northern Italy, where he drifted uneasily about, dreaming of a united nation. Nathaniel Hawthorne was rewarded for his campaign biography of Franklin Pierce by an appointment as American consul to Liverpool. The book which resulted (*Our Old Home*) wasn't very good. William Dean Howells was guilty of similar hackery on behalf of Abraham Lincoln, but fared better, obtaining a consulship in Venice. Beckett, Camus, and Calvino each fought nobly in the Resistance. Pérez Galdós wrote seventy-seven novels and twenty-one plays, and should have been jailed for dumping. He served, however, as a liberal delegate to his party. Blindness, the books say, put an end to his political career. Since when has this been an effective cause?

James Hogg stayed out of it by cultivating his garden. You could say the same of Quintus Fulvius Flaccus. Living on a government pension, Walter de la Mare wouldn't worry a breeze. But *hélas!* not Victor Hugo, whose vigorous opposition to Louis Napoleon sent him into exile in Guernsey, where he awaited, with the greening meadows and the cows, the advent of the Third

Republic. Returning, he was elected to the Senate, missing heaven by a single vote. His signet ring said EGO HUGO. That's nicely put. Which was what happened to Leigh Hunt—election, that is—after he was imprisoned for libeling the prince regent. Libel also put Zola on the run. Like so many Latin American writers—Carlos Fuentes, Pablo Neruda, Alfonso Reyes, Octavio Paz—Rubén Darío spent most of his life on the outside of his country, in distant places, playing diplomatic roles. Most of the others became exiles like Cabrera Infante, Reinaldo Arenas, and Severo Sarduy, to mention merely Cubans. However, Gavin Douglas, when kicked out of Scotland, went only as far as his favored England in order to die.

According to Augusto Roa Bastos, the entire country of Paraguay has exiled itself from the rest of Latin America by virtue of "its landlocked inaccessibility, characterized by territorial segregation, internal migration, emigration, and mass exoduses." When Roa Bastos returned to Paraguay after a thirty-five-year absence, he was shortly re-expelled from the country, and copies of the book by Jorge Canese he had come to help launch were destroyed. *Agarra los libros, que no muerden.* César Vallejo was imprisoned in Peru on trumped-up charges. He went to Paris upon his release, only to have his apartment there ransacked by the police because, they said, he was a member of the Communist party. Then he was ordered out of the country. He took up the Loyalist cause in the Spanish Civil War with a fervor hard to match, and, having returned to Paris, he begged money for the Republican side on the streets of Montparnasse.

Theodore Dreiser's first novel, *Sister Carrie,* had scarcely been released before it was suppressed by its publisher, Doublecross. Publishers didn't have the same success with the rest. Dryden has had his mention, but we should not omit Pope, who proves two related points: that hateful nastiness will add to your fame only if you know how to express it properly ("Flow, Wellsted, flow, like thine inspirer, beer," etc.), but also that a stupid thought will remain stupid however cleverly presented ("Whatever is, is right"). The Dumas pair had mostly monetary troubles, not affairs of state. Ibsen's exile was more up-to-date than most. Lack of funds and the determined indifference of the public kept him out-of-country for twenty-seven years. His impregnation at eighteen of a servant girl was politically conditioned, if not politically caused. Jonathan Oldstyle wrote satires on New York society, while Diedrich Knickerbocker authored a *History of New York* which had a style, tone, and subject matter suspiciously similar to those of Oldstyle's pieces; a few years later, Geoffrey Crayon hit it big with a volume appropriately called *The Sketch Book;* however, Washington Irving's diplomatic career was consummated under his own name.

Thomas Jefferson, Abraham Lincoln, and Teddy Roosevelt wrote rather well. None of them now would be elected. Ulysses S. Grant is another surprise. García Lorca was murdered by Falangists; and Juan Ramón Jiménez fled to Cuba, then to Puerto Rico. Flavius Josephus was born Joseph ben Matthias, which tells us a good deal about his character. As the governor of Galilee, he participated in the revolt of the Jews against the Romans. However, when his stronghold was overrun, he flattered his captor, Vespasian, by forecasting that brutal man's elevation to emperor. Josephus received a pension, safety, a home in Rome, and Vespasian's name, Flavius, for his trouble. Juvenal spent his life denouncing such Romans and their American-style lives, but James Joyce's departure from Ireland was merely a matter of prolonged good taste.

William Dunbar penned poems for James IV in return for a handsome life pension. *Timor Mortis conturbat me.* Jean Paul earned a Bavarian stipend and kept his nose clean. Rilke's wandering was self-imposed and nonpartisan, although he preferred castles to hotels. William Blake was too utopian to be truly engagé. Lord Dunsany spent most of his nonwriting life shooting grouse, Boers, and other game, but was otherwise, like most soldiers, unpolitical. On the other hand, Rimbaud ran guns and probably traded in slaves. To the degree religious revivals are political, Jonathan Edwards was a smoking pistol, describing, in *Sinners in the Hands of an Angry God,* how things would really be if the unjust were to get their just deserts. Nikos Kazantzakis studied philosophy under Henri Bergson but turned out all right anyway, doing much left-wing work and serving as the director of the Greek Ministry of Public Welfare. Occasionally the cloth redeems itself from the smirch of divinity. Charles Kingsley, for instance, took orders, but also founded the Christian Socialist movement. His attacks on Roman Catholicism provoked Cardinal Newman's justly famous response, *Apologia pro Vita Sua,* although Kingsley can't take all the credit. He was nearly alone among the clergy of his day in accepting Darwin's theory of evolution. Most still don't. Whittier wrote homespun, country-cousin verse, but earned many merit badges as an ardent abolitionist. Kipling wrote like a god and thought like the devil. One odd good thing about Kipling: he opposed sports.

Let us move on to Heinrich von Kleist, another nationalist. Napoleon's troops arrested him in Berlin as a spy and deported him to France for a year. When his politically inspired newspaper failed, he killed his lady friend at her request, and then himself on the romantic shores of the Wannsee. He died of gunpowder asphyxia, the doctors said. T. S. Eliot's politics, unlike Wyndham Lewis's or Ezra Pound's, were everywhere yet remote, like a distant smell or a sound of surf. Fontenelle's, however, were near at hand and loud, though mostly theoretical. He opposed authoritarianism, superstition, and myth while upholding science, sense, and reason. To tote him up: he was a model man and philosophe. The Dreyfus case made Anatole France angry, as it should have, and his prose grew a few teeth in response. He began as a narrow partisan, attacking the church, the army, and society, but later broadened the scope of his enemies to include man. Ben Franklin invented stoves, advised youths, drafted and signed the Declaration, spent a good part of his life in England and France, where he was minister to various love affairs. Admirable man and model philistine.

Ronsard was the court poet of Charles IX and a diplomat. He spent as much of his time in polemics as he did in poetry, but it is not clear, as it is not clear in so many other cases, whether the distractions which made up daily life and political duty actually deprived us of anything he might have written in their stead. La Bruyère could not have been more political, if we consider the cast and content of his work, which aphoristically exposed the cupidity, stupidity, hypocrisy, arrogance, and indolence of the upper classes. His only real punishment for this effrontery seems to have been a delay in his election to the French Academy. Philip Freneau, whose family was French Huguenot, was a sailor. Captured by the English, he wrote *The British Prison-Ship* in revenge and restitution, and, in consequence, became known as the Poet of the Revolution. That's the American Revolution. Choderlos de Laclos was arrested during the Terror and fled the country for a time. Back in Paris, he was detained again, but under Napoleon he became a general and died at Tarento, although his perspicacious cynicism seems to have predeceased him.

Both *Émile* and *Du contrat social* were censored by the authorities, and Rousseau felt compelled to live abroad in consequence. He believed that God, Man, and Nature—each and all—were good. Somehow only society, with its penchant for private property, was evil. Unfortunately, history, even in his own time, had already shown that God did not exist, Nature was indifferent, and Man was a murderous thug. Nevertheless, Rousseau is still read. There is always an accounting for bad taste. Ruskin, on our happier hand, is rarely read. Perhaps this is because he became a social reformer, and therefore a bore, with his later work, when he wrote imaginary letters to artisans and common laborers, advising them to unionize, establish a pension plan, and support a form of national education. Excellence is not always interesting. Bertrand Russell split his intellectual energies between logic, mathematics, epistemology, and a pacifist humanitarian social agenda—efforts for which he received misunderstanding, disbelief, or calumny. He died (only to write its name) at Penrhyndeudraeth.

Théophile Gautier neither gave nor received trouble from the State. He is on this meandering riverlike list because, in my opinion, the modern literary movement began with his attack upon the philistinism of the bourgeois in his famous preface to *Mademoiselle de Maupin* (1835). It was in "the age of cotton nightcaps," as Albert Guérard so aptly calls it, that Gautier, peeved to the point of plain speech, wrote: "There is nothing truly beautiful but that which can never be of any use whatever; everything useful is ugly, for it is the expression of some need, and man's needs are ignoble and disgusting like his own poor and infirm nature. The most useful place in a house is the water-closet."

Once upon a time, writers received their principal patronage from the church, and were often clerics of some kind themselves. Otherwise writers were attached to lowly feudal dukes, landlocked barons, or illiterate earls. They were secretaries, spies, diplomats, preachers, advisers, soldiers, politicians. Gibbon, for instance, was a captain in the grenadiers, but he was a member of Parliament by the time the first volumes of his *History* began to appear. Had he written his chapters on the history of Christianity a century before, he would surely have been incarcerated, and incinerated almost any time earlier. As it was, he only suffered notoriety, as David Hume would later.

The case of Thomas Sackville is exemplary. He is born to a well-placed family and is able to enter Parliament at the age of twenty-two. He finds favor (as they used to say) with Queen Elizabeth, who makes him a baron. With a friend, Thomas Norton, he writes what is often called the first Elizabethan tragedy, *Gorboduc*. He takes over the editorship of a verse series, *Mirror for Magistrates*, to which he contributes some important lyrics. His public career is distinguished to a fault: he is, in turn, an English emissary to other nations, a member of the Privy Council and Knight of the Garter, Oxford's chancellor, and eventually lord treasurer of the realm. He dies in harness, now the Earl of Dorset, at a council meeting in Whitehall. A career of this kind is, for a writer in any industrially advanced Western nation, nearly inconceivable now.

Dropouts became country curates. They didn't commit crimes, either of person or of poetry. They lived quietly, spoke softly, and specialized in rural themes. A few clerked or held small odd jobs. It did not do, like Burns, to be frolicsome. But most writers didn't choose writing as their profession. Writing was a hobby, undertaken as proof of one's breeding, sensitivity, and breadth, or because one felt the need to reflect on life as it had been led. Rarely did it turn into a career. And their attitude toward society was not determined by the fact that they believed themselves to be "artists." Nor was their experience of men, women, and the world postponed until they had received an advanced degree and gotten their first job. Gradually, the clergy's hold on the culture weakened, to be replaced by the overtly political—that is to say, by the new nation-state and its innumerable lackeys.

By the middle of the nineteenth century, however, when Sainte-Beuve was pursuing his career, bright young men were starting life at a later age, studying medicine or the law, and might—but only if they strayed from the course their family had appointed for them—consider writing as their vocation. Nevertheless, such a choice meant not only that you would probably end up a journalist, but that you would also suffer a concomitant fall in social estimation. Sainte-Beuve was exceptionally successful: he fell in with Hugo's crowd, published a scandalous novel, wrote an influential weekly newspaper column, became a powerful arbiter of public taste, and ended in the Senate.

When writing was a marginal activity of mainstream men, writing was the major medium of communication, and you could be punished for annoying the people in power; but when writing became the principal concern of marginal figures, it ceased to have the significance it once had. The word weighed when its writer weighed, and the writer was weighed in political pounds. Greek culture, being essentially oral, gave the word much emphasis; but the word was also as evanescent as an odor and had to be sensed, savored, saved, set down in the mind, for which reason poetry, oratory, and even argument emphasized sound, meter, and symmetry and peppered its passages with epithets and formulas. Writing gave the word permanence. What you said could not outlast living memory, but what you wrote could be held against you by generations yet to draw their genes. Printing allowed the word a width the word had never had. Nevertheless, the more words there were, the less value was given to any one of them. The word was worth most when it was incised on a tablet of clay; it was worth least when it announced bargains on a newspaper insert, through a radio ad, or in a throwaway.

The connection Socrates made between speaking and being could not be closer or more complete, and even in orators like Cicero and Quintilian, the breach between speech and business was as thin as a sibilant. With writing, the word became a means; its essence was soon separate from the sense it bore; and it fell into the callous hands of paraphrase. As eloquence declined, men possessed a poorer posture, became less elegant of voice and complex of character, while nature became a yawning bore. Nowadays, a belief in the power of the literary word is confined to backward countries and is a leading indicator of a less advanced society.

Latin American authors, as we have seen, are not strangers to diplomacy (and the citizens of their country honor them, listen to them, even pay them heed), even though the most notable live cautiously abroad. Soviet writers also had huge and eager audiences, even when what they were eager for was rarely received. In Africa too, liberation has so often been the door to tyranny, and the historical importance of the bard meant he would soon bear scars upon his back. A few avoided harm by escaping to the top, like heat up a flue. Léopold Sédar Senghor, for instance, labored for his country's freedom for twelve years, and when it was finally realized, he became president of the Senegalese Republic. Similarly, Agostinho Neto played the partisan's role. In the same year in which Senegal achieved its independence, Neto became the head of a movement for the liberation of Angola. He was almost immediately arrested, escaping confinement after two years in a Lisbon jail. Eventually he too would occupy a presidential chair. Ezekiel Mphahlele, forbidden to teach in his native South Africa, was forced into exile in Nigeria. He did not return to South Africa for twenty years. Likewise Alex La Guma and Dennis Brutus have seen the intestinal interiors of South African jails. Even in Senghor's Senegal, Sembène Ousmane's scripts and films have been torn by the censor's teeth. After his confinement during the Nigerian civil war, Wole Soyinka, like so many other African writers, chose exile in France before returning, after a lapse of years, to the country of his birth. Kofi Awoonor came back to Ghana after a distinguished career at SUNY, Stony Brook, only to be imprisoned a year for his alleged connection with an abortive coup. The authorities in Kenya did not trouble to try Ngugi wa Thiong'o. They merely put him away for a while to protect the public's ears from the harshly unpleasant sound of the truthful word.

In every country, in every clime, regarding any rank or race, at any time and with little excuse, orthodoxy will act evilly toward its enemies. Survival is its single aim—that is, to rigidify thought, sterilize doubt, cauterize criticism, and mobilize the many to brutalize the few who dare to dream beyond the borders of their village, the walls of their room, the conventions of their community, the givens of some god, the mother-smother of custom, or the regimen of an outmoded morality—and even the Greatest Good itself could not fail to be bruised by such handling, and rapidly rot where the bruise had been. One sign of a sound idea is its fearlessness. Protect the truth and you put it away in the same place you have put those enemies you have saved it from. And any time a zealot speaks against freedom on behalf of a sacred thought, we must always listen for the anxiety in the voice, for such a voice is worried only about itself: to protect the profits it presently enjoys, to prevent the losses it fears in the future, and to avoid the penalties which just such fanatics have paid in the past for their presumption.

Wang Meng can look back on a life of both servility and service, with his unpretentious short stories causing consternations at twenty-year intervals. In 1956 he published "The Young Newcomer in the Organization Department," a scathing picture of bureaucratic inertia which started a firestorm in the dry forest of officials. Wang Meng was pronounced a "rightist," and the Cultural Revolution swept him away to do menial work at Ili in Xinjiang. In 1976 he was repatriated and made a party member again. He immediately demonstrated his resiliency by writing "The Butterfly," the ironic tale of a time-serving bureaucrat who falls afoul of the young Turks in charge of purification and is publicly humiliated by his own boy, who boxes his ears and jeers as his father is banished to Mongolia. Yet in that barren backward place, the bureaucrat finds some meaning, a little love, and brief happiness—only, when abruptly restored to office, to return unimproved to his feebly inefficient and pampered ways. Widely admired for the staunchness of his character as well as the fearless honesty of his work, Wang Meng was made the minister of culture, only to be forced from his position by the party after the Tiananmen catastrophe. His most important recent story is called "Porridge," about an old man who refuses to eat his—once more upsetting the carts where all the apples are.

André Gide's defense of homosexuality (*Corydon*) created such a scandal, he sold his property and went to Africa. There, now politically alert, he was witness to the abuses of colonialism. Still politically alert, he was not taken in by the façades of fraternity and freedom erected around the USSR by its sycophants, or by its propanganda promises either, and was roundly criticized by the left for not sharing its inexcusably self-serving trust in what was always a dubious ideal. Gide sneaked back to France but only as far as Cannes. And kept his mouth shut.

The forces arrayed against the writer have so far been—in the order of their periods of domination—the Tribe; the Church; the Nation-State; society at large, or what is called Public Opinion; and the quieter, politer, more effective pressures of the marketplace, the so-called Commercial and Consumer World. The influence of the first is based upon accidents of birth, blood, and color; that of the second, on ignorance and fear expressed in superstitions; that of the third, on power, punishments, and prison; that of the fourth, on gossip, bigotry, pettiness, and parochialism; while that of the last is built on our faith in money, on "mememoreme" (in Joyce's coinage), and on the inexhaustible gullibility of greed. Now that all these fighters are noisily in the field, each contestant always endeavors to enlist (or, if not, discount) the influence and support of the others. In the tribal case, personal identity is a matter of family and race: we have the same nose length, hair kink, language habits, food fads, festivals, heroes, history, hates (I am a Serb). In the second, your creed counts: types of taboo, principal heresies, hierarchies, holy days and sacred relics, rationales, rites and routines, saints, symbols, and monetary contributions (I am a Sufi). In the third, patriotism, with its slogans and its flags, describes you: which includes all the grain which waves, the armies which bear the country's banner into battle—bless our boys!—the long and distinguished Past which chauvinism always creates to glorify the Nation (despite all the bad luck and betrayal it's suffered), yes, San Juan Hill defines you, Remember the *Maine*! and "The Marine's Hymn" define you too, somewhat the way you are defined by your town's baseball team (America First!). In the fourth, common concerns and the character of daily lives, inherited values, shared myths, convenient scapegoats, and conspiracies of blindness—a kind of stew made of the leftovers from the other four—do the literal trick (I am a Southerner). Lastly, in the Commercial World, the self is seen as a rack of clothes, as an address and a set of wheels, a position in the bank, a diet designed for our modern life, as a lot of fun-filled leisure activities, as a suitable set of sexual practices selected from Technicolor picture books (I am a playboy or his pliant and pettable bunny), each sale item understood to be a part of an installment lifestyle, naturally subject to change—to cite an instance, when I trade in my former personality for a later model, one with more options, more efficiency, more allure, more speed.

Jean Giraudoux served prewar France in the Ministry of Foreign Affairs, and during W.W.I was a soldier; then he spent W.W.II as the director of information for the French Republic, and finally worked for the Vichy government in the same capacity, slipping from one regime to another like the eloquent eel he was. George Gissing's subject was poverty, which he knew firsthand. You can write about poverty without being political, and a great many have, because poverty is fun to read about—full of human sentiments and local color. However, Gissing dealt with the *effects* of poverty, and no one cares to read about *that*—sordid stuff best left hidden behind the silence of neglect. People like Pater, Patmore, and Peacock did not drink from the bubbler of politics, whereas Peele (for we are somewhere in the *p*'s by now) appears to have abstained only from the vote, dying of drunkenness and syphilis so obscurely, the date of his death is a "circa." Dylan Thomas was also no slouch as a souse.

Killed or wounded in a war: Rupert Brooke, Wilfred Owen, Siegfried Sassoon, Charles Péguy, probably Ambrose Bierce, then Edward Thomas, Isaac Rosenberg, Henri Alain-Fournier, Guillaume Apollinaire—just a few from a long long list. Suicides: Sergei Esenin, who wrote his last poem with blood from his slit wrist before hanging himself; Walter Benjamin, in despair of escaping the Nazis; Paul Celan and Primo Levi, who postponed their deaths in the camps until later on in so-called "liberated" life; Gérard de Nerval, who hanged himself from a sewer grate by an apron string which he had bragged to his friends had been Madame de Maintenon's belt or was the garter of Marguerite de Valois; Hart Crane, who jumped from the stern of a ship, perhaps in despairing memory of the sailors who had beaten up and pleasured him; Chatterton, who could not have guessed that the manner of his death would make his literary career last a little longer than his life had; Virginia Woolf, pockets filled with stones to drag her body under, where her spirit was; José Silva, whose manuscript was shipwrecked; Cesare Pavese, communist in spite of himself, unable to commit to a world so woeful; and Mayakovski, the Soviets' first "poet laureate," who once wrote, in his poem to Pushkin, "I am now free from love and from posters," although, unfortunately, he was free of neither, writing poetry with one hand, propaganda with the other, and shooting himself in the heart to murder poetry when he should have shot himself through the poster and slowed for a moment another pitiless movement.

Alfred de Vigny's play *Chatterton* expressed the nineteenth-century writer's disillusionment with society and the values which gave it suck. His hardheaded rejection of political and religious solutions to Europe's problems unfortunately involved a sentimentalizing of the remote poet, the disinterested philosopher, the objective scientist. It may indeed be necessary to cleanse one's ideals of political and religious taints and preserve them in a protective solitude; however, if so distantly removed, they will shine only in emptiness, and no one shall see any better because of their light.

Lord Acton knew of the evils he warned his students about through his years of close acquaintance with the monied, privileged, and powerful. Although he never published his lectures during his lifetime, there are many posthumous collections. The correct version of his famous and frequently misquoted axiom is "Power tends to corrupt; absolute power corrupts absolutely." Has anyone composed an aphorism about what damage impotence does? or how good corruption feels? Are we to believe that passivity promotes virtue? Georg Büchner organized a revolutionary secret society and issued a fiery pamphlet called "The Hessian Courier," which got its message under way with the following wonderful sentence: "The life of the Aristocrats is a long Sunday: they live in beautiful houses, they wear elegant clothes, they have fat faces, and they speak a language of their own; whereas the people lie at their feet like manure on the fields." He was forced to vacate his native haunts and fled to Zurich, but contracted typhus there and died at the age of twenty-three without having heard a line of his mangled or seen any of his three plays performed.

Prison is a splendid place to put writers. Think of all the famous books which have been penned there, all the executions which have hastened undying lines into existence. But the jailers have few reasons to rejoice, for it is in their jails that men who had formerly no thought or sentiment to put on paper which could not be framed in dulcet words of love have composed their most politically inflammatory works. *Mein Kampf,* for instance. Nor, as this little run through history shows, have all of the jailed been jugged for literary reasons. Some were crooks, some spies, some were thought to be dangerous on other grounds, some backed the wrong pretender, some connived to the point of treason, a few were simply unlucky in their friends, or were caught in catastrophes too general to be choosy about who was carried down. And occasionally a government (even one of those) will feel sorry for some noxious fly in its ointment and pension the rascal, as the British crown did William Godwin in the twilight of his life and in the shadow of his bankruptcy. Godwin's feminist wife, Mary Wollstonecraft, died shortly after the birth of her first legitimate child, punished for her indelicate life and liberal leanings by Motherhood, society's heaviest club against women.

Consider the case of Matthew Prior, whose first writings were burlesques. His career as a diplomat was long and distinguished: a secretary to the English ambassador at The Hague, an aide at the negotiations for the Treaty of Ryswick, a member of Parliament, and a principal participant in framing the Treaty of Utrecht, called, on account of his role in it, "Matt's Peace." When Queen Anne, his protectress, died, he was put under house arrest, and in such restricted circumstances Prior returned to the writing of poetry, composing two long works which are today mostly forgotten, while the little scraps of lyric verse he jotted down in spare moments during his years at court and conference table are deliciously alive. Prison may prime the pen, but the sincerity of the writer's surroundings do not ensure success. Swift was another who had to leave England with the passing of Queen Anne and the fall of her party. Like many serious satirists, he was a Tory. He took no chances with *Gulliver's Travels,* which, he said, was written to "vex the world rather than divert it," and published it anonymously.

In men, talent and character are rarely in balance. Too often one trait is weak where the other is strong, and weakness (whose awesome power makes its name a misnomer) briefly wrestles with strength (whose deplorable flaws make its fall, like Samson's, as simple as a snip) only to find itself pinned to some pusillanimous page where it is permitted to squeak "uncle." Weakness, like a steady drip, wears confidence and skill and talent down though each be sturdy as a stone. When Gogol, a case in point, died, he owned only some old clothes (an overcoat, surely) and a couple hundred books; so the University of Moscow underwrote his funeral, a rite which did more damage to the State than his work managed. Admirers, passing his bier, pulled dead flowers from the dead man's hands, and the czar felt so threatened by the widespread display of grief, he kept any notice of Gogol's burial from appearing in the press. Turgenev was arrested for writing an obit.

In the same vein, the many minor virtues which de Tocqueville discovered in America could not make up for its major flaw, an inherently low level of creativity; and only in those cases where the writer is so gifted he can be a wastrel with his reason and pontificate to his heart's content, as Tolstoy did, or damage his prose without doing it utterly in, as Faulkner was inclined to (believing that a thinker won his Prize and not a word-drunk chronicler), can catastrophe be escaped. A woman may dare to remain both woman and writer if she is sufficiently resolute about her work as to overcome the need to verify herself by having children instead of books; for how many children had Lady Colette, or Stein, or Cather, or Eliot, or Woolf, or Porter, or Jewett, or Dickinson, or Bishop, or Moore, or Gabriela Mistral, or Flannery O'Connor? George Sand bore two before leaving them and her husband for freedom. Madame de Staël began by having affairs instead of kids, but then, in exile from the Terror, had two with her nobleman lover. However, she could turn their care over to her not inconsiderable household staff. Back in Paris she became the mistress of Benjamin Constant, but both were banished by Napoleon to her family estate on the shores of Lake Geneva. She certainly could never have been called Madame Constant, and eventually this husband was replaced by a strapping young soldier, as Madame usurped still another prerogative of the male. Benjamin consoled himself with a second wife (the first one he abandoned for de Staël) and continued that successful political career I spoke of earlier. However, the emperor he served remained of the dominant sex, and that emperor (once made sour, never to be sweetened) kept de Staël and her books out of France until he was forced from the throne and into exile himself.

If Godwin was given a pension when the government heard the reassuring rattle of his death and realized that retirement payments would not be perpetual, Carlo Goldoni lost his when the Terror took such support away from all the greencarders who had served the monarchy (Goldoni taught Italian to several Bourbon princesses). Thus rewarded, he died in Parisian poverty. On the other hand, a poet like Petrarch always had patrons and sailed over perilous political waters as if he were a seabird, not a ship. Patronage has always been a vexing problem, because patrons of the arts, whether private or public like our NEA, rarely realize that what they are supporting is the general possibilities of production in an artist's life, with its shifts of direction and qualitative ups and downs, not specific works with certifiable standards or previously approved points of view. That is, what is being encouraged is a certain kind of climate, not rain on a specific day.

Still, prison is a splendid place to put authors. It gives them a sense of grievance, and we know that grievances are among a writer's more powerful motives; it removes them from temptations, and we know how easily writers are tempted by bosom or bottle to imbibe; it eliminates distractions, that of the housewife among the more miserable, and makes pointless all the petty steps which must be taken in order to advance one's commercial, scholarly, or political career; it directs the mind to the main things: liberty, injustice, the misery of humankind, the irremediable loss of opportunity, man's vast immemorial waste of Time, now seen as not some abstract flow of tick to tock but as the lit wick of life itself blown out and the expired candle's timorous thread of smoke still unaccountably mistaken for the flame.

Pierre-Joseph Proudhon—now there is a name to remember with amusement—certainly occupies a place of distinction in Albert Guérard's gallery of philistines, along with Victor Hugo, Voltaire, and Ben Franklin (my nomination for the finest exemplar of the form). I should also like to recommend H. G. Wells, a splendid specimen. But Proudhon had as vapid a mind as has latterly been invented, and his inept poaching on revolutionary ground (he was prosecuted often and imprisoned on at least one occasion) drove Karl Marx to answer Proudhon's *The Philosophy of Misery* with a turnaround of his own, *The Misery of Philosophy.* Isaac Babel wasn't simply picked on either. He served in the czar's army, then in the revolutionary forces, and finally in the secret police. Or were these falsehoods placed upon the record by the Stalinist wretches who purged him? (Danilo Kis has written wonderfully about this sort of "documentary identity.") In any case, relatives and friends began immediately to erase the erroneous data and add their own air to an already clouded issue. He worked on a stud farm? yes or no. What counts, of course, is the reality of the evil tide which swept such a writer away. It was Proudhon who said, "Property is theft." Under Stalin, the person of the writer became the property of the State.

Putting writers in prison is preferable to putting them upon a pedestal. Giving an author influence is like giving him poison. His pen begins to froth at the nib. He not only continues to manufacture baloney; he begins to eat it himself. Soon, like Faulkner and Tolstoy, he is a victim of runaway megalomania. Alexander Solzhenitsyn's opinions are those of someone still in the pay of the czar.

Of course, when State oppression has reached its highest level of efficiency, walls will no longer be necessary; fear will put bars on every window, as Miklós Haraszti has so sardonically described in his analysis of its action in *The Velvet Prison.*

No, I say. Put 'em in the cold stone pokey. Make their suffering visible to themselves. They will be better for it. They will overcome adversity and triumph in the end. Censorship simply makes writers devious; it gives them a sense of importance; without oppression—without poverty and unhappiness—they would have nothing to write about, nothing to complain of, nothing to demand be changed. We wouldn't have *The Enormous Room* if the French military hadn't jailed E. E. Cummings by mistake for three months. Thomas Nashe was confined for his contribution to *The Isle of Dogs,* so that overly authored, weakly comic play cannot be called a jail's consequence but a jail's cause. Wilde's poem is quite another matter, of course. Jean Giono's sojourn in prison for pacifism seems not to have had any loud literary upshot; whereas Irina Ratushinskaya wrote poetry before, during, and after the KGB sent her into internal exile. That suffering ennobles, that oppression improves, is an old canard. Let us not worry about the evil effects of too much happiness. Happiness is not a habit of the human race. Misfortune is its forte.

We do not remember these writers for their political accomplishments, even if the Treaty of Utrecht was, for a time, called "Matt's Peace." The poet/politician produces two sorts of worldly effects: the document he signs, the plots for whose unmasking he plays the snitch, the preferments his flattery of the powerful obtains, the sagacious point of view his experience provides, the lessons his pupils learn (John Skelton was tutor to Henry VIII), the speeches he puts in the mouth of a monarch who otherwise would only mumble; *that,* on the one hand, while on the other there are the verses he indites, the plays he puts upon the stage, the lines which linger in the memory, thoughts which are carried by their ingenious rhymes into other countries and to other times. As the System sees it, that's the danger, for a sword thrust in some real Polonius' side releases only the poor man's blood, while the stage's imagined figure becomes proverbial, the meaning of his merely simulated death deep; because the reality of the work of art is what terrifies the tyrant who has so much terror of his own to spread; yet all of his effects are linear, and they begin to weaken the moment they begin to exist; whereas the merest phrase, turned on the tongue as though it were a lathe, outlasts and reappears, and is remembered—not Agincourt and what the English arrows did upon that field, but Shakespeare's speech in praise of Crispin's Day.

Words are persuasions poured into the ear, revelations delivered to the reading eye. Simple syllables can fasten darkness to a deed so firmly a bank of kliegs could not dispell it. Ironically, it is the Ruler's Law and its Officials who have thrown some wretch for theft or debt or slander into their keep, where they ignore the miscreant as if the world were asleep; it is the same daft set of bureaucrats who put a pen in the prisoner's feeble hand and then lend requested paper, before unwittingly releasing him later; subsequently the Tyrant can read of what his reign, his command of the country, has come to. It is therefore these same dunderheads who have made possible the text which they will have to condemn and ban, rail against and confiscate, on the shah's or the czar's behalf; since it is by means of such sequestered works that both they and the world learn what has been done, not just to one brief thief or pitiful pauper but—through an account of social inequity, corrupt officials, steep taxes, adventurous policies (I keep the list brief)—to an oppressed people; and consequently what the rule of such a Power-Poisoned Person and his Power-Poisoned Partisans has meant to an entire, now bankrupt, nation.

Yes, awake at last . . . the authorities . . . hurt, smarting from the imagined injustice of the latest libel (since authorities never see themselves as evil but only as vilely beset by it) . . . the authorities . . . a victim of exaggeration, surely, they say, yet fearful of these lies and their spread . . . the authorities . . . with futile efficiency act to alter the angry beat their beloved prison gave to the heart in its care—now much too late, well after the rhythm of the poet's lines has made their music growl if not sing in the souls of the Monarch's subjects (or perhaps they're called the Commonwealth's Citizens, Color's Brothers, or just Comrades of the Cause, anyone over whom the authorities presume to have a hold), the State will reply with much misleading rhetoric, a flurry of false reports, a campaign of sly innuendo, only to see how both their raucous rebuttals and their insistent whispers have perversely encouraged the people to refuse the colored shirt that's offered them, the mock military cap; now they won't wave symbol-bearing flags, or wear any armband other than one of mourning; they listen instead to the rhetoric of outrage, the pain-provoked words which are freeing them to feel the suffering, to share the courage, the verses contain, or the passion the prose holds, where resolution and disdain, or realization and rejection, live; for political power, though it can kill countless and maim more, is like water in the hand, and all its decrees are tardy. Nor will the fall of the State itself raise a spiff more dust than any other violent act; the noise of it will die away; but, like the body of Orpheus, torn to pieces, the poem will still find a head to sing through; and, though the poet's remains have been flung into the river, the poem will still contrive a way to float its song above the water; that is what galls the tyrant, stops every blue nose's nostrils with snot that his furious snorting can never clear, and drives him to his excesses: what does the sword say? the sword says *swat!* take that! bleed a lot! while the pen says— simply—that *it* is mightier, and proves its own point with the phrase.

That is how the myth runs, when written by the writer, of how it shall be with every society, every despot, who refuses to allow and to heed the free word.

After the Sharpeville Massacre in March 1960, Breyten Breytenbach had to become active in anti-apartheid activities. The South African government let him back into his country for a few months, but his subsequent book led them to regret it, so when he secretly returned, they arrested the renegade Afrikaner (whose visit was not quite secret enough), jailing him for seven years. *The True Confessions of an Albino Terrorist* made them pay for that, as has Breytenbach's lifetime of service to justice and moral decency.

Yet the confusions of history, which convulse every truth with the ailment of its opposite, cannot be escaped. Caprice is another king, Chance another feudal lord, Luck another castle. Irony is Sincerity's secret lover. Bruno Schulz wrote his stories and taught drawing in the boys' college at Drohobycz. It was not an easy life. His family responsibilities were heavy. Poor, he etched his drawings on spoiled photographic plates he was able to obtain from pharmacies. His work had won him prizes and some renown in Warsaw, but the drudgery of daily life had worn him down, and he had broken off a troubled engagement with a woman of another faith. First the Soviets, then the Germans, occupied his town. Fortune smiled its crooked smile. One of the Nazi officers admired his art, and took the Jew Bruno Schulz under his protective wing—the Jew Bruno Schulz, who, from caution, had ceased writing. One morning, Schulz was fetching home a loaf of bread when he was shot in the open street by a Gestapo agent who had a grudge against Schulz's "patron." The cemetery he was buried in has, itself, been liquidated. No account I've seen tells us where the bread fell when Bruno Schulz did. Clearly, the only writer present was the one killed.

The superiority of the word to the deed, which I've alleged, does not mean the word redeems the deed. The word redeems nothing, for nothing is redeemable. Is death to be praised for all the poems it has inspired denouncing it? When the *Deutschland* sank on its way to England, many drowned, among them five Franciscan nuns. Sad as the news was, as numerous the loss, it was the death of those nuns which provoked the imagination of Gerard Manley Hopkins. A priest, he had to ask permission to write a poem on the subject. This poem appears to have released his dark, nearly demented muse, to give us his major poems. Should nuns be ticketed on every overloaded ferry now, just in case?

Bertolt Brecht said he changed his country more often than his shoes, and demonstrated how unstable the real artist is, if you wish to build a political position on his ground; for his plays adhered too ardently to the particular to be trusted to support a slogan, and saw too far, and felt too much, to be satisfactory guides for action. His own Galileo puts it properly: "You have two rival spirits lodged inside you. You have got to have the pair. Stay disputed, undecided. Stay a whole, stay divided. Embrace the crude one, praise the pure. Be clean. Be obscene. Keep them bedded." Brecht spent W.W.II in Los Angeles, where his rented bungalow is on the expatriate-German culture tour (Schoenberg, the Manns, Adorno, and others). Your tour guide will also point out the house nearby which the FBI used to spy on him.

Juan Goytisolo had to prowl the peninsula of Spain while Franco ate the country. Driven into the arms of the left, as so many post–W.W.II writers were, he discovered no liberalities there, but all the ancient bigotries and the frightened bullying of the homophobes.

Our writers have been of every persuasion. Some have been foolish, others bright, a few upright, most rather average in that line, many mean and suspicious, a lot disloyal, unscrupulously ambitious, carpy, dishonest, hell-bent and promiscuous. Neither the High-Minded nor the High-Handed, neither Lowlifes nor Lowbrows, Wellborn nor Ne'er-Do-Wells, neither breasted nor balled, not the widely traveled nor the narrowly circumscribed, the broadly educated nor the specialized, are privileged to the literary life; and their various modes of existence are in no case safe indicators of the esthetic qualities of such texts as they may author. Remember, for instance, that Edmund Spenser supported England's oppressive policies in Ireland, where he lived most of his life until the Irish burned his Kilcolman castle in the Civil War. No, there isn't a single important point of view which has not been beautifully praised. There is scarcely an important truth which hasn't been brilliantly traduced. Sigh as one must at the medieval escapism of William Morris, yet don't let that color your appreciation of the common sense and sturdy prose of *News from Nowhere.* Despise mysticism as a positivist ought, but not the poems of Saint John of the Cross, who, as a Carmelite reformer, was kidnapped and imprisoned by members of his own sect. Doubt the truth of the pope's church from catacomb to spire, but do not doubt the honor of Robert Southwell, who was arrested while celebrating mass, wrestled to the Tower, and put upon the rack, where he refused to reveal the names of his fellow priests, though he lost his life at Tyburn for it; nor fail, either, to admire the beauty of his verse. The career of Sir Thomas More needs no recital. Politics, Moral Fiber, and Art may intertwine, but there is an essential difference between one vine and the other.

But this is not the popular opinion. George Meredith's first novel, *The Ordeal of Richard Feverel,* was withdrawn by its publishers as immoral. "O what a dusty answer gets the soul," he wrote, "when hot for certainties in this our life." Molière was hounded his entire career by religious zealots. Calderón de la Barca, on the other hand, began work as a playwright at the court of Philip IV and ended it writing *autos sacramentales.* Lope de Vega's problems were mainly personal. He was banished from Madrid for libeling his mistress. Nor did taking holy orders slow him down. His plays are estimated now to number fifteen hundred—many more than his mostly unfortunate affairs. Around men, women died in their birth beds. Copulation enslaves but breeding kills. Karl Kraus, the pacifist and Viennese Cassandra, was listened to, for he repeated the words of the politicians in the pages of *Die Fackel* and on the stage before thousands of entertained ears, reading the papers the way New York's Mayor La Guardia read the funnies, allowing everyone to see and smell the shit which came out of their leaders' mouths. Yet there was never enough irony, never enough outrage. Wars make splendid battlefields, Kraus suggested, and former battlefields are pleasant places to picnic. They listened. They laughed. They applauded. But they didn't change their ways. Thomas Bernhard castigated similar crowds, with the same mimsy result.

It may be difficult to admire the bourgeois sensibility behind Isaac Bickerstaff's *Tatler,* but if you wish to read a fine work rich in political observation, the recommendation here is Montesquieu's *Persian Letters.*

Hush, little baby, don't say a word, / Mama's going to buy you a mockingbird. Don't say this word; don't say that one; you might give offense; you might uncover to others a squalid condition, even of your own; you might affront, disturb, step on a toe, put a nose out of joint. In the same moment a word is banned, a thought denied utterance, a point of view shut down for the season, the writer has a holy obligation to search for a sentence which will contain it, seek a place to speak the thought raucously aloud, formulate the point of view, not as if it were his own but as eloquently as if it were his own.

What is unthinkable? Think it. What is unutterable? Utter it. What cannot be spelled without a dash? Fill in the dashes with doubts. What is obscene? Dream it. In all its tones, in seamy detail, at indelicate length. What is too horrible to contemplate? Describe it. With cool and indifferent interest. As though peeling a peach. You will not be the first, for the unthinkable has already been thought, the unutterable uttered innumerable times, God's various names have been taken in vain, the obscene has been enjoyed, the horrible carried out. This the value of Miller, Genet, Burroughs, de Sade, and Céline. Even the simplest thought, given the simplest form, must be uttered as though cast into a context which contains all of its conceivable opposites—not so that it will waffle and betray itself, but so it will be strong. But that means, for all those who lack confidence in the resilience of their ideas, that every fine line, even if it seems to be standing securely on your side, is open in its confident stride to every other pace, realizes the great range of human attitude and feeling on every issue, and invites these differences along; and what narrow mind or intolerant ear or suspicious eye wants that kind of crowd?

Writers constantly complain that political institutions fail, in the end, to improve mankind but, rather, encourage it in its foolhardy rush to the abyss and, if there's any hesitation at the brink, give the mugwump a hefty push. Rarely has contempt been so thoroughly earned as man's for man. Karl Kraus, even in 1914, which he called *"dieser grossen Zeit"* (these great times), said:

Mankind consists of customers. Behind flags and flames, heroes and helpers, behind all fatherlands an altar has been erected at which pious science wrings its hands: God created the consumer! Yet God did not create the consumer that he might prosper on earth but for something higher: that the dealer might prosper on earth, for the consumer was created naked and becomes a dealer only when he sells clothes.

> (*In These Great Times,* translated by Harry Zohn. Manchester: Carcanet, 1984, p. 73)

So all those guys who dealt Adam his first pair of pants (fuckfellows, now, with the politicos), in order to make one final sale, offer to us souvenirs of the last day, naturally in advance of the event.

In all fairness, though, shouldn't we ask how far up the slope of Mount Perfection our literature has helped us climb? Are we better now that Calvino has written? that Rilke has rhymed? that even as you read, on some machine beauty is being made? and do those great lines to which, a few pages previously, I made my bow, and praised for their power, their memorable nature, and their superiority to simple history . . . do they succeed in lessening our greediness, moderating our passions, and rendering less dull our sensitivity to suffering? Do we even want to be sensitized? Isn't there enough pain behind all our calluses already? when there's no longer anywhere to look away to, as some once looked away to Dixieland—no place to gaze without its being on a scene of grief?

I am asking for a list of great good things which we can tell the world were accomplished because Menander wrote a play, or Goethe made us weep at Werther's fate. Was I cleansed by Saint Genet? or even by my hero, Karl Kraus, was I rescued from any folly? for did I not do lunch one day at the peak of Pickett's charge? and look up from Jane Austen to bitch at my children? or yell "that-a-way" at a headline when we beat up on Iraq? and nod like a sage when I read what Pavese—another fallen hero—wrote: "One nail drives out another. But four nails make a cross"? One nod signifies agreement, two nods sleep. So can't we say to Mrs. Grundy: "Literature, lady, wets no underpants; don't blame us for your children's iniquities"? And can't we properly protest to the police that they are locking away innocence, for what book has brought a robber baron into being between its crafty pages? what steamy scene outheats the action in the slowest stew? No, my lord, literature is noble, therefore it desires to do nothing, does nothing, says nothing, is nothing, harms no one, opens not a single eye nor puts an untoward thought in any mind; and therefore writing should receive your scorn, perhaps, because a waste of words is the idlest of all voids, the dullest of deserts; but, sire, such vagrancy should not receive your prison's appointments when there's so much genuine demand, or your censor's attention either, when there's buggery going on in the bushes; no, let us writers write freely, prate away; we shall, if ignored, not even fright a gnat from its spoiling orange.

Imagine Montaigne as the mayor of Bordeaux, George Berkeley as a bishop, Richard Brinsley Sheridan as secretary to the Treasury, Sophocles a general, Yeats a senator, Mallarmé a schoolteacher, Voltaire amassing a fortune through a series of shrewd investments, O'Casey as a labor leader, Wallace Stevens behind an insurance adjuster's desk, Trollope as a postal inspector, Samuel Clemens a steamboat pilot, Disraeli a prime minister, Paul Valéry for twenty-two years a private secretary to the director of a news agency; and then imagine any contemporary writer in a similar position: what serious artist would now ally himself with the incarnation of Mammon, big business? what writer not simply wanting to promote himself would run for an important public office? or work, even for a time as West and Faulkner did, in Hollywood? or ever have the dubious opportunity to order soldiers "over the top"? What writing woman, perhaps as femme fatale, would enlist in the CIA? or would be allowed to take a turn as Emma Goldman or even run another Hull House? A lonely priest, perhaps, is still possible; a convict is more than likely; a whore, somebody deep in shopfront social work, an occasional physician or lawyer contemplating retirement, a guy running a gay gym; but a movie actor? a baseball player? a pipe fitter? a banker? That's why the recent election of Vaclav Havel, the candidacy of Mario Vargas Llosa, and the transnational threats to Salman Rushdie are so startling and unusual, and require our reconsideration of the entire relation between these two far different, much impinging realms. Because normally we teach; we serve as publishers' scouts; we edit a little; we pat backs, we puff; we hire out; we teach; we don't dabble anymore in diplomacy; we don't hold office, only office doors; we occasionally cover the news; we teach; now and then we still inherit, otherwise we teach; we run a dusty bookstore, drop out, push a private press; we teach; very occasionally we hit it big with a book, but otherwise we teach . . . oh . . . do we? do we teach? ah, but . . . my god . . . what? what do we teach? do we teach . . . technique? That's a matter even more puzzling. There are few vocations more dubious.

Unamuno was exiled to the Canaries for criticizing Spain's dictator, but returned when it was made a republic. An elected official for a while, the philosopher concluded his public career by denouncing both the republic and its opposition. That's the ticket. Imagine a philosopher today of Unamuno's range of experience, Unamuno's knowledge, Unamuno's depth of understanding, Unamuno's style, Unamuno's quality of mind, Unamuno's beautiful name.

Yes, how important we are, we argue when applying for government assistance; how impotent and barren we allege our efforts are when blamed for some abuse; and how much we should like to have it both ways. Yet writers get it both ways these days only from the religious right, who are adept at striking every cheek—

ass and face with the same slap—even if their adeptness tends to end with this one gesture, because the self-interest of the religious right is bent on remaining ignorant, in the dark, and unchanged, so that they can continue to believe that *Huckleberry Finn, Slaughterhouse Five,* and *Catcher in the Rye* corrupt their youth. They must therefore strike their enemies without looking at them, as it were, from their own blind side, and with blows which do not bruise even the bruises made by the stones they've thrown.

Yet the religious right, whether we are speaking of it as it operates here in the United States or as it exists in Moslem countries or in other benighted areas around the world, cannot make the least headway, as out-of-date as it is, blinded by fanaticism and crippled by superstition, if it does not have the quiet compliance and tacit assistance of many in the so-called open, liberal, and modern world. If the Salman Rushdie case teaches us anything, it should warn us of the immense submerged sympathy for the fatwa not only among the rest of the world's religions, who find here a common cause even if they lack the courage to claim it, but among every shrill and posturing minority, who fear for their feelings if not for anyone else's and who therefore sympathize with the tenderness of other skins, so long, of course, as such sensitivities offer no threat to themselves.

Vissi d'arte, vissi d'amore, the soprano sings. Work or world, the tenor might wonder. No one today talks much about the conflict between art and lawn mowing, art and childbirth, art and marital disorders, art and parenthood, art and car down payments. If a novel devotes itself to labor union organizing, munitions makers, or woolen manufacture, it would almost certainly be seen as a work of propaganda, perhaps high-minded but "committed" nevertheless, for why else would one write about such things? My parents, or yours, are unquestioned subjects, and if I have an ax to grind about my second marriage and the lout spouse I got stuck with, that's okay; what's fiction for? and if I write a series of lyrics about shopping at the supermarket, or planting a tree, or my vacation in the Rockies, these subjects aren't a problem either, my poems remain poems; but if I write another series on El Salvador, or about my sojourn in Siberia, my poems will inevitably be seen as political, partisan apologias for this view or that movement, which may be okay too, except that they cannot be approached merely as poems now and kissed upon their kindly open faces.

Once, as this recital suggests, art and the artist were part of the great world, but now art is only an alternative. Once, if a poet caused offense, it was as often as not for the way he had cast a vote or advised a prince; and once, if a poem offended, it was often because it charged the crown with a crime or called certain courtiers to account. In the West, at any rate, there are now no princes of note for poets to know, and no public which might know a poet and risk being moved. After the art, there is only the rest of the world. The rest of the world is nowadays roughly divided into two realms: the public and the private. The private is presumed to be art's special province, because the wide public world is far from any normal writer's ken, as remote as the High Command is for most of us.

The writer has the *Times* delivered daily, and there she can read about war and starvation and disease and the pillage of the planet, but what does she know firsthand about oiling an M-1 or international diplomacy or prison life in Sri Lanka? so, naturally, she is expected to write about what she knows best: getting a husband, keeping him happy, raising kids, getting on with the in-laws, aging without anxiety, going back to work, getting fat, finding time to read, burying her folks. And she frequently, dutifully does . . . write about that. However, when we observe that writers write about what most takes up their time, about what day to day impinges upon them most intimately, about what gets under their several skins—worries them, pleases, disappoints— we should also remember to place some considerable stress on the phrase "takes up their time." It would be a grave mistake to suppose that it was only public life which intruded on the writer's work, imperiled it with its oppositions, or lured an otherwise secure and faithful art onto the path of partisanship and entrapped it in the wiles of local social relevance, never to raise a worthy head again. Not only is "private" or domestic life larded throughout with public elements; it is as consuming as a fire, and composed of buttoning buttons, boiling water, cold toast eaten as if each chew were being counted, as well as long moments of mental vacancy filled by films, alcohol, hobbies, and other habits of escape, and family quarrels so silly they create their own anger—in sum, by total trivialities and the bourgeois comforts of the self—which is why Villiers de L'Isle-Adam remarked, "As for living, we'll let our servants do that for us." The writer's greatest enemy is her subject, which she writes about in order to stave off its demands, expose its nullity, control its course, explain its character, to justify a marriage, vilify a husband, understand a child; just as writers wrote, in greater days, of plots to overthrow thrones, ways to get ahead, as well as those ill-starred love affairs which deterred one, tragically, from greater goals.

When Zhang Jie wrote a few stories which championed romantic love over marriages which were traditionally arranged, the State chastised her, and such a cloud hung over her future, she needed to seek safety abroad. The relation runs equally strongly the other way: the public world is everywhere infected by the private, and some suspect that the politics of the family is only too often repeated in the hierarchies of the State. Many a dictator has been affectionately known as "little father."

How to measure the fear of imprisonment and the displeasure of the State against the distractions of one's household and the irritation of a spouse, as well as the anxieties produced when lives are joined and jointly threaten, when families are shattered by jail or divorce, children are orphaned or sent away, property is confiscated or divided, hopes are dimmed, and one is made homeless by events? Or the consequences of such distractions and such fears to the practice of one's art? A play is closed by the order of the king, and the playwright falls silent forever; a child dies, and the world receives an ode. For his nonpolitical position, Pasternak's poetry is banned, so he translates Shakespeare. During the war years, two volumes of poetry slip into print. But he is forced to decline the Nobel Prize, really given him for *Doctor Zhivago,* really given him for political reasons, a novel really written from private grief and shaped by history's course.

Francis Parkman was born to be a dilettante: rich, talented in an acceptably tepid way, with an unpleasant dependence on Haavaard and Baaston and tea well served, appropriately opposed to abolitionists, women's suffrage, the Democratic party, and moneygrubbing. He was, in these senses, dangerously parochial and a frightful snob; but instead of playing polo, he rode west, and saw what he saw with dispassionate clarity, and read what he read when he researched the French and Indian Wars with a devotion to fact which carried him straight through to values. His illness was his enemy, he said, but it freed him to be La Salle, Champlain, Montcalm. Proust didn't have a prince who would comfortably confine him, so he put himself out of harm's way; and who knows how many other tribulations have been literary blessings, and how many of Nobel's prizes, or similar successes, have wrought havoc and complaisance?

If you want to be made a fool of—take sides, and then let the side take you. This does not mean that all sides are, in moral sum, the same, for some are simply despicable, some are sordid, some are creatively stupid, many are criminally naive, most are poorly expressed, badly led, weakly implemented, and, underneath, up to no good the moment they get organized; but when the sides are as general and vague as "life" and "art" or "literature" and "politics," it may be useful to remember that coins and paper have sides but value and language haven't; there are no sides to a stew, either, only surfaces, ingredients, and flavors. Of course, seated before the fire in one's dressing gown wondering, as was Descartes' famous habit, whether one is awake or dreaming, a bit brandied and full of a fine dinner (perhaps it featured Brunswick stew), one is inclined to take Bobbie Burns' brief blunt way with things and say:

> The Kirk an' State may join, an' tell
>   To do sic things I mauna:
> The Kirk an' State may gae to hell
>   And I'll gae to my Anna.

Tribalism, Identity, and Ideology

On June 2, 1993, an Algerian journalist, poet, and novelist, Tahar Djaout, died of wounds he received when he was shot in the head near his home on the outskirts of Algiers by Moslem terrorists who objected to the attitude his newspaper took toward their fundamentalism. In humane terms, any crime of this kind is reprehensible, but culturally the loss is also considerable, because Tahar Djaout, thirty-nine when he died, was an accomplished writer whose novels, written in French, had received both prizes and acclaim. His murder got his ghost a brief and passing paragraph in several American newspapers.

Tahar Djaout's death was merely the first. At this writing fifty-six other journalists have been assassinated by bands of Islamic thugs.

Yes, we fanatics, we followers, we faithful, we patriots, we partisans: death is what we do best. We bear the body, beset the life, cause the corpse. The residue is huge: a heap wider than a wasteland, higher than a hill. Yet what have we made when we've made it? one more small circle of grief around a pile of sightless eyes. So many sick and shot and starved. So many women raped and widowed. So many children maimed and left alive to weep because they weren't among the fortunate who grew into their death like weeds into the ground.

Consequently, what call has Salman Rushdie—yes, a worthy man, immensely talented yet only a writer, and a citizen of another country, after all—what call has he on our attention when an entire world seems surfeited with suffering and we've lost count of even those still strong enough to scream? What scale can weigh his years of imprisonment within the hug of security police, where we must imagine his spirit being cautioned to skulk through the hallways of his own head? There is no way we can share these fears of a hidden gun held at the heart, as in a cruel game, to go off at a time unnumbered on any dial. What is one man's career supposed to mean to us, so safely situated, or his desire to be known for the excellence of his work rather than be notorious for the odd malice of his fate? What claim can any of this have on ears as continually beset as ours, where we hear howling everywhere, as if we each sat at the mouth of Hell itself? . . . and read or watched . . . were fed . . . the news?

What we now call Fundamentalism has been murdering its dissidents for millennia, and murdering them mostly with impunity—jailing them, threatening them, veiling their eyes with lies, denying them the world that's within their own language— but Fundamentalism is fighting for its life right now, and that means there will be many more murders; there will be more merciless minor wars; there will be more cleansing of countries at the expense of conscience; there will be more dogmatism, more oppression, more suffering, more fear. Fundamentalism is the tool of a social ideal which has been around perhaps even longer than orthodoxy has, and that ideal, for convenience, may be called Tribalism, which is one of the deeper roots of Racism, too. Our Old Testament is about very little else, Eastern religions are riddled with it (as our own are, of course), while Greek tragedy finds in it a fatal subject, frequently focusing on the conflict between the abstract ideal of citizenship, so necessary to the effectiveness of the city-state, and the loyalty of people to their relatives of blood, their ancestors even—to the tartan, to the mafia of an earlier age—to the frat, the clan, the club, the gang.

A tribe is a body made of family members. It tends to worship the seed which sustains it in being. Fathers are holy, but forefathers are even holier. Fathers exist to sire sons, to make war, in company with their sons, on other sons and other sons' fathers, to arrange profitable marriages for the daughters their wives have inopportunely borne, to ensure the integrity of the family line, and to issue orders whose character is never to be questioned and whose force is never to be opposed. In the tribe, obedience and morality are spoken together and spelled alike. One's essence is one's function: the same goes for the lung, the liver, or the eye. To be the father is to be the bull and bear the balls.

The conditions of life in a tribe are relatively the same for everybody, since everyone lives on the same mountainside, in the same snow or dust, or among the same creeping vines or steaming swamps. If tribes, through some catastrophe, are compelled to disperse and take up life in differing climes and countries, every effort must be made to retain unchanged all tribal ways: food, dress, shelter, worship, mores, metaphysical beliefs, the manners which grace human exchange, and most especially, the power of the family head.

Though tribes have strict rules about intermarriage, they rarely fuck far afield, and so the members of a tribe tend to look alike, speak the same tongue, eat the same meat and grain, believe the same beliefs, which are handed down like the skills of the hunt or the several ways to weave. Everyone who thinks as I do, feeds as I do, whistles the same tunes as I do, drives what I do, kneels as I do, hats his or her head as I do, votes or dances or loves as I do, confirms my mode of existence, validates the mess I have made of my life and makes it seem sensible and of value.

In the tribe, "purity" is a sacred word. Women must be pure to keep the male ownership of property secure and its transfer unencumbered. Thus tribal blood is not to be defiled, nor are minds and hearts to entertain impure thoughts or vile desires. Tribes adjust with difficulty and slowly to anything new, so they are happiest when life does not change. Sameness is safe if not saintly. Difference is despised. Behavior, religiously reenacted, becomes indiscernible from nature itself and soon resembles the instincts of the insect or the animal: the spider that repeatedly repairs its web, the birds that fly the same atmospheric lines to their former nests, the bears that slow their blood for winter's slumber and take to bed, each recurrent season, a store of fat they will consume though still asleep.

Each member of a tribe has a self which is the gift of the group: values, beliefs, directions of conduct, skills, speech, animosities which are part of the lifeblood of tribal history; so that methods of making and making do are inherited the way household goods and tools are, and memories too, of past triumphs or humiliations, the stain of their guilt and the gleam of their glory traveling along the family line the way a message enters and exits the telephone, inasmuch as there is no other learning allowed than that which passes from an elder's tongue to a youngster's ear—since order and obedience are one. Nothing in society is so serene as this passage of power.

Around the tribe, like twine that ties a package, like the protective paper too, superstition wraps its concealing self. Sometimes one superstition will find it expedient to be polite to another. As different as they often are, they have a common task, similar methods, an identical respect for hierarchy and its authority, frequently a text so sacred not even a comma can be canceled, a love of mumbo jumbo, pomp, and secret learning, a hatred of freedom, reason, and fact. Their function is the preservation of the group; therefore they find ways to mark its members, to glorify the group's past and promise it victory, to designate its enemies and vilify their qualities, to measure all such threats in order to exaggerate them, prescribe protective steps to remove the menace, and urge their prompt and ruthless undertaking.

Our world resembles the night sky, since all those stars we see shining together, and which seem to exist in the same plane as though painted on a plate, actually bring us their light from far different times—a few are thousands of light-years away, some are nearer, perhaps half a century off—and when we, often awestruck, gaze at them, we see this mottled past, and if we are wise, we try to correct for and understand the differences: not always easy, since the spangle of the skies does resemble, in its simultaneity and dazzling presence, Las Vegas' seductive signs. But the stars (or the light we admire in the stars' stead) do not constitute a community. The stars do not signify a heavenly society. The stars stand in a vast chill of indifference and send out for no reason their wholly lonely and utterly meaningless beams.

Sense is what *we* are supposed to make. Meaning is for man to manage, making mind out of all this "never matter." We ought always to have the gift of consciousness on our conscience. Who else can feel the warmth of someone's pleasure in a finger's touch? hear a voice rise like a slow bird from the meadow of the page?

So when, by threats or sophistries or betrayal's rewards, our liberty of thought and expression is constrained, our openness of action and free field of dreams impeded; when an unpleasant opinion, a vulgar expression, a disturbing incident, a troubling idea, a satiric skit, a peal of laughter, a hoot of derision, is foreclosed because this or that is not a laughing matter, is sacred as a cow may be, or king, or caste, or race, or flag, or god, or mother; when dirt's words are bottled up like bugs chloroformed in jars; when only the difference of local sameness is embraced, rather than difference itself; when the fascism of the left and the fascism of the right clasp underhands; then . . . then what? shall we toddle back to bed like chastened children, goblin cowed? shall we fail to render those in danger aid, though their plight is a plight of principle and not merely—not merely—a neighbor's need? shall we allow the very bases of all good life and all fine art to be besmirched, even removed, by sullen fanatics, by bewildered fools, by those who will surely lose their seat near God if they can't keep the rest of us away from the table?

The fatwa was pronounced against us all. It commanded the

murder of a mouth, yet issued from the mouth of a murderer. Although the act called for anger from us, an anger honest and righteous to stand against this fabricated and expedient pretense which fueled ignorant and distant mobs, the time for that feeling went pallidly past, and now the only object of anger ought to be ourselves for our slow, our wan, response, for our characteristic feeling of futility, our fears too, consequential as they may have been, since the question of the reality of the risk is irrelevant to principle.

Yet even if we believe no man is an island, even if we are all part of the main, there are so many in want, in danger, who have been, by their leaders and circumstances, betrayed; there are simply so many multitudes in pain; what can we say to ourselves on one man's behalf, or on the behalf of readers and writers, as if they were sufferers too, though most read only the papers, sign petitions, apply salves to their conscience, sit in meetings, pound an innocent table?

Only this, I think: There is a bond between us, readers and writers—an ancient tie as old as writing is, if not as old as speech itself, a pact, a promise which the act of setting down sentences in a moving way implicitly solidifies—that what we shall say shall be as true to things and to our own hearts as we can manage with our skills to make them; and that what we read shall be free and unforced and uttered out of the deepest respect for the humanity all language represents, whatever its content otherwise; and that this covenant (broken, tragically, every day which history has been there to mark) is the model for all exchange of thought and need and feeling, and that this community, the community of unveiled countenance and free speech, must be sustained if we are to continue, either in the harsh and unforgiving condition of survival or in terms of every genuine enterprise of the moral spirit—in short, so we can say, though we may be here by genetic accident or a god's decree, that we deserve to stay.

Our papers report that on account of the fatwa—out of a

hatred which would numb the tongue before its undoubted excision—editors, translators, readers, writers like Tahar Djaout, have been threatened, assaulted, wounded, murdered; but their victimizers cared nothing for their victims, not in the state of hate they represent; they care not a sweet plump fig for Salman Rushdie or his work or what it may say to them or to anyone, not in the condition of ignorance and fear which they embody; they seek an excuse to silence the mind, to blind the eyes, to stopper the free flow of feeling.

As recently as June 30, 2001, the *New York Times* reported that a Jordanian cleric, Sheik Abdel Moneim Abu Zant, called on Moslems in the United States "to unify against" Khalid Duran on account of his book *Children of Abraham,* alleged to be critical of Islam, and to punish him with death. Fundamentalists will not rest, for to rest, as with a cyclist, is to fall; to rest may be to realize that their light comes from a faraway star, that their mode of life has been dead for a long time, and the world in which they are busy killing and constraining is already a bier into which they, with their miseries, have been born.

The Shears of the Censor

A few weeks ago [March 1996] I had the pleasure of delivering the ecomium for Assia Djebar when this wonderful Algerian writer was awarded the Neustadt International Prize for Literature. Normally such a function would have been performed by the ambassador or a consul from the writer's country. The prize is that prestigious. Or it might have been undertaken by her host country, where she now lives and by which she is presently employed.

However, Assia Djebar's novels and stories concern themselves with the condition of women in her native land, a country from which she has been, by her pen, exiled. France, where she has found asylum, feared to anger Algeria, while I—an admirer, not a nation, and thus innocuous—was available and in every sense safe. Reading her, one realizes that censorship is not merely a media matter but takes many forms, including reluctance. Perhaps the most pernicious is the censorship of the body. If you put a person in prison because of her words, you are punishing her body only incidentally. You wish to stop her mouth from voicing her thoughts, thoughts which you would see silenced, frightened into formlessness. But women in many Moslem countries are persecuted precisely because they have bodies, because they have faces, breasts, thighs, because their private parts are prizes and may give pleasure to the male, provide him his heir, and sometimes—Allah forbid!—disgrace him.

Assia Djebar lays bare what has been concealed. She reverses the cut of the censor's shears. To expose . . . to lay bare . . . What an extraordinary and daring accomplishment. How many layers of concealment had to be removed—seven veils? And each one symbolic, through and through, of political, sexual, and educational enstiflement. Algerian women . . . their feelings held out of sight in their veiled heads, their ears allowed to hear prayers, their eyes given them to weep with, fists to beat upon their chests, their mouths for ritual wailing, their Arabic softened as when women speak to women; kept in closed compounds, weighed upon by husbands who've been arranged for them, so they may then be fondled like a pipe stem; their entire life and outlook surrounded by the plans of men and the cruel and stupid tyrannies of male "-isms," by a land, for women, empty of openness or opportunity; followed always by death as though they were a bone to a starved dog, by a death which will claim them when they become worn and ill and thin from bearing the children they will see sicken and die before they see their own death in the doorway . . . Algerian women: who shall break open their silk cells and let them fly in the light?

Once upon a time, women had their feet bound so tightly they could not grow properly, so they had to totter about like someone old with weak bones. They were like birds whose wings have been clipped, or animals who have been hamstrung. A passion for small feet, the fetish for high heels, remains. There are women whose necks have been stretched, whose skin has been scarred. Were they made of tree bark where "I love you" in a heart might be carved? "I love you" was hardly said. I own you. You are my sex toy, my brood sow, my wealth, as worthy of price as my cows.

Piercing and tattooing continue, but few give any thought to their original significance: the cicatrix as tribal trademark.

In Afghanistan unveiled women have been beaten with radio antennas ripped from parked cars. In Afghanistan adulterers will be stoned as in the good old days. Surgeons are now forbidden to operate upon female bodies, bodies which have been turned into sheeted ghosts more menacing than lepers. Women's schools are closed. And in Iran, bicycle seats, since they resemble saddles, are denied a woman's weight. And why are saddles denied them? They may not rise to such a height or ride astride a stallion. The gradient of oppression is long and steep; the climb, in those layered gowns, is difficult. In every country, someone no longer a child is swaddled, another injustice is suffered, varied tyrannies are endured.

When men hide their women away, they are also hiding something of themselves, and the cruelties they practice are cruel to them too. If I strike a tree stump often enough with an ax, I shall make muscle, not merely firewood; and if I am a jailer, I grow bars, and my heart is as hard as pavement, and I soon see only stone, the air is stale, and my food tastes of tin. How beautifully Assia Djebar presents these sour consequences, like a shining coin pressed painfully into a suppliant palm.

Decades ago, when I was a young and very junior ensign in our navy, I was ordered to censor the crew's mail before it left our ship. No one read what officers wrote, for officers were gentlemen and would not babble; but enlisted men (they were mostly draftees, actually) could not be trusted to be so discreet. At first I enjoyed the amused satisfaction a sense of superiority brings, because the men wrote clichés in childish hands, and expressed themselves awkwardly, and concluded their letters with rows of X's and O's—hugs and kisses, supposedly, but, according to the navy's fearful rules, possibly the ship's position or destination in a clever code. These I had to scissor out. Blotting would not be sufficient. X rays might reveal those treacherous kissy symbols in the act of spelling our deepest secrets beneath the censor's blurt of black ink.

This was not a delete key I was pressing. I watched my shears cut into the sheets and sentiments of these men. I was invading their feelings, first with my eyes, and then with my silly surgery. No hugs. No kisses. A sentence like "When we refueled at sea,

Mom, a new movie came aboard, the one you liked so much, remember, with Esther Williams," would be removed as if it were an inflamed appendix.

Some sailors will be salacious even when they know (perhaps because they know) a stranger will overread them, but that awareness had to inhibit many and stopper their feelings. An Algerian woman, if she spoke the truth to her husband ("Today I went out walking without my veil"), might very well be beaten. Nor do our sons say: "Sure, Dad, I was in the garage smoking pot," because the consequences will be unpleasant. The self censors itself because it does not want to receive or inflict pain. The truth, of course, is a casualty. "Do you love me?" a worried wife may ask. The husband gets out his tools. "No, dear, not a bit" is snipped. "I dunno, maybe" is rubbed out. "Haven't I always?" is considered. "Tons and tons, my dear" receives an enthusiastic hearing.

If I fear the superior sensuality of women, I can try to deny them their pleasures and soothe my nerves with a clitoridectomy. A woman can no longer withhold herself from me, for I have withheld her preemptively. Her sexuality has been censored. More and more my little navy scissors seemed obscene, my oversight mere peeping, my operations a form of malpractice. I cut along faintly blue-ruled lines. It was perhaps the pathetic paper, the cruel removal of a longing, a greeting, from the simplest message, that troubled me most. And the loved one or friend who received and read the letter, how would she feel when she saw after "Much love, John" that rectangular excision? So I just sealed and stamped PASSED, kept my scissors closed, my eyes averted, my time saved, and my conscience salved.

The censor cuts; the censor veils; the censor confines; the censor prevents, denies. All this is done for the sake of something higher: the stability, the good, of society. It is good to keep women in a harem and out of harm's way. It is good that they should remain ignorant of the male world and men's business. Ideas should on no account be put in their heads. But then, a cultivated ignorance, a denial of intellectual opportunity, and the cancellation of the ordinary citizen's capacities are typical aims of most ruling classes. Can anyone seriously believe that the will of Allah is the will of Allah and not the will of a bunch of wickedly conniving, cruel, and frightened men bent on preserving their miserable privileges? I, though a lowly ensign, barely twenty and as ignorant of life as a shadow not yet cast, had the power of the scissor; and I had the power of the scissor because others had power over me; so when it was discovered that I, the censor, was not censoring, I was confined to my quarters, dishonored, and believed shamed. I would spend much of my naval life in a relatively comfortable confinement called "hack"—finally feeling honorable for the first time, and reading quite a lot of William Faulkner.

When a person's position is based not upon some natural excellence or upon genuine services given freely to the community; when it is based instead upon an elaborate system of lies and evasions which that selfsame person, for the sake of success and to set a pious example, would be wise to believe with a fervor convincing to the public; then any fact, any alleged theory, any emotion, any desire or aspiration, which in the least threatens the ruling deceptions must be refused, resisted, ridiculed, and finally caused to disappear altogether. Dr. Soroush, a popular philosophy professor in Teheran who dared to suggest that perhaps a greater separation of mosque and state might strengthen Iranian democracy, was forcibly reminded that he was living in a theocracy when thugs mugged him on two separate occasions while he was lecturing.

The cowardly and hypocritical fatwa against Salman Rushdie continues its farcical tricks. Rushdie was recently awarded a Danish literature prize but banned from attendance at the ceremony on account of security concerns. Needless to say, he refused this troubled gift and doubtful honor. One can confidently guess that it was the cost of the security, and not its degree of difficulty, which counted.

It is not enough to have proper views. Any naive exercise of sight, of feeling, of thought, of imagination, strengthens gifts which will be less innocently employed elsewhere, at times when there is more at stake. Every free breath poisons the tyrant's atmosphere. Assia Djebar's fiction suggests that each block walked without the veil is a block walked away from the Prophet, and weakens his minions. They know that it is best the eye be kept closed and see nothing, the ear be shielded from every sound, the mouth be shut and silent altogether, since if one sense is allowed to be alert, clay feet may be sniffed, a king's clothes seen through clear to the clown's soul, the counterfeit coin bitten like rotten fruit and spat upon the ground.

So maintain women in ignorance; give them only a servant's skills; let them keep to courtyard and kitchen; let their girl children go unmentioned, the boys be taken away and sold to some ideology perhaps, like the protagonist of Ken Saro-Wiwa's powerful novel who becomes a sozaboy and fights to defend his jailer's right to jail him. They did dungeon the Nigerian Ken Saro-Wiwa. They imprisoned him because he saw and he spoke and he wrote of their injustice. He indicted his judges before they got round to indicting him. Writers must reveal and accuse. It will happen naturally. No need to aim at some selected target. Writing well will put the writing in the bull's-eye.

With a prescience both sad and ironic, Saro-Wiwa wrote a short story in the form of a letter from a confessed thief to a woman whom he fancied when they were both children. The letter, he tells her, will be smuggled from prison on the eve of his execution by a bribed guard "condemned," the prisoner writes, "to live, to play out his assigned role in your hell of a world." "Africa Kills Her Sun," the title of the story puns. The prisoner knows that his youthful flame will have read of his impending execution in the papers because "we saw it, thanks to our bribe-taking friend, the prison guard, who sent us a copy of the newspaper in which it was reported." Saro-Wiwa continues:

> Were it not in an unfeeling nation, among a people inured to evil and taking sadistic pleasure in the loss of life, some questions might have been asked. No doubt, many will ask the questions, but they will do it in the safety and comfort of their homes, over the interminable bottles of beer, uncomprehendingly watching their boring, cheap television programs, the rejects of Europe and America, imported to fill their vacuity. They will salve their conscience with more bottles of beer, wash the answers down their gullets and pass question, conscience and answer out as waste into their open sewers choking with concentrated filth and murk. And they will forget." (from the anthology *African Rhapsody*, edited by Nadezda Obradovic. New York: Anchor Books, 1994, p. 291)

The Nigerian government arrested and jailed Ken Saro-Wiwa. He had not only written worrisome things; he had organized public resistance to Shell Oil's systematic pollution of the Nigerian environment through massive natural gas burn-offs. Some time passed; protests were, of course, voiced; and then he was hanged.

The censor pretends he is protecting tender hearts, shielding children from sex and violence, keeping the righteous in the right path, guarding against temptation, preserving virtue. How? by burning books, tearing out tongues, stretching necks, stoning women; through torture and imprisonment; by threats of violence against the victim's friends and family; by force-feeding his own people a philosophy not only false and wicked now but false and wicked the day it was first announced by some imaginary lord and used to purchase or preserve his privileges and hoodwink the world.

Or by stealing the entire print run of the newspaper in which Berkeley students editorialized against affirmative action. Or by issuing idiotic accusations, such as that of philosophy professor

Sonia Harding, who insists that the laws of physics were constructed to maintain white male dominance, or posturing like the Afrocentric writer Hunter Adams, who boasted that the African people were "the wellspring of creativity and knowledge on which the foundation of all science, technology and engineering rest." The idea is to intimidate the politically incorrect and coerce them into rectitude.

When you cannot censor a position by removing its formulation, you can set up an alternative and opposite one which will then claim equal respect and attention, and compete for economic support. The National Institutes of Health, of all places, established an Office of Alternative Medicine to look into various magical cures such as Lakota medicine wheels and biofield therapeutics. The latter manipulates the patient's "aura" by scooping off negative energy. Congress likes to override institutional good sense, when it rarely occurs, by allowing some of its members to campaign for laetrile and other worthless nostrums.

What the lunatic fringe wants is credibility. This is the point of the push for prayer in the schools. Praying won't convert pupils, only bore them; but permitting prayer in State space will legitimize its message.

There is always a position of power and privilege which is at risk when the censor snips, for what stone tree would fear the woodcutter's tinny saw? Sometimes one has to fear a government, one as vicious as, presently, the Burmese. Sometimes one worries about what a brutal husband may do or a father or a teacher or a policeman or a soldier or a priest. In addition to their power, petty or profound, there is always a doctrine, a teaching, a set of rules, rites, and reverences, which secure that power and sustain its privileges, frequently by hiding the rulers' real aims behind benedictions, smiles of goodwill, even acts of kindness, shows of concern, promises of safety and salvation.

Freethinkers throughout history have sought to expose these deceitful practices and to tell the truth about the real enemies of the mind. From Socrates and Lucretius through Cicero to Bruno, Spinoza, Hume, Nietzsche, Marx, and Freud, that task has been bravely undertaken—the honor in their efforts can be proclaimed and celebrated.

Because so many dogmas are obvious fictions, they can be maintained only by means of patient and repeated indoctrination, promises of punishment, and prompt retaliation for any lapse. In addition to the sacred institution and its saving myths, then, there must be an investigatory and enforcing arm. It may be merely Dad's, beating his palm upon your bum. Thought cops will patrol and arrest, a gestapo will peer and pry, judges will serve a law which in turn will serve its lords.

One can identify falsehoods by finding the facts which tattle on them; but an equally good signal is the security which surrounds their insecurity: the walls and towers and guns and radio stations, the beating tom-toms, the pulsing pulpits, the political pronouncements, historical myths, martyred heroes, infallibles, and invincibilities upon whose shields the enemy's missiles must harmlessly ring and clatter to a holy ground.

The most efficient control is achieved when society is of relatively one race and one opinion, and when its ignorance of its own ignorance has been made a part of the catechism. Society will therefore sanction (in the word's positive sense) some beliefs, some actions, while at the same time sanctioning (in its negative sense) all others. Sour looks, injured feelings, disappointment and disapproval, with the few rewards they signify, will be enough to control contrary opinions and keep them beneath the breath, in a straightened chest. Then we shall need no watchmen asking what of the night, for it will be daytime though it be dark, and no one will wonder why the dogs don't bark, because there won't be any beggars to bark at—no foreigners, no heresies, no differences. There will be only false alarms, pointless excursions, malfunctioning equipment.

Once the right ideas (through what will be benevolently called education) have been firmly fixed in every youthful head and have achieved the serene status of "family values," so they may age till blue like old cheese; then the empty field that the mind of the citizen has become (all is known, no further action is necessary) needs to be filled with plays of thought resembling games of golf, with a pleasant pointlessness which brings on sleep as easily as ale in the afternoon, or Saro-Wiwa's beer and bottled American sitcoms. "The sleep of reason breeds monsters," Goya wrote beneath one of his grimmer etchings. But societies have been known to sleep for centuries. In quiet disregard of reality. In a peaceful equipoise disturbed only by a storm of sand sometimes which buries even pyramids.

Each culture will produce its own pap. One may fill the days of its citizens with holy memories, and every hour will be a word in a sacred sentence. Another may put on parades and headlight the heavens, flank paths with bands and banners, put its citizens in snazzy uniforms, issue certificates for admirable performance, award medals to sneaks for snitching on their fellows, buss both cheeks of the worker who exceeded his quota this month in the production of military weapons. Our pap is pop. The commercial world we live in does not need to stoop to such amateur measures as Mariolatry or medals. Playing golf, I may strike the ball as hard as I like, because I am only trying to hole out; and playing rock, I may wiggle and moan as much as my mighty meaning means to, until there's not enough silence to entertain another thought in. Violence on the screen conceals the real thing behind a cartoon; eyesores are only images; theft is merely a modeling of Play-Doh; the shock a little cruel nudity creates is no more than the buzz my dope brings to my harnessed head. Dope is good because dope keeps dopes out of my harm's way, and in theirs. Dope and dumbness keep the competition down. Let them love Elvis. Throw them a pair of Levi's, and let them eat Macs. Rap on their bars. In a world where money mostly matters, money buys mostly amusement. Waiting for the end through a double feature. The poppy of the people.

There is no single Evil Empire. Every empire can play the villain. We serve as many another nation's goblin, good for scaring kids and arming soldiers.

Work occupies, amusement preoccupies, promises attract, threats distract, rigamarolic rites reassure, dogmas deaden and disguise. When all is well, everyone is ill but will not know it. If you and I are "good," we are pious; we are patriots; we are dutiful; and we are purchasers. We'll not feel the price, because its payment has been deferred till after our brave death in defense of our glorious country; and we can't discover how we were diddled and do something about it, because we won't be around, but moldering in the ground; unless, of course, the other guys were right, and we are getting our damned infidel deserts: fire and ice each day, and the Three Stooges for a thousand thousand nights.

The chief mode of censorship in a commercial society is, naturally enough, the marketplace. It is not that we suppress serious books entirely. But in capitalist countries, only on the margins can excellence be located. Poetry and most significant fiction have to find a few little magazines to appear in, or an occasional small press which may be prepared to nourish them. However, those obscure mags are read only by their editors; the presses are being pennied to death; while their distributors go bankrupt. The government supports the arts so modestly, the endowments are as virginal as onceuponatime brides. The State spends less on literature than on its military bands. Back when the NEA had a budget, only 3 percent of it went to literature; the rest was targeted for public spectacles of one sort or other. Now, quite predictably, funds must come from the private sector—that is, once again, from business, which wants a gangbang for its buck.

Ideally, magazines should be supported by their subscribers. But our educational system doesn't produce such audiences. We publish poetry; we don't read it. We like it performed for us so that it will, with the poet, take the plane. And we like our few books autographed, because they will, one day, be worth more to our heirs and our assigns.

The varieties of censoriousness are many. What will the book-store stock, the library lend, the papers report, the publishers publish? Chains are now reading manuscripts in order to advise publishers what books they might like to see on their shelves. Pad a palm and it will put a handsome stack in the window. But they had better sell. Pancakes are given a slower turnover. My book was almost here today; how can it be so thoroughly gone tomorrow?

Library budgets are squeezed by popular taste on the one hand and rising costs on the other. The mayor of one French provincial town complained about what his city's library didn't stock, not about what it did: there weren't enough right-wing works among its holdings. Maybe there was no card for *The Protocols of the Elders of Zion* or *Quisling: Norway's Unsung Hero*. We know the protocols are lies, but falsehood is every censor's excuse. As librarians, do we select what we believe is best? what the reading public appears to want? what is cheap and at a discount? what will placate special interests and deflate pressure groups? Do we stock a little of this and less of that? At one university the navy made me attend, I took out a Chaucer which had lines scissored out (that implement again), and I was refused access to Lawrence's *Lady Chatterley,* despite its assignment, on the ground that if this dirty book ought to be locked up, it ought not to be—forgive the pun—lackadaisically paroled. The same response was given me by my public librarian when, at fourteen, I requested *Ulysses.* Did she actually think I'd get so far as the juicy parts? Or did she fear I'd be found out by my parents, and that she might be called on the carpet in consequence?

A book may have been published, but it is not available if I don't know it exists; if it costs more than I can afford; if it is locked up and out of reach; if I am illiterate, or ashamed of bookishness, or teased or told I am uppity if I want to rise above my fellows. Entire societies are devoted to keeping their citizens ignorant, unskilled, unschooled, fanatical in support of their own stupidity and of the forces which would switch off every intellectual light. Don't tell me such societies aren't evil, that every way of life is right, or even that it once was and they must have time to catch up; because such societies always were—were evil—from the first, and every footfall after is toward doomsday.

Places, sometimes euphemistically called "archives," can be used to imprison texts. The author may be as dead as Lenin, but the texts are alive and must be confined. Recently, a number of documents by V. I. Lenin were published by the Western press. The *New York Times* reports that "there is likely to be more material in the secret vaults of the Presidential Archive, which is controlled by the Kremlin." Lenin, who always wrote and spoke like a conspirator, probably would have approved his own suppression. Nixon may have thought every one of his words was wondrous, but he didn't want them all known, any more than the Texaco CEOs who planned on shredding evidence which might reveal the company's discriminatory policies. A tape caught each of them and shredded their innocence.

How to disgrace that great anthology, the Bible: tell us it is holy and nothing but the truth, for if I believe that, my brains will have been cut out and carried away to be fried.

The only holy word is the free word. May they all be pronounced from every peak and steeple. The democracy of the word requires that all words be deemed equal. In any language, in any dialect, in any argot, in any slur or drawl or stammer. Good manners may suggest that in place of saying to a lady of doubtful character, "I see you are a slut," you should say, "I see you have a free and easy spirit." This inner check is self-censorship, usually thought to be of the best sort; but there are those, especially in these dim days, who fling their sensibilities like a rug in front of all feet and then cry out when trod upon. In a free society, we should be free to give offense as well as take it; we should be allowed to be boors, if boors we are, so others may be warned; we should be permitted crudeness for the same reasons; and playing the fool has always drawn crowds, applause, and remuneration.

Stupidity is not my strong suit, Paul Valéry said. Today, to attack reason is the pastime of professionals, of academicians who are busy betraying their calling, committing once again "the treason of the clerks." Well, one must bear it, bear the name-calling and the posturing and the hypocrisy of those who would curry favor with cliques and clubs and tribes of all kind. Scott Momaday tells us that the Indians who object to scientific examination of the bones of their ancestors are not fearful of what the scientists will find out about their origins—they are confident they came from the cave of the bear—but are simply upset by the desecration of their sacred grounds. The rest of us are supposed to say, "Well and good," respect these customs, and accede to these desires. The worship of old bones is an established human habit. Moreover, we are not supposed to think that a person who believes he came from the cave of his clan's bear is a dunce. All right. We shall fold back our inclinations and censor our good sense.

To be polite. I believe in politeness as I believe in neatness, but both censor thoughts and conditions. A smile greases the wheels the smile wants to see revolve; redding, cleaning, picking up, removes evidence and restores the status quo. Good oh. Here's a bit of tidying: the pope has decided that the teaching of evolution no longer contradicts the teachings of the Catholic church. He's got to be kidding. So please. A polite smile.

Even in the church the truth changes.

I shall be taught forbearance and acceptance by the sophists who presently police the academy (and like police most places, a mite short on human kindness). We must endeavor to understand how inevitable such practices (name your tune) were in the society of this or that time and in this or that place. We must further realize that our pulpit, from which we preach our values and pronounce our judgments, is no different from any other—just another soapbox from which we shout our slogans and puff our prides. And then we shall be able to excuse if not accept other rites and religions, differing dogmas and political aims. Our society will realize it is one among many, no more than that, modest, understanding, liberal, up-to-date.

Here what is cut is the connection between the excuse which is to be given to the agents of social action (they could not do otherwise) and the nature of the actions themselves. For I do understand why the fatwa was pronounced upon Salman Rushdie. I do understand why society's scissors are used to cut a woman's hair, or nose, or clit. I do understand why criminals were drawn and quartered and their heads mounted at the four points of the compass. I do understand why tribes fall upon and rape and murder one another. I understand why heretics were burnt, why witches were too, why widows went up in smoke along with the dead husband's furniture. I understand why Africans were sold into slavery, why Jews are persecuted, why the KKK is the KKK. So it's okay? Or shall I still say: "Cut it out"?

When Karl Kraus criticized his Austrian society, when he wrote in support of pacifism and against the follies of the First World War, he was not merely being admirably brave. He was right. And he found a moral place in that society from which he could launch his criticisms. Sophists support the status quo until it changes. Then they support the new status quo. They are the friend of every place of power. And are beloved by regimes large and small because they can offer no reasons for change. Except they aren't fast friends. They wiggle with the wind. And every tribal law is right—but only inside the tribe.

So we are surrounded by censorship of all kinds, some of it desirable. The Fates could tell me the hour of my own death, but I don't want to know. The future veils itself to protect us from its often awful look. But why should I want to stop a lot of falsehoods from being bandied about? Because others, not as smart as I am, may fall for them. So what? Let others live in ignorance. I know I am one of the elect. And they don't have a vote. But if I know what is good for others, haven't I a moral obligation to see that quality served? Plato thought so. One may smile at the pope but not at Plato. But only after careful and democratic debate should fluorides be added to our water. We can warn smokers about the dangers of their habit; we can even decide not to help fund the repairs they will one day have to have made; but can we ban the habit, stop word of mouth, pull up the offending plants? Most areas of real ethical debate are gray, and all our decisions should be cautious and considerate and, where possible, reversible.

The forms of censorship that concern most of us in this country (which is fortunately free of many of the worst kinds) are those that involve efforts to remove books from public libraries, newsstands, bookstores, and school curricula. Primary- and secondary-school education, many believe, should be controlled by the community in which the children are being taught and brought up. This point of view, I think, has many merits, though perhaps not enough of them to deny our need for national standards. Nor can we be certain our own hands will remain clean. Do we really want racist novels read in our schools? to kids in their formative years? especially in a society already poisoned by bigotry and distrust? Are we being morally responsible when we permit creationist nonsense the pretense of equality with the views of science, or are we merely being cowardly? for we frequently refuse to stand up for rational principles out of a misguided sense of fairness and freedom.

At the heart of the problem, I think, is a distinction we ought to make between two ways in which people customarily believe their beliefs, and here I am not talking about how we ought to arrive at them—certainly a significant matter too. The difference I have in mind can be illustrated quite simply. If I was born in Poland, then my birthplace is a nonideological fact. If I then say I am Polish, I am adding to that fact a cultural commitment. I am allowing Polishness to define me. Actually, I was born in North Dakota. I am a citizen of the United States. I reside and vote in Missouri. Do these truths make me an American? Not if I can help it, because I do not choose to be defined by a set of senti-ments. To behave as a citizen ought is quite enough.

I can believe that life on this earth probably goes back 3.85 bil-lion years because I just read a scientific report to that effect in the *New York Times*. Weeks or months from now, scientists may change their minds, and their mind-change may change mine. But were I a short-termer, and believed life started only a brief while ago (in Biblical terms) (and because this point of view is part of a system of ideas which I have allowed to define me), then it is not open to me so easily to alter my opinions, since to do so is to alter myself.

In short, the question is: do I own my beliefs, or do they own me? If they own me, then the institutions which formulate and guard and sanctify these notions own me. I have joined a group. I have become an elbow or an arm—a member. "I am a philatelist and a member of the stamp club" says one thing. "I love to collect stamps and I attend meetings of the stamp club" says quite another.

When I am owned by an ideology, I am going to favor its defense as if I were being defended, because that's what will be happening. The free mind can open its fingers and let fall ill-favored fruit. Other ideas are always welcome. What are not wel-come are views which hinder sight, which are themselves fists, which possess our souls like a disease, which say—as Satan did to Faust after their bargain—"Now you are mine!"

I want to conclude by returning to the wisdom of Ken Saro-Wiwa, commenting on his country's condition but referring to us all.

The men who ordain and supervise this show of shame, this tragic charade, are frightened by the word, the power of ideas, the power of the pen; by the demands of social justice and the rights of man. Nor do they have a sense of history. They are so scared of the power of the word, that they do not read. And that is their funeral.   ("Africa Kills Her Sun," p. 293)

Were There Anything in the World Worth Worship

Were there anything in the world worth worship . . . were there anything in the world worth worship . . . what would it be? Would it be me? . . . me? ah, no, not I, for I was old at every age, and wrinkled, thin and skinny, skinny of eye, thin of thought, bald beneath my arms, loud only in empty halls, scarcely present for anybody, since I was hid by me in a faraway look, a look slightly, prudently ashamed; I was an ash deposited in a trouser cuff, left by myself on a closet shelf—a fucked sock, cast out—me, yes, me, I do, I do, I think about me, feel me, row of low hills, fat as an inflated figure, profit without honor, a cost of no account, but I can't say I even hate myself correctly, bent in the shape of a Z, teeny, like the last letter in "guilt," *t*? no, not me, or *e,* as in the end of "dirty shame"; naaaah, as we crooned in third grade, naaaaah, I grew up and out of all that, made a name out of last letters, ate grease, played the game, got burnt when I burned with a bright gemlike flame, knew nothing in life would be worse than the breathing of it, inasmuch as breathing is a leaving, exhalation, sigh of the behind; ah, what an ass she had, and was that ass worthy of worship? were there anything in the world worth worship, would it be that ass? not a dimple in it, smooth and hard in jog style, softball size, a single seam, but mere appearance, lacking a before or after, cool as marble, veined with steel, of no prominence, boyish, one cheek cozy only to its other, worthy of notice, worth a licked lip, one tongue run through a small mouth. Not more.

So what, then? some other part of speech? the bust? ofttimes
lauded, especially by the painters and the poets, one with a wide
aureole, how about it? among all soft things the nub and bubble
of comfort, asking to be nipped, and is that it? a little nip? perhaps it's liquor, aforebed, more warmth on the tongue where it
goes to stir itself around than on any teat of any animal. Numb,
it falls over speechspace like a smatter of sun. There's a god in it,
some say. There's life in it. There's truth too. Enuff said. Before
bed it does you in. Does you. So you don't care that nothing's
done. Does you dumb. That's worth something, worth a friendly
nod, worth a hug, worth a firm shake, toast, a cheer, and the light
in the glass is aglow with goodness—is it an ad? false as fever,
cold to come.

Yes, there are many things in this world of which to be wary, no
doubt, and the worst ones, wanting the wiliest of wariness—
unwearing watchfulness—are just exactly those which for a
moment seem, for a while appear, to be, possibly, worthy of worship. Mother of misery the bottle-ended bosom is. Butts will land
you in the crack of indifference. Do not go to ego, either, for every
my is a me, each me a mirror where we lie like an island in a
mountain lake surrounded by stills and other bits of pictured
scenery. The firs. Mist. Shroudy peaks. Where the eagle shits.

So what's it to be? to bring us to our knee? an empty blue steel-
eyed sky? not an evil in it, not a whisk of cloud, not a speck of
smoke, emptiness altogether thrilling through and through, azure
here my dear have a lap on me. O stratosphere! clear to the moon,
made of the dust of dead loves and other apostrophes. Let us
spoon a tune. With what sad steps thou climbst the sky, Diana,
huntress, chaste and fair.

Still a dull rock, after all, and wholly unresponsive, because, I
wonder, would we worship without expecting payment for our
prayers, our abasements, our grovelings, our fear, gimme god,
gimme Jesus, gimme a room at the inn in Super Bowl City,
gimme a tip on the races, lotsa luck, gimme gangsters, gimme

famine, gimme guts in a pail, gimme damnation. Silky Satin in the sixth race. Worth a bob. Might do. Evil is a successful operation. Pain is its own penalty even if virtue ain't its own reward. Do our dailies backward then. Fart just ahead of feasting. Barf before the beer. Sicken at the sight of her. I do. Merits has its. Stirem. But worship? Life backward won't be any better. Sure, you won't suffer the snake's sting, but you'll get the rattle.

It's death's doing, you say? is that the reason all is ash, and nuthin's worthy of such high regard as worship asks for? Comes to a gopher gone to ground, it does, but even passing passes, dust becomes dust, and the earth will fetch up in a hole the size of its own self.

Of course there are ideas. They have advantages. Best of parents: the friends of the Forms. If I love the laws of motion and you love the laws of motion, there is no love lost, no cause for consternation, jealousy is not an issue, for ideas can be shared without diminution or division. You move. I move. We move in sync, you up, me down, down me, down she, upon cue. We have societies for shared enthusiasms of this kind, but of clubs composed of Janet's lovers who carry on convivial discussions of the slope of her back, or share anxious queries concerning the commercial name of her lipstick, there are none. Just coins and stamps. Furthermore, as worship knows, it is better to love than be loved, far, far, for to be loved is to be consumed, supped upon, had; but to love ideas . . . that love is safe from all response, the ideas remain unmoved, they repay devotion without the least sense of duty, just by being themselves (which anyway they can't help), repaying our pursuit by improving the length of our lope, the ease of our breathing even after a long run, our legs too, as strong as a barrel stave, yes, they sharpen our smarts, it's good just to be in their company on account of how they are all— what? .... true.

That's a joke. It's good to be in their company because they are chummy ghosts. Ideas have no home and no substantiality. No truth either, with little *t* or tall. They cannot call out. Their touch cannot be felt. The idea of man as a featherless biped, ant animal, hive and tribal wiseguy, yields a certain pleasure, calm to calm repose, yet does not work away in Fred's breast the way his heart does, or let Frank breathe better, or ease Hal's pee, or pay attention to her hair—who?—Beatrice of the beastly thighs. Not an element in anything. Not so much wrong as irrelevant. Theory, dearie, won't get you laid. Idea of man as two-legged locust. Image of man as solar parasite. Worthy, surely, but not worthy of worship. Like cards, these ideas want to be played.

Candidates come forward. What do we have? movie stars, ballplayers, politicians, fake saints, sentimental artists, pocket-padding preachers, soldiers of fortune, gunrunners, dope peddlers, junk dealers, false promisers and other promoters, emissaries of ethnicity and blind-eyed bigots, fact farts, professional liars and whiners, shit salesmen, beaters of diseased meat, gangsters, cheats, slumlords, sanitary-napkin salesmen, usurers, bluenoses, party poops, white trash, performers of the slotease . . .

Pretty sight. Were there anyone worthy of worship, we wouldn't recrucify him the way we were supposed to grill Jesus or anybody whose good was really good, no, no, he'd be on the air everywhere making fistfuls of money, saving the souls of millions, creating lakes for their tears, with a golf course and cottages at seasonal rents.

If not a nipple, then your dick. Worship is a waste of energy, cuts into sales, except for stained glass and those little caps and the money Bible paper people make along with the Mecca rug companies and the Zion cartridge crusaders, guns for God and all that, something there, perhaps in pew wood, begging bowls, collectibles of all kinds, stigmata nails, Magdalen mascara, mystic moments incorp.

Sure, there are good things, lots, sure, blow jobs, chocolate mousse, winning streaks, the warm fire in your enemy's house, good book, hunk of cheese, flagon of ale, office raise, championship ring, the misfortunes of others, sure, good things, beyond count, queens, kings, old clocks, comfy clothes, lots, innumerable items in stock, baseball cards and bingo buttons, pot-au-feu, listen, we could go on and on like a long speech, sure, it's a great world, sights to see, canyons full of canyon, corn on the cob, the eroded great pyramids, contaminated towns, eroded hillsides, deleafed trees, those whitened limbs stark and noble in the evening light, geeeez, what gobs of good things, no shit, service elevators, what would we do without, and all the inventions of man, Krazy Glue and food fights, girls wrestling amid mounds of Jell-O, drafts of dark beer, no end of blue sea, formerly full of fish, eroded hopes, eruptions of joy, because we're winning, have won, won, won what? the . . . the Title.

But not worshipworthy. Not sufficiently shapely for such on-the-knees kiss-my-feet praise, like scrub-cloth loo-lid toiletries to take out sin and feed stains, laaaah deeee, they do a good job, but not that good, not ogle and aaaah; but suppose there were, there were something worthy, worthy of worship, just suppose, then what would it be, that thought, that thing, that consummate connection? Holy trophy? Being beyond Being, the Lonely Alone, long time no see.

It is common knowledge—no, if it is common, it isn't knowledge—it is widely bruited abroad that worshippers exist, by the tens, the thousands, loyal to the law, as patriotic as a standing prick, full of cross-my-heart-and-hope-you-die desires, pious folks who do indeed adopt an attitude of worship, light candles, tell beads, go about in a beanie, can you imagine? wear black and bind their breasts, cover their lips, let only their eyes peek upon the world, bind feet, circumcise, scarify, flagellate, fire rifles at the sky, eat only vegetation, only meat, only blood sausage, water their wine, catsup their fries, religiously wipe their ass with soft quilty clouds of pillow feathers, wouldn't be caught dead in curlers, and they, those who have such a bent, they, since they worship, by the tens, the thousands, in the morning, in the evening, kneeling east, praying may God kill everyone who ain't like me, doesn't like me, slay those who believe Darwin, read Freud, think Marx, feel de Sade, O Lord, salt their earth, sterilize their cattle, dewomb their wives, dedickie an entire generation of their hairy males, X out their smart-ass sugar-mouthed kids, and so on . . . well, will He? will He who is worshipped smite? will He come in a cloud full of acid rain to do His will? God's tender bowels run out streams of grace. Well, I say, where was He when the massacres of his believers occurred, when they died of badly consecrated wine, when they trudged across the alleys of L.A. seeking a future home, when they were captivated by Mammon's neat pitch, led on by Belial's sleek sermonizing, shackled to shekels, lied to, by false promises bought? He was in His Underwear Somewhere. He was looking in windows. He was overthinking our thoughts. He was inventing AIDS, a new strain of influenza, bombs which burst the air. He was trying to persuade Bertrand Russell He had powers, He had foresight, He had innumerable perfections . . . one of which was He was everywhere at once like atmosphere, so He was there when the Gandhi was kaputted, and à Becket got the business; He was there when the canisters of Zyklon B fizzed into cells so small so crowded they'd have one by one died anyway, climbing one another if not the walls. He invented kitsch, and the motorcycle after all, He can do, be, see, anything. Imagine, just imagine, if such a He existed.

Heaven is the most painful part of Hell, the saddest idea mankind ever held out hope for. And monotheism is religion's most vicious form. When poly was holding Olympus, then the manifest and myriad evils of this world could be blamed on inattentive supervision, on quarrels, on pique, on a petty god's spite—life and nature made sense—things were as bad up there in the snow and fog as down here in the snow and fog. A deity could be deceived, outrun, outfoxed, opposed by another. Deities had smallish dominions, washed their hands of a lot, let Poseidon do it, were too busy pitching woo, changing their shape, conniving, getting even. And you might want to placate them, get on their good side, enlist their help, sacrifice a tough old cock, make the requested gestures of obedience, observe birthdays, utter formulas of petition and gratitude; but you didn't worship the smooth ivory-hipped shits, even if they were splendidly bummed or fully breasted, toga'd to beat shucks, no, they were simply the aristocracy of the sky or the lords of the earth and had their own interests, pursued their own quite fallible plans, and rarely wanted to rule their bit of land like a feudal lord, lay down laws like mines, exercise presumptive rights (except for a few carnal ones); no, they were too busy kissing their neighbor's wife or fucking some hairy-flanked satyr in the dell.

And nobody—but nobody—disgraced the mind with dogmas and tenets and taboos. Nobody needed a metaphysics to explain how Zeus got into Leda's pants or knocked up Europa. Nobody consequently needed to be killed because they didn't think a small swallow of thin wine was God's blood and a dry cracker anybody's body. Nobody had to take arms against a sea of infidels, sack cities, commission crucifixions, schedule time on the rack, build bonfires for heretics. Occasionally a human sacrifice. Nobody's perfect. If you have some pocket-sized god of your own to present, why, he/she/it is welcome in poly, pull up a throne and have a seat. No need to draw and quarter, try by ordeal, accuse crones of bewitchments. No need to have a holy book, because there aren't that many secrets. The deity (when he got to be the One Big Guy) became an imaginary dictator with oh god real clerical bureaucrats doing his pretend bidding. Working in a holy world is like living in a post office. This is a worshipworthy situation? Some may still be impatient to die for the emperor, but the chief point in life is to die *of* something and never *for* something if it can be helped.

Polys had golden calves to suck up to. The golden calf is a good joe; he doesn't need feed; he doesn't do doodoo, or moo morosely, or low like a languishing lover; he can't require much dough, upkeep is minimal. I guess you'd have to guard against theft and now and then polish the animal. Good glow. Over Jehovah and the rest of the monomolochs, he has the further advantage of actually existing and being really worth something if sent to market or auctioned at Sotheby's.

They say He's always watching, but Allah is a snooze. They say He can get out tough stains, but the Almighty won't rubadubdub his nighties on river rocks, or work out at the club after a hard eon at the Holy Office, or get tough when the toughs get going. They say He has so many good qualities He's lost count, but there's no more tickle to Him than a French feather.

Faithifizers are dangerous. History tells us so. Nevertheless, people ought to be allowed to play the fool, since multitudes subscribe to foolishness as if it were *Vogue*. They outnumber the rational by several billion. Which must prove they're right, right? except they disagree among themselves on most major and every minor point, and hate one another with a heartfelt hate, and hope to interfere with every other life, and despise themselves since they cannot avoid hypocrisy, falls from grace, and other humpty-dumps, deviations from rule, large lapses in what they call love. Once they are dead, they say, they shall be saved.

They shall rot. Rather.

Our only chance is to allow them to remain full of balderdash, bitter and divided. Use their beliefs in universal peace to carve up one another.

A question remains: why do so many believe in such beliefless stuff? toss their wives on the pyre they go to a coil of smoke in? avoid perfectly good grub? mutilate themselves? starve? deny? wear a permanent pout? think the earth will open to let their corpses out? Power, possibly. Women in purdah, what a place. Privilege, possibly. Feeding at the coffers of the church. Fear, principally. Of leaving their mostly lousy life. Trading it in for an imaginary model. To survive. Enduring the pains of each day in the hope of a carefree and happy tomorrow. If there is anything certainly true, it is that everything alive dies. How stupid to deny it. If there is anything certainly true, it is that we must fuck to breed. Yet against all rhyme and reason, the Fictionful let a maidenheaded girl conceive. Why didn't God just come down out of a cloud and say: Hey, here I am? watch me put Spam in a can without opening the tin. Why knock up some innocent kid and ruin her reputation?

Still . . . still, even for a lowlife and soulless nonbeliever (many of whom are as nuts as their opposition), there must be something worthy of worship, a poem perhaps, a chapel ceiling, a symphony, a play, a novel, a diamond tiara, a designer gown, some dancer's gay physique. No. Surely the *Duino Elegies*. No. Not even. Good things, like the truth and good sense and moderation and generosity and kindness and peacefulness and honesty and intelligence and forbearance, must not be worshipped, for worship makes good things into bad things as if they turned on a dime. So even if there were a poem by Yeats that was worthy of worship, we shouldn't give it its perhaps due; even if we have a hairless stripling in plain sight, a youth with a bonny little willie, we mustn't dirty our BVDs; because the good things of the world need also to be questioned, laughed at, mocked, so that our love of them will remain pure, beyond the sound of canons, out of scholarship's soiling reach, free from the possessive grip of idolaters who will squabble them to death; because death, though denied, is the sacred's most sacred precinct; there hubris has hurled many a fine idea, good life, thrillchilling scene, bouncing baby, touching aria, blissful kiss.

Says Satan to his disciples: organize, dogmatize, stigmatize, and send the sorry result to the Devil.

Were there anything worthy of worship, then, we should ignore it; look at it, if we must, cockeyed; keep clear; never let on; invent no curses which employ and preserve its name; await the time when the vines of all our lives will grow over and hide it so it may lie safe like a city left empty and forgotten, silent inside us, solely in the deeps of us, so we might wonder about it like some wonder about Atlantis and, lost and alone, so it may remain worthy of worship, and a star shining in the midst of our dirty earth.

How German Are We?

It was 1981 and a windy wet spring in Cologne. My photographs of the cathedral look as dark as its dizzying façade did on the day I was to lecture at the Amerika Haus. Boys rode their bicycles so swiftly up a length of builder's plywood, which they'd strategically placed against the cathedral's steps, that the bikes leaped into the air at the first landing, and the kids whooped and wildly waved one arm as though they were busting broncs in the movies of the American West.

After visiting the incongruously modern museum which now squats next to the church, the American cultural attaché led my wife and I off to a nearby restaurant for lunch. We entered a large rectangular room which contained a banquette and two or three rows of linen-layered tables. I was struck by the absence of anything Germanic. The room was light and open, the china shone as it should, goblets held the diners' napkins as if they were flowers, and the walls were bare of boars' heads or braggy coats of arms.

I remember little about the meal except that it was pleasant enough. The dining room was reasonably full, and there was a nice buzz of chew-softened talk which surrounded and secured the privacy of our own conversation. The patrons were adult families, shopping companions, friends, not businessmen or -women, I thought. We were nearly finished, very likely nibbling on a tart of local fruit, when the singing began. It arrived with an almost belligerent bluntness, one voice, two, then nearly the

entire room was singing something, not a timid rondelet either—
no shy rendition, this. It wasn't long before the whole room
rocked, and women I had taken to be ladies looking for sales on
frocks were striking the cloth with the palms of their hands, and
male faces had reddened with a menacing joviality.

This wasn't a *Bierstube* at ten p.m., and I looked at the cultural
attaché with undisguised amazement. He appeared to be as dis-
concerted as my wife and I were. We sat through the din as
though in chains, for clearly we could not leave in the midst of
such hearty happiness, or call for our check or make an American
move. Spoons were rapped on wood in some sort of rhythm. We
had to hear more than one verse, I suppose, of more than one
song before finding a space between tunes in which to make our
red-eared way *aus*. Out of the corner of my eye I saw a waiter lift
the upper layer of our linen like a shaken rug. "That couldn't have
been for us," I wondered when we were out on the street. "What
were they singing? I didn't recognize it." Our guide said simply
that it didn't matter, but he was clearly as out of answers as we
were, though I don't know whether his blood had run as cold
as mine in response to this noisy fat-cheeked sample of
Gemütlichkeit; because that was how I heard it, saw them, then,
plump and red and boisterous, vulgarly out of place in that time
and setting, but I also felt bullied by the bonding that was going
on. We walked briskly away, my wife and I holding hands, the
attaché silent. I mustered up a German phrase. *"Wie deutsch ist
es,"* I said.

Later, at our hotel, Mary and I reminisced about our first meeting with Walter Abish and his wife, Cecile, in Virginia, when
Walter's wonderful and disturbing novel *How German Is It* was
awarded the PEN/Faulkner prize. Much later still, when I taught
the novel, I read with deeper understanding the quote from Jean-
Luc Godard on the title page: "What is really at stake is one's
image of oneself." My image had received a shake. I had thought
I had gotten over the reluctance which had kept me out of Ger-

many for so many years. What was the source of so personal a revulsion? I had nothing particularly German in my past—only a name shortened from *Gasse,* "alley," and a fondness for smelly cheese and fermented sauerkraut.

Like most Americans, I thought I knew only movie Nazis. And was thrilled against my will when the blond boy sang his Brownshirt song in *Cabaret,* or when Robert Shaw and his men stomped out "Das Panzerlied" in *Battle of the Bulge.*

I cannot date the day when I first heard my father refer to his president as "that rich Jew Rosenfeld." I had no idea what he was talking about. My father was a patriot, and never spoke proudly of the Germans. He'd been, he claimed, wounded in the First World War, even though he'd been injured by the flu in Texas, where surgeons had removed a few of his ribs in the course of their treatment of his subsequent empyema. Nothing much pleased him, but he was majestically elated on the day Max Schmeling defeated Joe Louis.

In 1935 that other father, the father who wasn't my own, Father Coughlin, came to my eleven-year-old attention. (I thought he ought to be called "cough lin" as though he were, as he was, a syrup.) Father Coughlin had recently founded the National Union for Social Justice, a group whose acronym I judged ugly, but whose one-dollar donation, warm support for Huey Long, Gene Talmadge, and Mussolini, along with the organization's inspiring hatred of labor unions, particularly the United Mine Workers' leader, John L. Lewis, compelled my dad, though he had let his Catholicism lapse, to look upon the group with favor. When the political party Coughlin's ugly acronym formed named Bill Lemke of North Dakota (my father's native state) their candidate for president, and subsequently gained the support of Francis Townsend's pensioners and Gerald L. K. Smith's bunch of Share-the-Wealth reformers, my father finally felt a strong tug of allegiance.

Lemke didn't draw enough votes to get the bucket wet,

because Americans normally don't like to waste their vote just to protest; they'd rather stay home, or elect the leastworst. And Coughlin was soon out of the kingmaking business—even, for a while, off the air. However, the Catholic church knew a good voice when others applauded it, allowing Coughlin to return, provided he could avoid party politics.

Well, anti-Semitism isn't politics, is it? He organized the Christian Front; his pro-Fascist magazine, *Social Justice,* spread racial smut in the manner of *Der Stürmer;* he put bullies with clubs and pamphlets in the street; he reprinted the *Protocols of the Elders of Zion,* which must have pleased Henry Ford; he rallied his embittered little forces, which, by then, were composed, in addition to leftover Townsendites and Gerald Smithslimes, of "discontented reliefers" (as Wallace Stegner put it), "the patriotic riffraff, the belligerently 'American,' the haters of foreigners and Jews, and borderline tough guys, and the hoodlum offspring of broken and disorganized homes" (*The Aspirin Age,* edited by Isabel Leighton. New York: Simon and Schuster, 1949, p. 250). When thugs of the Christian Front beat up New York or Boston Jews, the Irish cops, the victims complained, looked the other way.

I also remember the frequent assemblies of the German-American Bund, a Coughlin ally. Movietone newsreeled their rallies. They wore proper dun-colored shirts, with big belts and proper ties, and made that odd salute seem less silly than no doubt it was, because they gave it so smartly they had to mean it and not simply be acting in a play. Another group was called the Silver Shirts, a spiffier color. Few people in the world I knew approved of these angry ninnies, but in time Americans would learn how to be fascist by following German fashion, just as Germans would wallow in Karl May's Zane Grey West.

Wallace Stegner wisely warns that

it would be well to ponder the enormous following he [Coughlin] had at his peak. It would be well to consider how vague, misty, unformed, contradictory, and insincere his program was, and yet how it won the unstinting belief of hundreds of thousands, even millions. It would be well to remember that even a people like the Americans, supposedly politically mature and with a long tradition of very great personal liberty, can be brought to the point where millions of them will beg to be led, and will blindly follow when a leader steps forward. . . .

It is not likely that Father Coughlin or any of his American imitators can ever again be more than public nuisances, vermin in the national woodwork. But let conditions again become as bad as they did in the deep thirties, and the vermin will reappear. (*The Aspirin Age,* p. 257)

Though conditions are not nearly as economically awful as they were in the thirties, nor as evil as they were during the Red scares of the fifties, the nineties see us surrounded by extremist groups of every persuasion, armed to the height of their ignorance, as venomous with bitter belief as any snake, showing every cap, kind, and color—divisive, simpleminded, and murderous.

Prejudice is everybody's peanut butter, but prejudice in the steel town where I grew up appeared to be climate controlled, and directed at the southern immigrant, whether from Alabama or Italy. It was the spick, the bohunk, the eytie, the shine, who were despised; not the Junker, not those of the disciplined, Protestant, work-oriented North. I dislike the drawl to this day, and have no tolerance for slurred speech. Although the Hun has been our hated opponent during two world wars, and especially suffered from bigotry's lash during the First, the German remains someone to be trusted and admired: private, God-fearing, principled, productive, and even peaceful in the next-door–borrow-a-cup-of-sugar sense. Nor did the Germans sniff at us like the English, Spanish, or French, who founded this country by fighting over it and snuffing the natives, yet after our independence never migrated in great numbers from their homeland to ours, only sent castoffs like contemporary Cuba, or profiteers who were just visiting the Yankee dollar. The Germans, on the other hand, arrived in two great waves during the 1820s and 1850s. So Germans were okay. They founded orchestras, newspapers, and Schiller societies. They kept Missouri in the Union. They read Marx. They loved Hegel. Even German belligerence was quietly esteemed. After all, where could you find a more aggressive bunch than a group of American boys on a hunt or on the town or—yippee!—on the trail?

My father was a member of the American Legion, and when there was a sufficiently serious public ceremony, or if one of the Legion had died, he would dress in his jodhpurs, puttees, belt, and boots, strap on his polished metal hat, sling his rifle over one shoulder, and try to get the valves on his cornet unstuck. Off these otherwise grown men would march to toot taps in fragile unison, get photo'd by fans of military bands, and toss a few down to honor better times and more virtuous lives.

I used to regard these activities as innocent enough, but I know now that nothing, ever, has been innocent. In this world, even The Good itself is guilty.

Much later on in life, I moved to Indiana, where I made the acquaintance of the Ku Klux Klan, the Knights of the Golden Circle, and the John Birch Society. I learned that the Klan's anthem was "The Old Rugged Cross." So those were rugged crosses they had burned, and were burning. I enjoyed the pornographic revelations of ex-priests collected in sleazy mimeographed packs, which could still be found in dusty stalls in forgotten towns where the Klan had held forth and passed their truths around. While in Indiana I began to write a novel about what I would call (to save confusion, and avoid the shame of not knowing, when I was asked what the book was about) "the fascism of the heart," because my experience of my homeland had considerable resemblance to my experience of home—home where the fascist heart was, land of the scared and suspicious, the piously denied and dominated, the resentful and sore. "That Rosenfeld," my father said, "it hurts my ears to hear his shitty chat."

Still later yet, I restarted life in St. Louis and learned about Satanic rites and survival cults. For a few moments the State considered allowing citizens to carry concealed weapons. People (men again, mostly) collect guns and hide them in the woods while pretending they are protecting their homeland. Our pop-kult kulchur (from scat to rap and swing to rock) appeals to permanent thirteen-year-olds. Brutality we embrace like a temple whore. Everywhere I hear racist slogans; I see tribal totems; I feel the heat of puritan fury. Moreover, we prefer to believe that in our frequent wars, unlike other nations, we remain without blame (for Iraq restored our pride after our pride took a fall in Vietnam). Nor have we German guilt to give us pause.

Anecdotes, of course, aren't history, aren't evidence, are only rarely even amusing. Yet anecdotes are all most of us have: lore and gossip and libelous tales, movie myths and racial stereotypes, nuggets of news, political ploys, memories as triumphantly ragged as Fort Sumter's tattered flag.

I thought I could smell the atmosphere of my hometown in more corners of the country than I cared to: dust-bowl desperation, the Depression's melancholy, cynicism's hopelessness, a vengefulness which felt fully justified in being enacted. Let us have windows through which relatives of the slain may watch the murderer die. Our Rambo kills in a good cause, saving the very nation which has abandoned and betrayed him. The cowboy hero must watch his house burn, his children die, his wife endure her rape, before he can, in our clear conscience, collect his tormentors' scalps.

For twenty-five years I have been writing about resentment, and maybe I am now ill of my occupation. Yet I cannot help noticing how much of the initial response to *The Tunnel* has spoken of my narrator as a man so monstrous as to bear no resemblance to anyone they know, only to Nazis and other ancient historical figures. When he invents a political group, which he calls the Party of the Disappointed People, his creation is taken as a sign of his crazed and cranky condition. And my precursors in the growing of sour grapes are said to be Swift, Dostoevsky, Wyndam Lewis, and Céline, each of course more justified and better at it than I. No one drops Sinclair Lewis' name (his style and artistic intentions seem so far from mine), yet in 1935 Lewis was imagining a political party and a candidate too—fascist to a fare-thee-well—to respond to the naive confidence that our American way of life was immune to dictatorship, and that fascism couldn't happen here.

The hell it can't! Why, there's no country in the world that can get more hysterical—yes, or more obsequious!—than America. Look how Huey Long became absolute monarch over Louisiana, and how the Right Honorable Mr. Senator Berzelius Windrip owns *his* State. Listen to Bishop Prang and Father Coughlin on the radio—divine oracles, to millions. Remember how casually most Americans have accepted Tammany grafting and Chicago gangs and the crookedness of so many of President Harding's appointees? Could Hitler's bunch, or Windrip's, be worse? Remember the Kuklux Klan? Remember our war hysteria, when we called sauerkraut "Liberty cabbage" and somebody actually proposed calling German measles "Liberty measles"? And wartime censorship of honest papers? Bad as Russia! Remember our kissing the—well, the feet of Billy Sunday, the million-dollar evangelist, and of Aimée McPherson, who swam from the Pacific Ocean clean into the Arizona desert and got away with it? Remember Voliva and Mother Eddy? . . . Remember our Red scares and our Catholic scares, when all well-informed people knew that the

O.G.P.U. were hiding out in Oskaloosa, and the Republicans campaigning against Al Smith told the Carolina mountaineers that if Al won the Pope would illegitimatize their children? Remember when the hick legislators in certain states, in obedience to William Jennings Bryan, who learned his biology from his pious old grandma, set up shop as scientific experts and made the whole world laugh itself sick by forbidding the teaching of evolution? . . . Remember the Kentucky night-riders? Remember how trainloads of people have gone to enjoy lynchings? Not happen here? (*It Can't Happen Here,* chap. 2)

Could Hitler's bunch be worse? Well, they were worse, because they had the opportunity. And opportunity is what another year like 1935 might provide. For now there is no more American way of life to protect the way Sinclair Lewis wanted to protect it. Richard Blackmur, commenting on the utopianism of Lewis' novel, observes that "there is a history of terror in the bowels of every nation only awaiting the moment's impetus to be articulated and made general" (in *Sinclair Lewis, a Collection of Critical Essays* by various authors on Lewis' novels, edited by Mark Schorer. New York: Prentice Hall, 1962, p. 109). My narrator (and there are so many millions like him, to my mind, that if he is a monster, what are we to call man?) is sorrowful, without hope; he no longer bides his time. He cannot be confident that the markets will collapse, that inflation will run away with all our wealth, that the national ego will fail to survive another blow, that a series of natural disasters will empower his attitudes, that the middle class will at last rise to resist one more reduction of their heartfelt hopes; but he is there, waiting, nevertheless, just underground, rather quiet, like the web worm in the sod, on the off chance, in case.

For me, the principal question is a variant of Walter Abish's, but I think equally pertinent and important. It is "How German are we?" and I think it is appropriate to put it in these prejudicial terms (based as it is on a Germany one hopes is history) because German culture—its marvelous music, its profound philosophy, its adept science, its great literature, its industry and discipline—remains problematic; because it was, though higher than the Alps, a culture which did not prevent the world's worst moral catastrophe. And that catastrophe casts doubt on the character of our every success, and makes suspicious even our simplest, plainest, most innocent-seeming acts. How German are we? my novel asks. Its answer has pleased few. Its answer is—very.

THE STUTTGART
SEMINAR LECTURES

*The Stuttgart Seminar in Cultural Studies, organized
and directed by Professor Heidi Ziegler, then president of
the University of Stuttgart, was held for two and half
weeks in a parklike resort just outside Ludwigsburg called
Mon Repos, usually during alternate Augusts. The fellows
were generally young faculty drawn from European uni-
versities, though occasionally Taiwan, the Republic of
South Africa, and the United States or Canada were represented. The faculty consisted of writers and scholars
largely from the United States, and all sessions were conducted in English. I had the privilege and pleasure, during the years of the Seminar's existence, of taking part in
these immensely stimulating exchanges. I felt it also gave
me the opportunity to compose some lectures that dared
to fly a few feet from convention. Their markedly different
natures reflect the changeable climate of my intellectual
life. Yet their themes, attitudes, and ideas also reiterate the
past, prolong the present, and project themselves
unabashedly into future projects. Alas, I see no help for it.
In any case, here are three of them.*

Quotations from Chairman Flaubert

Heinrich Zeitung Muller-Müller sat silently in the speeding cab and tried not to overhear let alone to listen to his wife complaining about the risk inherent in wet roads, about the traffic, heavy already although it was early in the day, about the draft the driver had created by cracking his window, and the smoke of his cigarette, which was inconsiderately circulating across the backseat before finding its way out into the street. "So you say," she said, though he had said nothing. She regularly read his mind as if it were in print, as so much of it unfortunately was; for if he had not written at such length about his life in East Germany, he would not now be defending himself in the press, whose schadenfreude at the present turn of events was not sufficient to satisfy them. They wanted—their readers' wanted—endlessly, more: more dirt, more tarnish to the silver of his reputation. On second thought, perhaps he should upgrade his image so that the gloss, when it went, would be gone from something grander—how about gold? Gold, after all, was the metal in the medal he didn't get on account of the political imbroglio he found himself in, and dingy was indeed the life he now led. "See," his wife boasted, "it's just as I said: *they* can smoke up the taxi like a stupid tune on their radio, while *we* must sit and inhale it as if we were some bug on a bush being poisoned as a pest; but if *we* want to smoke in this public conveyance, *they'll* complain as if speaking for their lungs, and lah-dee-dah their concerns about cancer louder than the tinny tunes *they're* listening to."

The smoke, he thought, is trying to escape to the West. "The driver can hear you, dear," he tried to say mildly but sharply said.

"He doesn't understand a word; they make no effort; *ich weiss nicht* is all they know in any language; isn't that the same shop we passed a while back? is he really taking us to the airport? these people are all alike, at least in New York they get lost now out of ignorance. In New York they drive their cabs straight off the boat and still think they're in Moscow or Cairo or someplace, and hang a left like they hung their last left-wing leader. But here, they think they know every cinder in the street. Look how he's shaving the paint from those parked cars; you'd think he was in the refinishing business." How, Heinrich Zeitung Muller-Müller wondered, was he supposed to sense the soul of society in the throes of its sweaty changes when he spent his time holding his nose so he wouldn't hear his wife's laments which were, by now, as redolent with repetition as ripe cheese?

What was the appropriate quotation from Chairman Flaubert?

#12. Practical life is loathsome to me; the mere necessity of sitting down in a dining-room at fixed hours fills my soul with a feeling of wretchedness.*

Trapped in the taxi, inhaling his wife's words as he so often had to, Muller-Müller was nevertheless comforted by the verification which events were providing him. The Chairman was always correct. In a world where all the trees had been felled, Flaubert's stump was at least larger than the others. The cab shimmied down the off-ramp toward the airfield, and his wife squealed almost audibly. I guess I should thank god she's only imaginary, Muller-Müller thought; still, she does carry on like a cartoon. I'll have to do something to deepen her nature, even if that means

---

*All Flaubert quotations have been gratefully taken from Francis Steegmuller's translation of the author's letters. (Cambridge: Harvard University Press, 1982)

giving in to the feminists. "I'm made-up, that's what you mean," his wife said, as if she were reading over his shoulder. "You can't pretend that reality is a fiction just because you lie about life all the time." Oh, she would like to take the Chairman's place, if she were given the chance, and put her own pronouncements in his position of authority; but Muller-Müller was determined on that score. Of all the *chers maîtres,* Gustave was the *cher*iest.

The wipers wiped away, somewhat smearily, and the rain pattered upon the roof of the cab, sort of gently, and his wife would be required to say as they slid to a stop in front of TWA: "Well, we left the States without an umbrella to our name, and it's rained the whole d— time we've been in Berlin, god, it's as gray here as Vienna is, and I thought Vienna was the grayest gray place I've ever been, and now we're going to get soaked again getting out of this car." Who said writing is the best revenge? What good is a revenge which has to be taken again and again like a photographer from the press? a press which had been particularly annoying, flashing their pans at his person, blocking his path, the lights laughing at the hat he held over his face. "So I suppose they'll all be here," his wife said, "waiting like worms in their moist spoil of dirt." It scarcely mattered to his wife that he made her out to be a nag. "Once I get going," she said, "you" (meaning Muller-Müller) "have nothing to say." He sat silently in the cab for a moment, fishing with his forefinger among his German change for pieces of the right size. Anything, a character (as the folksy old critics called it), or a situation, or a thought, a word, an expression like "German change," might cause a text to turn a corner and disappear into significance, such as "the Unification of the *Reich*"— that was certainly a change, even if it was like remarrying your ex-wife. "Unification"—yes, there was a term which might scare the pants off most writers, and what were you supposed to do after your pants had been frightened into fleeing: run faster, screw, shower, sit on the stool? how long had it been since they had been unified, he and she? longer than Germany had been happily divorced; boy, some people learn none of the lessons of

Heraclitus, namely, you can't marry the same woman twice and expect to live any way after that except sappily.

He felt his wife's impatience like another passenger. She wouldn't get out of the car ahead of him but would wait for her husband (him) to hold the door and hand her over the curb like a date at a dance. Just an old-fashioned girl, aren't you, hon, he'd sometimes say. Go to h— she would habitually respond. Flaubert bragged in—was it #35?—that in some recent work of his

> There are only two or three repetitions of the same word which must be removed, and two turns of phrase that are still too much alike.

Where were the reporters he feared would be waiting, or did such things happen only in that other—that nearly unmentionable medium—the one in which photos of photographers photographing photogenic moments were so popular? ganging up on some guy as he comes out of court or emerges from a cab to tackle a staircase which has occupied its life collecting steps, mike in his mouth, the newsies following him tread after tread, hounding him, holding the hem of his trousers in their teeth, cameras aimed like Uzis, and that mesh-covered earmuff, initialed by a network, pushed in his face, the instrument to which he mutters, "No comment at this time," and so forth. "Are you going to get the bags," his wife commands. "No comment at this time," he says, then *"Danke* something *schön,"* I think, to the driver, whose cigarette lets go its ash that instant on his valise: should he compare that small pale fall to the errant plop of some pigeon or directly to the character and consistency of his consumed life?

Was the Chairman simply upset with the banal repetitions which make up day-to-day existence—in contrast with the belly dancers he observed in Egypt, where the rippling rolls of fat seemed freshly jiggled just for his tourist's eye? How different Constantinople and Damascus were from his tidy environment at Croisset, his blessed bachelor digs; but didn't he desire such a pallid, undemanding, day-to-day existence, so that his imagination might run undistracted and unimpeded to its goal? Because nothing interferes with creative work more than phones and children. The misery of millions is inspiring. A flat tire ruins the day. Louise Colet wanted to wring a little passion out of Gustave; she wanted to feel his heart ache for her; she, after all, was his true love, wasn't she? No. Of course not. A stupid question. Work was his one true love, of course, and her cunt a convenience. Can't be kind and survive. Flaubert conferred his letters on her, a gift which Rilke's epistolary ladies understood far better than Louise, who was, after all, a dunce—never mind the desperate bios that made her out to be the master's victim.

Couldn't I contrive a Croisset for myself in the Hamptons maybe, or on a street in Queens? a walk-up apartment over a pants-press store, possibly, where they'd never find me, neither newshounds nor police? Who would expect anyone to live in Queens who had any control over their fate, Heinrich figures. Or maybe the Chairman is concerned because the French language, so vowel-heavy it will blow away in a Boche breeze, or be intimidated by a rapid and guttural polonaise, doesn't dare any more repetition than is already built into it—*oh* and *ah* and *aay* and *eee* everywhere like cattle lowing on the lea?

I know you can't hurt language. It can absorb every stink-footed invader and turn them, in time, into model citizens. Sure, we should treat our own language well, for it is, after all, our only muse, but each of us has a somewhat different tongue. My American, my vocabulary, the syntax of my mind, is not the same as Frank Sinatra's, or anyone else you might mention. Henry James does not have the word "snot" in his vocabulary. No. Inaccurate. He knows what "snot" means. Probably he more than once thought, of a drama critic, "that snot-nose," but it is not a word one of his stripe writes or utters. He is a gentleman. Dare we say "of the old school"? He does not write sentences like "Geez, Louise, it's okay, play with yourself if you wanna."

We have to do more than differentiate between *langue* and *parole*. There is, of course, the historical language, packed in the volumes of its dictionaries, and there is that same language as it is used now. Within the current tongue, there are all the regionalisms and dialects, funny ethnic mixes, slanguage and the argot of the gangs. Then there is the speech of you and me, and if any one of us is to have a muse, and a source of inspiration, it will be shaped by our style. Without one—if our pages are indistinguishable from the pages of who knows how many other scribblers—if Jackson Pollock's drips are no different from mine—if my leaps would satisfy Balanchine—if wines were as standardized as pop—if the grass is never greener on the other side—if our fingerprints, at least, our scars, our moles, our genes, don't distinguish us—then we are without an identity, without a trade, without a soul; for there will be no way for us to prove we are we when one we can do the work of another—another? what other?—because even a stop sign should say STOP in its own way, and at its own corner, if it wishes to be regarded as real, because the individual is everything, isn't it? isn't she? and that's why the Wall had to come down, and why Mozart couldn't be Haydn, and why—if your sentences read like a cereal box or announcements on the sides of trucks—a chill should run hickory-dickory up and down your now anonymous spine, since sameness is death, and why it is vital to understand that Muller-Müller's lies were indisputably his, had his touch, and were undeniably deserving of praise.

She always packs too much, Muller-Müller shouldn't have thought (taking the bags one by one from the sullen cabby, sullen not because of an insufficient tip, Muller-Müller didn't suppose, but because the driver dimly knew he had been talked about, heard himself slandered in that American soldier-boy tongue, the shadow of the sense showing, even if he couldn't see its substance); no, Heinrich can't have M and M (as Muller-Müller was surreptitiously called) think his sweet wife carted too many clothes about, because to think so would have been to have committed another cliché, supported one more stereotype, and made his prose predictable; nor would he have made such a common-place complaint if he were writing her up fairly, because she packed with rare wisdom for a wife, and never brought winter clothes on safari or bought heavy things you had to haul home in sacks whose strength was every moment waning, and lug aboard the plane like a bum and his bag lady . . . embarrassing . . . well . . . he could see their reflections as he turned, valise under his left arm, garment bag hung around his neck and slung over his right shoulder by a strap, the small case swinging from his left fist so it whacked his knee when he walked, the large bag scud-ding along the cement (lending the illusion of precision to the prose) . . . wait—where is the wife? she's into the airport clickety-split, are any of these damn doors—whadyacallit?—seeing-eye, as if they had dogs by their sides barking once for open, twice for shut . . . yup, there's the wife, she's yattering with the press already; she pretends to hate the Filth Estate (as she calls them), says she despises journalists and loathes interroga-tions, when actually she eats them up . . . eats them up, when she wouldn't eat what she called "those calorie-coated German cutlets" we were everywhere hospitably offered, making a lunch out of nothing but beets once, their juice like a ring of blood around her mouth. . . .

Indeed, it was a dreadful mistake making up a name like Muller-Müller even if it sounded everso genuine, and even if the explanation of the hyphen, too, had the smell of the true-blue to it: my mother, Sophie Muller, Muller-Müller would, with a sober smile, explain, married Hans Müller, hence the umlaut over Heinrich's old man's *u* like a tiara and the absence of one in his mother's *nom de née;* but nobody bought that story, except for *Stimme,* the German magazine, which apparently will print any-thing, especially if you allow them to pay exorbitantly for it. Muller-Müller prepares himself once again to tell the press, who now are buzzing about like a bunch of ponces wanting to sell him a good time on their Rieperbahn, that he was really Fred Miller from Arkansas, and that he gave himself the name they knew him by (and sold his story to *Stimme* for an entire opera, man, not for a single song) in order to find out how it would feel to write under political oppression and public opprobrium, because he'd heard that such restrictions were great spurs to the imagination, that you had to suffer to create, and that once people believed he'd lived in Potsdam most of his life (though he did consider residing in Dresden) and was a Stasi spy from the age of five, when he turned his mother in for cooking cabbage according to a capitalist recipe; then, richly disgraced, he would compose, first, a reply, then a defense, finally an admission—each in inspired prose, and for an equivalent profit. In short, the works of Guilt would be followed by the works of Remorse, but these could be surpassed later by those which celebrated his rediscovery of God and the church, whether Catholic or Lutheran he hadn't decided yet. But there was no need to get ahead of history, and Muller-Müller was happy to leave unchosen his future faith.

> #40. A proper name is extremely important in a novel—crucial. It is no more possible to give a character a new name than a new skin; it's like wanting to turn a Negro white.

However, though the wily Heinrich had been tripped up and exposed before he had got fairly started down the road of his ruse, things did seem to work out for the best, because Heinrich Zeitung Muller-Müller became famous as a fraud of an especially intriguing kind: as a non-German who had climbed the Wall from West to East to take up residence in a country covered by thick clouds even on a clear day, rather than being merely another native-born police spy in a left-wing Nazi state where there would have been more spies than victims spied upon if most of the spies hadn't been spying on other spies, which is always a necessity, since once you decide to be a spy, I don't care if it's for God, you have sold your soul simply to fill a file, and will consequently make mischief for the rest of your life as if it were your profession.

Fortunately Fred Miller was only a liar and a cheat, a con artist with inadequate skills, and aims quite beyond his reach, so he could be viewed with amused sympathy, and even with some surprise, because (though he had finally been forced to admit that he wasn't German, hadn't climbed the Wall from West to East, hadn't lived in Potsdam or considered residing in Dresden either, had spied on no one, turned up no secret traitors to the State, couldn't even speak the language, having had his Ozark-smoked American prose put into not very convincing Plattdeutsch by an old school chum, Trevor-Groper, who himself was no bargain, a klutz in fact, who wrote German with an English accent because he thought it lent his fibs about being a Rhodes scholar and an Oxford don a whiff, like mint, of verisimilitude) . . . yes, because Muller-Müller had expressed the East German's initial idealism and told a sympathetic story of progressive involvement, disillusionment, and betrayal so convincingly, he became a hometown hit, representing brilliantly the pain of confronting the truth at last and then writing (as he alleged) those daring subversive works which circulated only in manuscript (since, even if they were merely imaginary manuscripts, their readership was real enough)—the story of the peasant who builds a hutch for his rabbits, for instance, a story so plainly put, so simply arranged, but told nevertheless in such an Aesopian way that the reader understands the hutch to be society itself and each little round rabbit-dropping a bureaucrat—each of his brave tales passing from furtive hand to furtive hand, causing the anger of the populace to rise like yeast; and then, in the last act, with the authorities in furious though futile pursuit, the author bravely escaping to the West disguised as a steamer trunk. It was a saga to be cherished, and, as always, the truth had nothing to do with it.

#1. By now I have come to look on the world as a spectacle, and to laugh at it. What is the world to me? I shall ask little of it, I'll let myself float on the current of my heart and my imagination, and if anyone shouts too loudly perhaps I shall turn like Phocion, and say, "What is that cawing of crows?"

Indeed, one thing which M and M discovered when he encouraged his imagination to go over the Wall to the East and take up residence in the mind and heart, not to say belly and loins, of a German writer was the dread which he knew the feeling of his new importance should engender in him. As hard as he tried, and as many words as he wasted endeavoring to create the condition, he never really felt threatened by his imaginary manuscripts. He could put himself in the place of someone who watched his words in the workplace, lest he get reported to his superiors (that was like avoiding boy-girl jokes in the USA), or he could identify with someone who kept his political nose clean in order to keep his job and avoid contretemps (if you were gay in the USA, you remained in the closet, because society would now pretend to tolerate fairies if, like fairies, they were mostly invisible and very quiet and not inclined to flutter); but that a line of verse or a little scene in a small hotel (where Lilly reveals the secrets of left-wing sex to Karl by making him a present of her manifestos) might excite anybody's political libido was a fact his inner self could not believe in.

It was true that, in the States, if you wrote about kikes and niggers or your characters beat up women, you would get a lot of flak, and maybe face a lawsuit—nowadays only fat white balding old-boy Prots with a classical education are fair game—but a little legal wrangling over a case you might just win was scarcely the same as a life and a livelihood which might be suddenly snuffed; nor would your friends fall under suspicion if you spoke your mind, as if you'd been corrupted by them, and although your wife might not be kept on at the day-care center, she wouldn't just disappear one day in a puff of police.

If being offensive to folks was the only way to get attention back home (being offensive had become almost a moral obligation) and being inoffensive was the surest way to stay out of the State's sight in the East, neither was, strictly speaking, connected to writing well.

#3. An artist who is truly an artist, who works for himself alone, unconcerned with all else—that would be a wonderful thing; such an artist would perhaps know immense joy.

You can help your neighbor mow her lawn, but can you really help your fellow man? No one, however strong, can do that alone, which is why we join parties and form groups and enlist aid and support some cause. Nor are such things always futile. I know of a few old buildings which have been saved that way, of improvements made to parks and a few restrictive laws changed. But the truth is destroyed when you organize it, as are good intentions too. A writer should be wary of the world, as if it were a place of poisonous ivies and venomous snakes.

The problem with repression and threats to one's life, like the cowardly and self-serving fatwa against Salman Rushdie, dependent as they all are on the devoted ignorance and murderous compliance of the masses, was the persistent distraction which distressed the soul, the obsessive thoughts of fear and revenge which possessed the mind, especially for those to whom politics had always been important, and religion too, so that they were already weakened by the need for belief, with the consequence that to sit down to write was to sit down to brood, to mull over, ruminate, only to throw up, like a cat, the grass just chewed.

#30. In our day I believe that a thinker (and what is an artist if not a triple thinker?) should have neither religion, country, nor even any social conviction. Absolute doubt now seems to me so completely substantiated that it would be almost silly to seek to formulate it.

Muller-Müller's wife—what was he calling her today? Louise?—was now really miffed, because the little crowd of cameras she had so winsomely approached were merely waiting to make a raincoat commercial. Herr Muller-Müller was no longer news, nor was Fred Miller either. He was being kicked, but not escorted, out. He would not have to recite his intentions again. And at the airline counter there was a long sloppy line of sad, disgruntled, or impatient faces. He found the queue's frazzled terminus and let down his bags between spots of umbrella water. Louise lurked a little way off, perhaps signifying her disdain for the loser to whom, alas, she felt she was linked by loops of stale leftover love, or maybe she was just dismayed by the line, or still annoyed by their total fall from fame and the embarrassment of her mistake.

"Why don't you change our marks back into money?" he semi-shouted at her, pointing to an icon which directed tourists to a currency counter.

"Our dough doesn't rise, now you want me to punch it down, nevertheless," Louise said, snatching his billfold from his proffered hand. "That's all you've got left? I've most of my money in my purse, where it will stay."

"Hey, I always pay for everything," Fred said. "I'm still playing the captain of this houseboat." Louise's look said she was totally tired of his whiny badinage. She had once characterized his usual frame of mind as one of "smug self-pity," but he had rejected this description, calling it a psychological contradiction. Actually, it was peculiar to be pestered by a person who was so completely in your power that you could alter her breast size with a word. "Small" would do. "Diminutive."

Lines made Miller gloomy. He always ruminated while standing in them, staring into the space he hoped to reach, counting the backs ahead of him without really noticing what he was doing. At first it was the petty patter of his wife, then it was the failure of the press to hound him, maybe the rain, and now this line of lumpen luggage bearers which had lowered his nose to the level of his socks. There he saw a pair of bright yellow pumps with high heels, a sturdy walking sandal whose wool sock oozed between its thongs like molecular pudding, a badly bitten bluish ankle, and lots of little wheels on which trunks trundled, or larger ones, their rims wrapped with rubber, which racked bags and robbed porters of their livelihood.

> #4. To be stupid and selfish and to have good health are the three requirements for happiness, though if stupidity is lacking, the others are useless.

Louise was at the airport bank exchanging one kind of money for another, which wasn't what he wanted to call creativity. Nor was it creative to jimmy a pfennig or two from the transaction. Fred felt about bankers the way everybody who wasn't a banker felt about bankers. You were only creative if you added new life to life. Otherwise, you might be inventive. But by "new life," Fred didn't mean new like the two tykes who troubled his sight, both military brats, their mother a Gretchen, their father a Yank in mufti, or the babe in arms up the line he would certainly be seated by and expected to coo at too, as if kids were some sort of blessing instead of one of the world's many plagues. No, by "new" he didn't mean additional. More people meant more pain, more strife. Nowadays, you had to earn the right to nibble at the celery. And Fred Miller wanted desperately to prove he deserved to be, as if existence were a prize handed out in advance of the deed. However, his desperation frequently led him to do things like lie, commit fraud, write slop, look for an angle, call himself Muller-Müller, cultivate critics, bad-mouth the competition which denied him his just deserts, which yielded him at best but external goods: a few bucks, a bit of glory, a moment of renown, a session in the sack with some young climber who took him for a sturdy rung on the ladder of literature—and left him feeling guilty and a failure because, of course, that's what he was. He was another lout in this unmoving line.

The only encouraging thing was that people were piling up behind him now. But what sort of encouragement was that, to be scum, not dregs; to be a pissy writer, not a shitty one? Everybody had a manner. He could see that by examining the fellow sufferers standing stupidly ahead of him, beginning to become impatient, some more immediately than others, some voices raised, some higher, some thinner, a few rapid with complaint, others chatty, apparently oblivious to their circumstances, engrossed in their narrations: the purchase of a piece of the Wall, their reasons for returning to the States, the way the kids had behaved on the trip, their comfortable shoes, the wretched weather, the cost of everything. There was nothing unusual in all this. He had heard these voices, logged their messages, and observed such lines over and over again. "Marie! Stay close to Mommy, honey." He and Louise were no exceptions, typical tourists, entering this tired sentence like two worn-out words.

How often had he remarked the short skirt stretched to the point of pain across an immense haunch, only in this instance it wasn't pink, it was robin's-egg, the pink was farther along toward the head of the line, on a scarf; and the man with the mustache he tended like a garden was present again, but this time the fuzz was on a fuller face. How could he miss the kid with the half-head of bald hair who was everywhere, even in his dreams, as was the aluminum rack on the back of that young girl, as fresh-faced as a cola ad, her bedroll as predictable as the pace of the line which was now inching forward so that he had to shove his baggage ahead with his shoe. A habit of his. Miller began to undress her, starting with the pack. He would pitch the pup tent, unroll the roll, before undoing her shirt. Immediately in front of him were two young men—college students—as trim as lean meat, in German sweaters straight from a shop in Prague, judging by the knit, and because they were worn over Havel tees, which helped him make the inference, for when the silent one suddenly pulled his sweater off over his head, there the tee shirt was. The crowd was warming up the hall. Here, dear, let me unhook you, he tried to pretend. Down on the soft Black Forest floor. Louise handed him some money in familiar denominations. Twenties. Tens. Oh to be twenty again, hiking in the mountains with a merry maid, trying to find a way to make out in a hostel, putting calamine on bee bites, suffering through the inevitable irregularity of meals, hitchhiking for hours on a hot highway, house on one's back like a mortgage, a stolen apple hiding in your pocket, the bite you'd try before flinging the fruit from you, as green and bitter as grass.

A sentence, he said to himself. I am sentenced. And all of us are simply clots of words, groups we've formed and will form again, wandering, waiting, wallflowered, some like old folks out of relatives and friends, words entering and exiting rooms, walking halls, strolling in gardens, through neighborhoods, milling about with other words, forming lines, disappearing into books. Look here, an unfamiliar one has now appeared alongside my two students, eastern seaboard by the speech of them, but not the new fellow, greasy as a spoon, twelve kinky clumps of hair tousling his big fat head. It seems that they know one another. Small talk. Shove ahead. The line has moved. The boys before me too, in syntactical talk, shaped like a short phrase which qualifies our collection of bags and worries, the heaviness of our columnar bodies, yes, they constitute a clause; and then, stretching to the counter where a young pale lady leans to listen to language she cannot understand, to a question she will answer anyway, *that*— her narrow pale face with its fiery lips—is the head of the sentence we are all standing in, each term of us moving toward her features, her red mouth, to modify a meaning no one in the line will know. Before long, all of us will be rearranged in other collections, connected by diversified spaces, making meanings of a mundane kind, no doubt, only to drift again in a northerly direction; each of us minutely altered by our interaction, our exchanges, so that over time our significance will almost insensibly shift, or we will become archaic—i.e., dead.

For the real writer, life does more than accept or resemble language; it coughs up words like gobs of bloody spit, suggests them, insists, and every one is more historical than history, deep beyond diving, wide beyond reach. Lovemaking used to be thoughtless;

limb rubbed limb without a line between them; the inarticulate cry was the body's talk; but as our senses dulled to one another, the familiar was forgotten, and words rose in the mind where reality had been, reminders to touch this nip, that flat stretch of skin, to moan as if out of one's head, until sex became manipulation and performance; well, words everywhere interpose themselves between our jam-spread toast and our closing teeth, our footfalls and the walk they fall on, our clothes of wool and silk and an equally swaddled world. What justifies Fred's wait in his airline line? for who has shown up to enliven his tedium but the sweaty fat guy with a cartload of clothes who has parked alongside his friends now, all of them chatting like birds; yes, he's playing the friendship card but planning to break the queue—that's what the shit is up to: he intends to slip into the line far ahead of his turn. Furthermore, the implication drawn like a baby tooth from Fat Boy's machinations has angered Fred, who is already annoyed by wife and life and lies and loss of attention, as well as the slow line itself, inefficiency's consequence, looping behind him as he turns to look and measure the extent of Fat Kink's crime. What justifies any of this but its description?

The two Americans and their greaseball queue crasher are pretending to be oblivious to everything but their happy chitchat; nevertheless, chitchat or chatchit, Fred knows that Herr Ratteficken is figuring out when to edge his cart . . . ah, now, there it goes, a foot forward into the queue at an insidious angle, and to Fred it is the spear which pierced his so-called savior's side.

#14. Let us love the muse and love her and love her. The child that may be born is of minor importance: the purest pleasure is in the kissing.

Louise said. What did Louise say? Nod. Smile in her direction. But her face is turned away. Fred and Louise still conjoined by the ubiquitous conjunction. They rode inside several sentences through the rain to the railroad station, and now they are waiting

in this aforementioned line to purchase a seat in a first-class carriage. Off to Lyon to eat snails. Haven't lied to anyone at all. Are
twenty-five and thirty, fit as fiddles, in constant touch, a look
here, a sniff there, a bit of pressure on the arm, a brush of bum,
murmur of endearment, an odor of sexual satisfaction rising from
them like a smug fog. No. Fog settles. It's mist that rises. Fuck it.
Also not in Master James, who ducked it. Nor did he rhyme.

Fred is debating with himself. He is basically a patsy, easily
pushed hither, even more readily pushed yon. He hates scenes,
that's why he is somewhat surprised by his reaction to the East
Germans' accusations: he was pleased with himself; talked back
in a confident, even arrogant, way; enjoyed their annoyment . . .
no, annoyance . . . the magazine's discomfiture too, because
they'd been taken in, conned, fooled by a fellow from—where is
Fred from, Kansas? Iowa? Iowa City, sure, every writer in America is from Iowa City, where poetry looks the same as prose but
sounds sleepier, the way, among states, Iowa is supposed to be.
He had them buffaloed, which means, more likely, Wyoming or
Colorado. Some cowboy place. In America everybody wants to
know, first off, where you're from, as if it mattered, when it clearly
doesn't, as in this case. Louise is from Florida. Fred is from Cali-
fornia. Two states which have no natives. Only immigrant trash
from New York and North Dakota.

Anyway, Fred is debating with himself. Should he do more
than glare at the Fatsweat Ratfuck? He is doing that now. And
Fatsweat Kinkhead Ratfuck is giving him the corner of his right
eye. Uneasy, shifty, symbolically shouldering Fred aside but clip-
ping Fred's furious glances to paste in his scrapbook. Certainly,
Fred's glare is collectible; it is a glare which would melt fat. And
certainly, Herr Ratteficken is as moist as a greasy spoon's dish
towel. His shirt (what difference does it make if it's blue?) has
fled the wide embrace of his belt and has bloomered a bit. Or
should Fred suddenly shout at the fellow, pop the question: are
you trying to break this queue, young man? Is that ratsweat I per-

ceive on your swarthy ethnical brow, you Allah-worshipping author-threatener? Or should he simply point with a stern finger to the rear of the line, now full of Hong Kong Chinese or some other sort of rich refugee. Hey, see the other immigrants back there—that's where you belong—end of the line.

The thought that Herr Ratteficken's attempt to inveigle himself and his rack of rags into the line—a line which begins with a pale-faced female functionary who has highly visible reddened red lips, and ends with a clutter of Gucci-baggaged Chinese money launderers—is symbolic of some international condition: that unpleasant thought will occur to Mr. Miller much later. In, as we say, retrospect. When he is Mr. Miller once again.

> #21. The entire value of my book, if it has any, will consist of my having known how to walk straight ahead on a hair, balanced above the two abysses of lyricism and vulgarity (which I seek to fuse in analytical narrative). When I think of what it can be I am dazzled.

Standing there, sore-footed from a week of gawking about and running from the police, Fred is falling further and further into the dumps. He doesn't denounce the interloper, who is still chatting away with his pretend friends while eyeing Fred warily, sliding his cart into the queue as it makes its way briskly forward now, since other uniformed and lipsticked ladies have arrived, and, yes, now there is a middle-aged, rust-thatched, bark-skinned man with a clipboard made of Masonite moving back along the line (shall I say, querying people in the queue?), asking a woman, whose splendid bustline has been hidden from Fred's scrutiny before this moment, whether she has packed her bags herself or had her Palestinian maid do it, and whether she owns a hair dryer (she does) or any other object shaped like a .45 (she doesn't), but her hair dryer isn't in her luggage, she says, see, I've got it in my capacious purse, she says, pulling the dryer out and pointing it at the clipboard-carrying chap, who is taken aback, whereupon three members of the security forces who have been lurking behind some arras or other rush forward, Uzis at the ready . . . Uzis blazing, shooting the clipboard from the functionary's fingers . . .

Basket that.

#10. For my part, until someone comes along and separates for me the form and the substance of a given sentence, I shall continue to maintain that those two terms are meaningless. Every beautiful thought has a beautiful form, and vice versa. In the world of Art, form exudes Beauty; just as in our world it exudes temptation and love.

Of course, the Master means to refer to well-shaped sentences, not to the noxious pages which Fred's rivals wipe across their cracks and hope will count as writing. The symmetry of the lady is astounding, Fred thinks, examining her as if she were a paragraph. She is also interestingly irregular in the right way, for there's a wry twist to her full lips, a slight lean to a weaker left leg, an ear which has been allowed to escape her hair where it's been swept like a surfer's wave to one side.

Just as you cannot remove from a physical body the qualities that constitute it—color, extension, solidity—without reducing it to a hollow abstraction, without destroying it, so you cannot remove the form from the Idea, because the Idea exists only by virtue of its form. Imagine an idea that has no form—such a thing is impossible, just as a form that does not express an idea. Such concepts are stupidities on which literary criticism feeds.

No one in this line, which has so far had to stand for the ineptness of our airlines, the docility of the populace, the mixture of peoples, the profit in tourist and travel trappings, the present pecking order in advanced societies, the moral degeneracy of some races, the ineradicable salaciousness of the male eye, and the nature of sentential functions; no one in this line . . . what? Fred's gaze wanders from woman to woman, young to old. Wonder of wonders: they all hadhave form. Louise, he was sure, did not put a check beside every male she saw: yes, no, maybe, or good, better, best, as in his case. Fred had never eaten an ear of corn he didn't like.

It's born in you, Fred felt, this passion for form.

#5. What I love above all else is form, provided it be beautiful, and nothing else beyond it.

This sad string of souls, for instance—inching toward nothing more than check-in, just as, even more imperceptibly, each member of it is slipping away toward checkout too—this line possesses a low level of organization, a bit better than a pile—which is held together by the similarity of its occupants and their common location like a heap of stones, heap of potatoes, heap o' livin'—because there is also, in every one of its elements, a shared aim: to receive the A-okay of Miss Red Lips and get let into the flight lounge.

#16. When, in a big way or a small one, one wishes to meddle with God's works, one must begin—if only from the hygienic point of view—by putting one's self in such a position that one cannot be made a fool of.

A dunce among these dumbos, if I were merely passing by, a new arrival maybe, on my way downtown, then perhaps I could call this queue by its right name.

You can depict wine, love, women, and great exploits on the condition that you are not a drunkard, a lover, a husband, or a hero. If you are involved in life, you see it badly; your sight is affected either by suffering or by enjoyment. The artist, in my way of thinking, is a monstrosity, something outside nature.

Oh, to be an artist. Oh, to be outside Nature. Where I could render Herr Ratteficken as the Ratfuck he really is.

What? Hair as rubber red as a pencil eraser. Yes, that's why we've been standing for a period approaching forever in this line, Louise replies. What? His speech seems as thin as he is; it emerges like a soft whistle, made mostly of air. I packed all of these bags personally, every piece, Louise answers, pretending to read her exchange receipt. What? Fred can't make him out, but Louise always answers, even if tartly. Most sentences are like this line, where words have come together willy-nilly, only a few have known one another before—Fred and Louise (that conjunction again), the family groups, a few friends, Herr Ratteficken and his pretend pals (have you asked *him* your questions? Fred says, nodding at Ratteficken's fat back) (he's a queue breaker, Fred wants to say, and queue breakers murder their mothers and blow up planes)—a sentence made of strangers, then, held together here during these few disagreeable moments like an utterance, like an expletive (hardly creative: fuck you, Ficken, you fucker!), and then to part to become a passenger list, a weary bunch waiting for their luggage, followed by dispersal, scarcely a goodbye, never to come together again, and everyone grateful for it; although similar sentences will be formed day after day in airports all over the world, and many of these poor words will find themselves in similar sorry sentences countless times in a shabby, queue-cursed life.

The voice of the clipboard carrier, coming from behind Fred now, was more understandable overheard than heard. He was asking people to fill out a few forms, help the airline do a better job; he hoped to enroll them in a frequent-flier plan, lure them from one line into another. He wasn't the security interrogator after all. What had Louise been saying to this guy, then? As a matter of fact, Louise had been speaking for some time of a skirt she had seen in a chic shopwindow, and she was wishing she had given in to her impulse to

The trouble with the line was exactly its fragility, its slender hold on existence, its inherent evanescence, even if it gave the impression of being eternal. It was too loosely formed. Even when its members were all seated uncomfortably in the airplane's cabin, their arrangement (though some had chosen aisle when asked, and others had pleaded to be put in the last three rows near the johns, where smoking was permitted and the stewardesses sat to chat), their configuration, was fundamentally random, even though the syntax of the cabin was stingy and rigid, every proper name belted in place. More of that anon. The aim of art, and something which could not be imagined in advance, was a line so perfectly interconnected, it generated its own personality; a line so fulfilling of every term, none of its elements would want to leave; a line one would defend against any change, a place where Fred and Louise would be frozen forever, as if they were carved on Keats' urn, and finally at peace too, however gravelike and stony, because Fred's otherwise overly loud clan-plaid shirt rhymed with the tan tam on the kid with the bad limp the kid had probably had from birth. Yes, weren't those corrective tennis shoes?

> #25. What a bitch of a thing prose is! It is never finished; there is always something to be done over. Still, I think it is possible to give it the consistency of verse. A good prose sentence should be like a good line of poetry—unchangeable, just as rhythmic, just as sonorous.

Fred Miller began his career as a novelist by memorizing *The Selected Letters of Gustave Flaubert*; however, this feat, which measured his fanaticism and spoke well of his work habits, did not significantly involve his writing skill, which, according to some of his critics, left everything to be desired. Fred remembered an appropriate quotation, #29, commencing, *Nothing great is ever done without fanaticism* . . . but now the line had reached its delta and tended to flow out of control. There were two podia (was that the plural?) in front of them, manned by a pair of hostess-haired young women trying to be twins. At this point the line frayed, Herr Ratteficken pushed his cart around the couple in front of him and rushed the left-hand lady, eager to be questioned about his bag-packing habits and whether he took gifts without examining the state of their teeth. #22 came to Miller's maddened mind:

> I am leading a stern existence, stripped of all external pleasure, and am sustained only by a kind of permanent rage . . .

His tongue touched the moist edges of her podia.

Louise was repeating her litany about yes, she had, and, no, she hadn't. Red Mouth was well in sight now, like the promised land, peering at passports with a smile so complete it parted all her lips. Soon they would be checked in and could wait sitting down instead of standing up. Soon they would have their bored bodies tickled by invisible rays, and soon a boarding announcement would be made. Fred wondered whether he should then pretend to be blind or lame so as to get let on early.

2

Why do I always have to sit in the center seat? Louise wondered. Fred knows women have smaller bladders. I'll have to crawl over him while he's asleep or make him stand up while he's having a drink, and that'll annoy him—what doesn't?—now all he has on his mind is that guy who weaseled his way into the line ahead of us. It's our bad luck the sweaty squit had to sit near us where Fred can death-ray his rear, really the back of his neck, I guess. Men. So he should have told him off when he broke the queue if it was so important. First he'll stew about it for a while and I'll have to endure his ill humor, then he'll plan to put the creep into a book, into some story or other. I always thought that was the way you immortalized somebody—put them into a book—but it turns out that's what you do to get even. I don't dare divorce him. He'll make public our lack of private life, and I'll be a laughing-stock. He's probably done it to me a dozen times. It's a good thing I don't read what he writes. It's a good thing nobody does. What's so important about writing? Actually, it gets in the way of every-thing. I'd rather listen to the singing strings.

As Fred begins to doze he holds Herr Ratteficken's fat neck in his sights. If I were the victim of a disease or had suffered the right sort of psychic wound, maybe my work would be better and I wouldn't spend so much of my time hating the world and my life, strapped into Procrustean seats like these—a symbolic set-ting, surely, from the squeeze of the armrests to the tray I have to eat from, little squiffs of stale air periodically puffed in my face through a nozzle I can scarcely reach and never can properly adjust. What's she saying the movie is? the who? the what? *The Mighty Ducks*? Sure, one might write a little happy lyric about—oh, someone, who? what?—kingfishers catching fire, yes, Hop-kins is pure pleasure, where elsewhere on earth than in lines like his are such riches offered to the ear? and that's where inspiration comes from, the deliriously great way it has sometimes been done, word attracting word the way Herr Ratteficken flung his singulating self into the queue, cart first, heavy with his belong-ings, and one knew then, watching his layered, self-indulgent self shove himself ahead of Fairness and Patience and Boredom's Dulled Pain to put himself, without a flag which proclaimed him standard-bearer, into—not even the van, where he might come under fire, but into the soft undefended middle, where the gate to the line was being guarded by a wimp. Ah, a wimp, yes; but a wimp (don't I wish?) of God.

Fred used to fall off her like that and go to sleep as his cliché said he should and, having shot his wad, simply await the arrival of the reload like a rifle leaning again a wall; well, a nice trick, Louise thought, envying his ease, and in fact she used to eye him with a little, soft-as-lotion love, in his baby snooze, back in the beginning of their nighttime days, thankful he'd finished before her own nerves had begun to tingle, so she could enjoy sliding downward to darkness, wasn't it? on this plane's—she hoped—still-extended wings.

Well, Fred dimly thought, okay, once in a while the poet might write to praise the world—*rühmen, dass ist*—but most of the time even Hopkins was singing a doleful tune. No worse, there is none. That's the central string of the muse's lyre. Pitched past pitch of grief: that's where the poet's soul is thrown.

The fact is, and Louise knew the facts, had a head for figures, called a spade a spade, even when it wasn't trumps, so Louise knew, confidently knew, that her fond spouse Fred wouldn't have been quite so put out by the breaking of the queue had it occurred behind him instead of immediately ahead, smack in his face, delaying *him,* even by a little, as if Fate knew Fred was just another Abject of Allah and would merely glare and inwardly fume but accept the role he was given. These days, everything evil looked Middle Eastern. That guy probably had a bomb in his bowel. His stupidly greedy kind could be counted on to buy fraudulently labeled bargains from the duty-free shop, and Louise had seen him looking through the plane's catalogue of color-coded crud before he'd had time to settle his fat behind into his squeeze-your-ass seat, though he was already surrounded by sealed duty-waived bags, their plastic handles stretched by a big bottle of scotch for Uncle Ahmad no doubt (drink that Allah had forbidden) and five pounds of chocolate-covered cherries for Aunt Anahita (treats her doc had nixed), an aunt whose name Louise remembered from *The Satanic Verses* (may its copies multiply and lay waste the earth), and who knew how many cartons of Marlboros for his friends who liked to drink and smoke during those inattentive times when Allah was visiting his concubines.

"THE CAPTAIN HAS TURNED THE SEAT BELT SIGN ON." The announcement nudged Fred woozily awake. We are about to serve you one of our miserable meals, so we expect rough air; we expect you to tear futilely at the plastic mustard with which you would like to cover your slab of dry ham; we expect coffee to slosh out of your cup when we hit a cloud, and fake sugar to shoot from the packet you have finally with pain ripped in two; we expect mayonnaise to smear a page of that book you bought in Berlin, and ooze like pus from the dry bread we brought all the way from the USA in order to avoid your having to eat anything either decent or foreign on this plane; because you're home now, ain't ya? on sacred airborne ground, and we expect every passenger to do hizzurher duty, that is to say: sit. So Herr Ratteficken stands up to fetch something from the overhead, shirttail totally untucked, and with difficulty pulls down one of his large floral and cloth-covered valises—it looked like a large purse—plopping it on his seat, where, after taking more pains to get it open, he begins to rummage. Fred had not missed the fact that Herr Ratteficken had carried on four bags, one in each hand and one under each arm, bumping awkwardly down the aisle, against the airline's rules, of course (not the bumping, which was mandatory), and storing three above and one below his seat, heaving and squeezing while clogging the aisle so that other passengers were forced to wait behind him, he apparently oblivious of the gridlock he was causing, perspiring copiously, color suffusing his face, a kind of stubborn sulky determination composing his doughy features.

Louise felt Fred should do better by her, after all she was his wife, but once again he was devoting his language to another of his created creatures, most of them cartoons anyway, exaggerated to the point of parody; though she also had the wit to remember how many of his descriptions of her were of the same sort—mean and humiliating—poking fun at her rockabyebaby walk on account of the high heels she insisted on traveling in, or her forthright point of view on all things, which he always made both frank and simpleminded—he was such a missoge—only being nice when he wanted a feel-up; because, although Fred was always quoting his Führer, Flaubert, on the true artist's godlike detachment—for instance:

#26. Art is not interested in the personality of the artist. So much the worse for him if he doesn't like red or green or yellow: all colors are beautiful, and his task is to use them . . .

—he was nevertheless nothing but what he wrote. It was odd. Fred was what he wrote because he wrote it, while she was what he wrote because she was what he wrote about. He did himself by doing; she was done by what was done. In short: he creates himself by creating me. So both of us are fictions, she thought. But I am the prior and more important one. That was a kind of comfort. Louise opened her magazine. My god, she thought, he's given me *Redbook.*

Fred felt fulfilled, felt real, only when facing the page, for in that space he seemed supreme. Oh, there were difficulties galore, of course, the page was a pain; yet here, he would say to himself, here I am free, nagless, invincible to others, only my own limitations limit me, and all my endeavors are like isometric exercises, the angel I wrestle is myself, and my struggles make me stronger.

Mister Duckfuck is fighting his luggage, he thinks, but it is really himself in those big bumbles of borrowed baggage, because what Middle Eastern man would choose to lug large roses—were they?—leaves as green as spinach, purple and pink petals on a scuffed black ground—what male mahout would disgrace his sex by showing himself to the world with luggage like that, as if in an old maid's company? But that, Fred began to believe, was the secret of Duckfuck's invincibility. He had taught himself not to care for the world's opinion. He pursued his passions and satisfied himself without regard for the rights, views, values, of others. Just go get it. (Actually, it was exactly the right attitude for the writer.) He was like a submarine, mostly submerged. He probably broke only small laws: parked his car in handicapped spaces, didn't tip even decent service or return his grocery cart to its storage space, took more than his share of popcorn, pie, or cake, hogged the limelight, whatever there was, farted like a punctured tire, hurled himself into crowded subway cars while thinking only, "I want to go where I want to go, and I want to go now."

So when Flaubert famously said, "Madame Bovary, *c'est moi*," what he meant was that *Madame Bovary* made him into the master we admire, just as Sir Walter Scott became "the author of *Waverley*," a writer we may not esteem as highly, although knighted by his queen and turned into what logicians call "a definite description." Instead of being modestly defined as a Frenchman, writer, bachelor, romancer, scoffer, misogynist (and who would say "merely" to any of these) (certainly he was never laird or lord), Flaubert became the author of . . . not detective stories, bodice rippers, porno pleasers, or costumed adventures churned out to pay the bills, like Scott, Dumas, or a dozen others did . . . but the author of *Madame Bovary,* the author of excellence, the author of *Bouvard et Pécuchet;* so that the man who, at the same time, remained a rather coarse hail-and-well-met fellow, insensitive and selfish, morose and cynical, was made by his night-by-night work, by his fanatical verbal fastidiousness, into a scrupulous perceiver of the world, since he had to choose his adjectives carefully, pick his prepositions like a chef selects fresh ingredients, sort his nouns like a jeweler choosing among common stones the true gems, and cut malignant growths from his prose as ruthlessly as a surgeon removes a discovered tumor; he had to fill himself with subtle and tender anticipations in order to wring every drop of significance from his fiction's dirty laundry; striving patiently to overcome his weaknesses, persevering when both world and writing seemed to oppose him, ready to redo everything or begin again, seeking a loveliness he could not divine ahead of time; until his hard soul was softened by his own prose, until he was sometimes so surprised by the skill he had acquired, so moved by the beauty of what he had written, that, as he says, in

> #22: Sometimes, when I am empty, when words don't come, when I find I haven't written a single sentence after scribbling whole pages, I collapse on my couch and lie there dazed, bogged in a swamp of despair, hating myself and blaming myself for this demented pride which makes me pant after a chimera. A quarter of an hour later everything changes; my heart is pounding with joy. Last Wednesday I had to get up and fetch my handkerchief; tears were streaming down my face. I had been moved by my own writing; the emotion I had conceived, the phrase that rendered it, and the satisfaction of having found the phrase—all were causing me to experience the most exquisite pleasure.

The emotion, its phrase, its finding, the pleasure: these are one thing, created and discovered in a single act of execution.

The plane makes its passenger. Writing makes the writer. We shouldn't be surprised. A weight lifter does not earn his muscles by dreaming of them first and then pressing two hundred pounds. Nor does a chess player improve by imagining himself a champion, but only by playing one. So if a society were to want writers, it would encourage reading of the right sort, the sort that would teach quality not quantity, innovation not convention, subtlety not glibness, contemplation not instruction, challenge not amusement, permanence not the nonce, reality not its representation. So if a society wished to inhibit the development of its writers, keeping youngsters out of the company of good books would be a splendid beginning.

Let them read instead trash which is locally treasured. Let them take pride in being Scots, or Samoans, and memorize epics in meters beaten by oars upon ocean waters. Let them grow up stupid, Fred thought; it cuts the competition. Let them listen only to their peers. Let them aim to make the movies.

Reading of the right sort realizes that writing, like culture in general, is a matter of making choices; it is a matter of discrimination and selection; it must be free of any ideological interference; and it must cast upon the page a passionately formal eye, for that is where the art lies. According to Master F and me. Quality depends upon the realization, within a chosen medium, of the right relations, and upon the understanding and acceptance of the consequences of such connections.

Reading of the right sort . . . (My ass is paralyzed) . . . would include the reception and interpretation of social signs . . . (I'm clenching my butt muscles as a form of exercise) . . . since the meaning of things and actions is the first language: voice, dress, manners, taste, discernment, choice, the way Herr Ratteficken drops his valise into the seat rather than places it there, the way he opens the clasp of the carpetbag so his fist has to force its way through a reluctant opening, and how his hand mills about out of sight inside, feeling for what it eventually draws out: a spiral-bound, letter-size manual of some kind, which he tucks in the netting where the airline magazine, airsick sack, and Technicolor catalogues of midbrow knickknacks and clutteralls are kept— pics of clocks set in golf balls, ads for laser disc racks, and other marvels. . . .

Chin Chin spreads his gaze about the cabin. Louise has decided on Chin Chin as her name for him. Chin Chin is not a very imaginative choice, and suggests someone vaguely Chinese. Chin Chin is wary of being watched. When Chin Chin's attention returns to his bag, his jaw drops with his glance, and folds of fat appear like a ruff around his neck. Chin Chin's ears have large lobes like fruit you might harvest. She has noticed that he gives strangers a slightly curious yet distasteful look, as if he'd just inhaled them. Louise is going to use Chin Chin's name a lot right now in order to get into the habit. Otherwise she might forget. It.

The first language, the social tongue, gives the writer words, and this is what he takes from reality. The most refined and illuminating perceptions of the world are worthless to the writer unless they lead him to write something. The second text depends upon the ear. For that's what a writer writes with—not the pen, the keyboard, or the screen—not by running with the bulls in Pamplona, not by beating up boyos in bars, not by enjoying an unfortunate marriage, dealing with leaks, clogs, dirt, and three kids, not by holding the thinning fingers of your AIDS-eaten friend, alas, though it feels sad enough to be inspiring, for that kind of thematic content counts for nothing; not through persecution at the hands of an evil State, either, which is why Heinrich Zeitung Muller-Müller was so hard on his imaginary East Germans, giving them no excuse, even as he understood their circumstances; because the apples in Cézanne's baskets, the pears on his plates, are as important as women, maybe Sabines, raped.

Perhaps the Chairman's most notorious pronouncement expressed the artist's aim exactly.

> #20. What seems beautiful to me, what I should like to write, is a book about nothing, a book dependent on nothing external, which would be held together by the strength of its style, just as the earth, suspended in the void, depends on nothing external for its support.

"Dependent on nothing external" is the key phrase here. Herr Ratteficken's voice is high, with a guttural emphasis on consonants. Because Ratfuck is a Ratfuck, nobody gives a rat's fuck whether he speaks with a squeak like a mouse or roars like a lion. Therefore this detail does not bring to the text any strength borrowed from its being a brute matter of fact. Since the aforesaid vocal quality does not belong to any Ratfuck in the real world, Fred is at liberty to describe its effect on others in any way the text requires. Picasso felt free to move the eyes in one of his outlined faces wherever his work wished, thereby demonstrating once and let's hope forever that art isn't anatomy. To be liberated from the claims of the referent is not to become a loose cannon on the canvas or the page. In the material world things connect with things; across musical space notes call to notes; in the mathematical realm, numbers take their place among other numbers; and even if we could collect Ratfuck's daily sweat and weigh it, even if we sing out "Chillicothe" as the train pulls in, even if we can describe our summer vacation for our grade school teacher, these useful facilities do not determine the validity of addition, the tunefulness of the town, the quality of our summertime fun, or the artistic excellence of any expression.

It is for this reason, the Chairman writes to Louise Colet, stringing his girlfriend along with artificial pearls,

> there are no noble subjects or ignoble subjects; from the standpoint of pure Art one might almost establish the axiom that there is no such thing as subject, style in itself being an absolute manner of seeing things.

And that's why right reading (through which the writer begins to learn the trade) must be for relations, continuities, balances, breaks, disembowelments of design, surprising restitutions of order; and that is also why oppressive governments regularly attack texts for the messages they imagine texts contain, when it is their form which can be subversive. Unless the shape of the State is changed, the new bureaucrats the revolution brings in will function precisely as the old 'crats did, and the awfulness of life will go on as before; and there will be queues for food, and queues for the phone, and queues for the use of the latrine, and queues for falling down, and queues for breaking faith; you will have to get in line to lie; and there will be others for chunks of coal, jars of cooking oil and fuel, queues for the use of the bed, for weeping as if alone, for fucking as if together, since there will be no really private life; only queues and the Red Lips who lick them so the end of the line will glisten and beckon; only queues calling for Herren Ratteficken to violate them; queues we form out of unhappy habit, as if one wizened cucumber or dried-up turnip were worth its penny purchase, even if it were imagined stuffed up some huffy functionary's ass.

Huge ears, large lobes, coarse black kinky hair, striped shirt, fat Semitic face, thick glasses in heavy frames, coat pocket full of pencils like a clerk. When Chin Chin sits down, she saw, he sits as if on tiptoe. From time to time he rests from his bizarre work by tilting his head back and staring at the gridded ceiling of the plane as though staring at the stars. Louise had watched with fascination as Chin Chin fairly forced his big bag back into the overhead, stopping to give the cabin a challenging inspection, but she missed the large shiny stainless-steel scissors he also took from the valise when he unpacked the notebook. Fred had seen a glinty something thrust by Herr Ratteficken behind the waistband of his trousers, and Fred's stomach had grown cold and seemed suddenly swollen, as if he had swallowed a bit of iceberg along with his lousy lettuce. But before Herr Ratteficken sat down, the scissors—clearly shears—appeared. He even snicked them twice to see if they still worked, but with a bit of braggadocio in the gesture which felt to Fred like the twirl of a pistol.

Yes, Fred thought, this plane is like the modern State, all right. From flight to flight the passengers will change, the crews and pilots too, even the mechanics who service the ship, and the handlers who crush the baggage, or the film that's sometimes shown, as well as the plane's destinations; but the seats will retain their numbers, the galleys will malfunction as they always have, the engines will rev, air will lamely circulate, miserable meals will be served; meanwhile, the entire structure is growing older, of course, dirtier, more stressed, rivets as loose as change, the machine now on the chance edge of a flaming crash. If we were all words in the right sentence, then it would matter to the jet's engines that Louise was aboard, the rattle of the liquor miniatures in the drawer of the drink trolley would tell a tale, and the toilets would tremble at the thought of the attentions of Herr

Ratteficken, who has his spiral open on his tray table and is glaring nearsightedly at it.

Why is this shit in *my* stream of consciousness? Louise wonders. This stuff belongs in Fred's head. He is always talking about the language the real writer writes in. Real writer! What was real about H. Z. Muller-Müller? What a mess! what a scandal! what an embarrassment! to be kicked out of a country that no longer exists. To find the hounds of the press baying beneath another tree. Then to have one's head tormented by theoretical thoughts like these, and one's eyes soiled by the sight of Chin Chin taking a roll of cellophane tape from his jacket pocket. Better to be bothered by fears of flying. Yes, death was the driver, wasn't it, the driver which drove these writers on, writers like Fred? each book a piece of memorial stone, as if their consciousness would continue to have a life between such sheets. Good writing depends on the mastery and integration in one instrument of all the levels of the learned language . . . Oh dear and damn, Louise said, I hate it when our heads get mixed . . . the heard, the read, the written . . . Louise would have walked about the cabin, fled these intruders, but she didn't want to disturb Fred, who was pretending to be asleep . . . writing written to be read, read to be heard, heard to be fully felt, felt to be remembered, remembered to be repeated, repeated to become a part of one's self, lines on one's soul like the lines of the face . . . Louise hated her lines, of course, wrinkles made of age and alcohol, work and marriage . . . lines like that of the Chairman's, Fred recalled, #23, for instance: *If you put the sun inside your trousers, all you do is burn your trousers and wet the sun,* lines which furrow the brow, lines which speak to the world of pain and its perseverance, pleasure and its price . . . what the hell is the sheep lover doing now?

He is scissoring strips from one page of the spiral, trimming each edge, and retaping them—some of them—onto other sheets. He manipulates the scissors and the tape with a surgeon's surety and swiftness, automatically, with flawless skill, his thoughts, so it seems, on the result of these recombinations, not on either cut or paste. The paper he would waste is crumbled in his left fist and stuffed behind the webbing where the flight-safety card lives its useless life. Didn't William Burroughs scissor that way for a while? Ransom notes were collaged—yes, you could hardly say "composed"—in such a fashion, and page lay-outs too; he was possibly such a person, magazine menial, but no, not working from a notebook like that; by golly, sometimes he simply tears off a strip; Fred is transfixed, the rip is rapid and pre-cise and can be heard, whereas the scissors are silent, the snicks too slowly made to send a signal. A few of the bands are wide, but most are as large as a line and pasted down with a tape so broad it must cover them. As with flies in amber, now only light can reach the symbols.

Fred is transfixed and Louise languid, lulled by the loud mur-mur of the plane and by the two scotches she has put away. A blade slides through a page as though cutting pie. Louise has placed a pillow against the window from which Fred would have admired the tops of clouds and there dreamed a world as pure as the snow of the poles. Now her head presses her curls into the plastic foam, layer after layer—pane, pillow, hank of hair, scalp shampooed to dryness, thin carpet of flesh before the bone—lying between stratospheric cold and drowsy consciousness, more than a cushion, these many barriers keeping thought from acidifying the passing clouds, and cold from compressing every feeling like a fistful of frozen fingers.

Fred stands in the aisle and, by stretching, pretends to stretch, when in fact he is spying on Herr Ratteficken and on Ratfuck's rapid pasting. What is he doing? what is he reading? what the fuck? Rat's scissors snick. Fred's curiosity is not quite out of con-trol, but it has driven him to the edge of simply asking. He draws back in time, however, and instead leans obviously forward but behind the Rat's back and sees rows of differential equations—strange brackets and symbols shaped like banister knurls—what the hell!—and at the top of the page being sliced eager blades are separating WAVE from PACKETS. The guy is cutting up a text in quantum mechanics.

Failing in physics, was he? Fred wanted to think, returning to his seat not quite at the speed of light. But the kid would have to be a graduate student, too old to be anything less. "Rochester," hadn't Fred heard his companions say? so he was a student at the university, or perhaps he worked at Eastman Kodak; he was possibly some electronics whiz, that might excuse him—weren't whizzes notoriously sloppy in their personal habits, lost in the stars, or in among the protons, quarking away without regard for normal niceties? But this plane was a nonstop to Chicago. You wouldn't go that route to . . . wait . . . it would have to be Rochester, Minnesota. That would be on the way. But what was in Rochester, Minnesota, besides Swedes? An institute, that famous hospital, what? not Sloan-Kettering, no, New York, the cancer college . . . clinic . . . the Mayo Clinic, that was it; but wave packets . . . ?

The fellow was obviously plugged into the Comedy Channel, because he would giggle now and then while he cut up equations. Normal expository procedures were being rearranged before Fred's very eyes the way he had once hoped to rearrange the narrative flow—so it wouldn't flow anymore—so it would pile up in one place, so that space would replace time in importance, and the movement of the line supplant the course of common action, prose would ponder its point, not run and leap and pounce, to pursue an end which he now renounced, an illusion which belonged to an outworn providential view of history and not to the contemporary world of . . . well . . . wave packets, black holes, and chance. That fellow, Fred thought, he and I probably understand the geometric bridge between art and science. We—our minds—probably belong to the world of today. The difficulty was that the world of today was thinly populated. Most everybody's thinking about things seemed to be at least five hundred years in arrears.

"Years in arrears—oh dear—years in arrears." Well, friends, have few fears, I have no intention of violating the maxims of my masters, Bouvard and Pécuchet, and shall soon remove, with a pair of shears, the offending phrase, "years in arrears," since it is clear its skim-milk-melody offends the ear; but why, we must ask Flaubert, do words which jingle, jangle? What is the precise character of his complaint? I'll bet the answer is that such singsong-along is childish and out-of-date; that it is suitable for Dr. Seuss, but that as we mature our speech should match our age. To continue with the Chairman at

> #22: The time for beauty is over. Mankind may return to it, but it has no use for it at present. The more Art develops, the more scientific it will be, just as science will become artistic. Separated in their early stages, the two will become one again when both reach their culmination. It is beyond the power of human thought today to foresee in what a dazzling intellectual light the works of the future will flower.

Putting wastepaper and his own notes in his neighbor's vacated seat, the physicist walks down the flight aisle to chat with other passengers he seems to know—how is this?—carrying his paper coffee cup like a blessing rattle. Σ So he is probably an Iranian studying physics in the States in order to go home and build bombs. Σ But he might appreciate the point that the art of any art is abstract, since Islamic art is free of graven images and often contents itself with creating fields of polygonal interlacing, highly rhythmical and continuous, though not without their significance, either, since the center of such a system is, like Allah, unseen, though the web is indeed a web, with a quality of relentless inevitability due to its repetitive interconnections and a sense of quiet repose in the harmony of its geometric regularities.

A young woman with a heavy mop of blue-black hair whom Fred had not noticed before (why not? she was rather good-looking) rose from her seat near the front of the cabin and turned to face the physicist, who greeted her with a salute from his paper

cup. "Ah, Melachrinos, there you are," she said in a loud penetrating voice, whereupon the physicist bobbed his head and
laughed a rather rich warm laugh like an unrolling rug. Good
God, Fred thought, the guy is Greek.

And a quantum mechanic. Who might have imagined? Fred
remembered that on one of the few occasions in which he had
actually tried to teach writing (down on his luck in those days,
though less down than these), he had placed a printed card above
the door of the room in which his workshop was to be held. On it
he had printed his favorite Platonism: LET NO ONE ENTER HERE
WHO IS IGNORANT OF GEOMETRY. And not a single student had
enrolled.

**This is a Reader's Alert. An Advisory follows: Observe that
these paragraphs have suddenly become several sentences
shorter than they once were, and take appropriate measures.**

Fred began to realize with some shame that his estimation of
the physicist had changed. Was he such a snob as that: to forgive
Ratfuck his fucking rat's race if he was found to be cutting apart
wave packets on an airplane? even if he did ostentatiously pick
his nose, and even if he was still overweight and freely perspired
and tended to leave signs of his presence everywhere he went like
an elephant foraging through undergrowth? Because an attractive
young woman had greeted Ratfuck, saying, "Ah, Melachrinos,
there you are," did the physicist now deserve a diction drawn
from Henry James, even if Fred's reservations about him
remained? The qualities which constituted Melachrinos' appearance hadn't changed, but their relationship to one another had. It
was as if Fred had simply read further on in the text, because as
one did so, each verbal combination shifted too ("Melachrinos"—
"Melachrinos" was the name of someone he knew once), constantly redefining every relation, as well as one's sense of the
significance of the whole.

That is the real secret of the art, Fred confided to himself as he
wobbled his way toward the lavatory, looking for one of the first

words you learned in any language: "OCUPADO." Fred preferred the phrase "in use," though it had lost out long ago. Yet "in use" had some smell of the urinal to it still. You had to have the nose to catch even the slightest whiff from a word. You had to have a tongue which had tongued them and a memory for their tastes. How else could you hope to combine ingredients with some stew of success? No. "Stew" was a commoner's term for a commoner's dish. How about *"fromage,"* "some *fromage* of . . ." No, "some *gâteau,"* then, "some *gâteau* of success." Yes. Fred smiled at the sight of his salacious soul and said again: "You have to have the tongue to tongue them." No better but more fun. Melachrinos was a poet's name. Fred felt in vain for the connection. Like a gnat it eluded him.

He didn't realize Louise was right behind him. "I've needed to go since we got on," she said, tapping his shoulder and speaking softly to his ear. Suppose he denied her her desire? But Louise pushed past him, and the VACANT sign de-lit. In a moment he heard her bolt the door, and the letters of OCCUPIED grew bright. She'll take for-fucking-ever, Fred thought, and sighed. Stood a moment. Sighed again.

#43. In a work whose parts fit precisely, which is composed of rare elements, whose surface is polished, and which is a harmonious whole, is there not an intrinsic virtue, a kind of divine force, something as eternal as a principle? If this were not so, why should the right word be necessarily the musical word? Or why should great compression of thought always result in a line of poetry? Feelings and images are thus governed by the law of numbers, and what seems to be outward form is actually essence.

A perfect spot for contemplating important if not eternal truths, Fred felt: in front of an airplane's unisex toilet, thirty-five thousand feet in the air, over a world of very cold water, by a mind bored as fully as its bladder. Here I am, like a text, Fred says to

Fred, standing between need and relief, between aim and target, thought and its object. I'm in another goddamn queue. Waiting on wife—what's new? I transform everything I see and hear and feel into language, that's how I work when I am Text with a capital *T*; but not simply into language, any words, or any order syntax insists on; no, but into a specific flow of ideas; because it is impossible to reproduce this cabin I know lies behind me, even if I simply reeled off the lettered numbers of its seats, and recited the names of their occupants, and noted whether they were awake or asleep; my list wouldn't really resemble it at all; and when my head said "chair," it would say to itself, "That's 'flesh' in French." "My flesh is sad, alas, and I have read all the books," it would quote. The reality is, my flesh is full of piss. My head has nothing on its mind but jet stream. There are two johns here. Why doesn't someone come out of one, and like my mama give me comfort?

Every phrase forms a unit, each sentence is a system, and interconnects objects by means of their names, and these with concepts by means of their symbols, uniting *res extensa* and *res cogitans* at last, despite their irreconcilable differences, more firmly than Descartes did, through mere marks—amazing—with hushed sounds, sounds sometimes hidden out of anybody's hearing in the head, sounds chosen for their unimportance, marks selected for their ease of manufacture, since any five-year-old can write "pee" on a piece of paper and snicker like the candy. So suddenly, you see, both matter and mind are music. And as each new note arrives, sounding or shining—VACANT, for instance, like a sign in the sky—it rearranges everything; because a text, as it unfolds, first gathers its elements into its arms, making a unity, and then lets go its load like an armful of logs just to order up another, a more inclusive whole now, only to watch that combination erode, puddle, or explode, depending on the strategy . . . "explode" is the right word, hey, the sign says VACANT, why is no one coming out? hey, hey, a head, the head of a sallow-faced lank-haired juvenile (probably been whacking off, which might account for his sheepish grin), is appearing, easing its following body out like a bathrobe slipped from a hanger; hey, kid, outta the way; how do these damn latches work, I always—oh god—I always push them the wrong direction, hah, good, I am OCCU-PIED . . .

Some physicist, standing where Fred is standing, probably heard the hollow sucking roar the toilet makes when the flat metal flap falls after you flush, as Fred just did, and said, "That's matter entering a black hole . . . *saaaaaauck* . . . just like that . . . *whoooooosh,"* and lives now like a slow fat cat on the proceeds of his Nobel Prize.

A perfect passage has a perfect pulse, and the final resolution, when it comes, consists not only of the ultimate order and concluding significance which its nervously strung-out words have realized, but also of the rate of dissolution and recombination the text has passed through like another rhythm; consequently, one has to understand the initial positioning of the words as provisional, for they are everywhere at once, though making their modifications sometimes only in combinations and acting, through the reader's obedient eye, mostly at a distance, simultaneously with others, creating an incredible vibration in the work as it rests so serenely on its page, with the result that the sound of the text, when its signs are properly recited, will seem made by the very shivering of the sense inside the line.

Relief at last, Louise thought, tilting her seatback into another passenger's dinky space and packing a couple of pillows behind her head. Maybe now I can enjoy the ride. Chin Chin was still standing in the aisle, engaged in an intense conversation with another, much older man. They were examining a book, and Chin Chin was pointing at something on one of its pages.

Crystals of Fred's uric acid had been added to the atmosphere. He was not amused by the noise, which had always seemed threatening to him, as if the suction should reach up like Satan to claim his soul and he would be left standing in front of the john as empty of self as of the self's piss and vinegar. There was no way of estimating the cost to his career of the catastrophic East German adventure. Once again, he had bladdered his work away, compromising it with worldly aims. If he understood writing correctly, there was no method for calculating the nature and course of even so much as a sentence in advance. The sentence had, as it came into being, a vaguely known function to perform, for there was nearly always a task under way which the fresh bit of text was expected to help complete; but what form that sentence would finally take or what new impulses it might instigate could scarcely be imagined. Fred invariably had a Project, a Commission, some Plan; there was inevitably an Occasion on which something about someone had to be said; so he had never allowed the medium to be his muse.

And that medium: wasn't it the whole history of man, all his evil errors, his few victories and occasional decencies, packed into the language he has used? buried in it like murdered bodies are in weedy fields, or gold bars in piratical chests, or dance cards and kids' games boxed and carried to the attic? . . . or maybe Thoreau alone in his woods, tending his journal like a field, writing words there wiser than the words of God?

Had not the Chairman written: *Yes, you must work; love art. Of all lies art is the least lying*? Well, he had worked, all right, but only to raise the wrong crop. He had felt unrecognized and put upon and had written to settle scores; he had taken a few stray causes home and fed them so well they stayed; he had lusted after fame and the feeling of triumph; and he had courted readers like a whore. *Try to love it with a love that is exclusive, ardent, devoted. It will not fail you.* But Fred had forced forms upon his material as if it were cookie dough fated to celebrate Christmas. He knew that some of his narratives had a shape similar to the airplane's cabin, with labeled places where his characters were required to sit in fuddled puddles of stale air, mostly asleep, and with little room to act even during those marshmallow moments when they were awake. *Only the idea is eternal and necessary.* Amen to that, he said, remembering to zip his pants.

The physicist still had his big butt parked in the aisle where he was haranguing someone. Fred could see him pushing his cart pell-mell toward O'Hare Airport's interterminal trains, though there wasn't any need to hurry. To reach Rochester, Minnesota? What was a sentence like, Fred asked himself one more time: a sentence was like a packet of waves.

> There are no more artists as they once existed, artists whose loves and minds were the blind instruments of the appetite for the Beautiful, God's organs by means of which He demonstrated to Himself His own existence.

For his part, Fred knew he was himself only when he was writing well, a rare experience these days when he was flopping about like a fish in a net. Do not touch the Times and maybe the Times will not touch you. Was that Thoreau talking? Fred felt his presence more and more as the plane flew over Maine and headed down the Saint Lawrence. Fred plopped into his seat beside his wife and opened the airline's magazine. He had nothing but scorn for its contents. He had written for it once. He had nothing but scorn for himself. The pay . . . hadn't the pay been good?

Not really.

> For such artists the world did not exist; no one has ever known anything of their sufferings; each night they lay down in sadness, and they looked at human life with astonished gaze, as we contemplate anthills.

That was the conclusion of quotation #6. The seat belt sign went on, and a stewardess' semi-seductive voice warned of turbulence ahead. Fat Butt continued talking, punching a calculator he held in his hand and literally putting his head in the crack of his new companion's book. Fred wondered if his wife would ever kiss him again. No. Fred wondered whether his wife would . . . What did wave packets tell Fat Butt about the human condition and the nature of man? Or why, having traveled this far, one would want to complete the journey, or, having gone, to go again, or, having been, to continue to be?

There Was an Old Woman Who

There was an old woman who lived in a shoe,
She had so many children she didn't know what to do;
She gave them some broth without any bread;
She whipped them all soundly and put them to bed.

lived in a shoe. Well, it wasn't a shoe, really, it was a commercial building put up in L.A. during the twenties and designed to look like a high-topped shoe, laces and all, although there was a door in the toe and windows at the ankle. It was intended that shoes would be sold in this shoe. The Brown Derby was directly down the street, and there was a Frosty Freeze nearby in the shape of an overturned custard cone. A hamburger stand was roofed by a bun, and the meat beneath was window glass. So when the Depression sent the footware business in for repairs, and when, some said, cutesie-pie buildings went out of fashion, the shoe was left empty and sullen like something lost along the road—a shoe, for instance. Soon (the exact week or hour has not been fixed) an old woman took up residence there. If it is possible to squat in a shoe, she did—she and a passel of kids. Actually, she wasn't that ancient either; she only seemed, in her rags and rug-thick babushka, to be old. Records relevant to the time indicate that she was thirty-six, and the number of children living with her beneath the laces was then reliably estimated at between twelve and twenty-two. With that many kids to take care of, and times so lean, it could well be she didn't know what to do, but that would be an interpretation.

As the days and then years of the Depression passed, people who frequented the street noticed that the number of children seemed steadily, if gradually, to decrease, and they commented on the fact that, although times were hard and the old woman seemed to do nothing more than live in her shoe, the kids appeared healthy enough, pink-cheeked and laughing, sliding like seals over the old toe and having a high time, childhoodwise. Suspicions were aroused by certain odors, however, which were so pungent and persistent and fundamentally sickening that finally social workers, health inspectors, telephone repairmen, and other Paul Prys—thin-skinned folks wearing thin cloth masks—gained entrance to the shoe through a crack in the hide. Many remarked on the stench. Inside they discovered large kettles caked with grease, closets full of kiddie clothes, heaps of human bones—one, under an eyelet, 1.7 meters high. These facts have been photographed. Records and reports can be consulted. The number of the bones, the bags of hair, the jugs of blood, have been tabulated. The old woman freely admitted to having eaten quite a few kids over the years. The entire family had, she said. Quite tasty, some of them, she claimed, although Gertrude and Freddie remained bad to the last bite, as tough on the plate as they'd been rude and mean in life. This was, of course, only her opinion. A number of back teeth had been made into serviceable dice.

There was, as you might expect, a considerable hue and cry. Outrages were released like steam into the L.A. air, threats were expressed with hisses, opinion polls invented to answer certain questions. The following facts were verified: most of the children were waifs and strays, but six or seven were her own. Children weren't eaten all the time, only on festival occasions, such as were birthdays, Mother's Day, and Christmas. The victims (as common opinion called them) were chosen quite at random and for no reason: whoever came in range of the cleaver at "market" time. They were sometimes roasted, sometimes boiled, frequently fried. Hands, feet, and organs were pickled to prevent spoilage, the way we soak pigs and smoke hams. A collection of handwritten recipes—which some say they have held before their own violated eyes, and read, and even copied—has never turned up.

These and other details, hypotheses, and conjectures then current can be found in the first of the many volumes devoted to the Crime of the Century (as it was mistakenly called, for people are inclined to brag). The first *Shoe Box Book* (such is the title of the series) contains the rather complete results of a forensic and pathological investigation into whether the Old Lady had served up only children not her own or had cannibalized willy as well as nilly. Concerning the fathers of her numerous kids, the otherwise cooperative Old Lady remained stubbornly mum. But bones believed to belong to adults were found among the mortar and the rolling pins. One fact considered significant at the time was the absence at the scene of any copy of Jonathan Swift's "A Modest Proposal," an absence widely felt to be surprising, since the Old Lady's name was discovered to be Hanna O'Hare. On the other hand, a volume containing Oliver Goldsmith's *The Deserted Village* was found in her possession, its pages considerably eared. Many nevertheless insisted that her barbarism had to be another one of Literature's perfidious consequences. Copies of Mother Goose were seized by school boards in some communities—northern Mississippi, I believe, southern Indiana—but those traditional rhymes were later cleared of any meaning and thereby vindicated. The press also compared this tragedy to the Manson case and to the suicides at Jonestown. Because these catastrophes had not yet occurred, the imaginations of the writers had obviously soared.

As the bones were counted and the shoe explored, other discoveries were reported. Many of the walls of the interior—dare we call them "rooms"?—anyway, locations so high as to be above the tongue of the house—were decorated with drawings done in brown monochrome, and Sir Bernard Barrenman, brought to the scene to practice his expertise, pronounced them drawn in plum jam by a natural master. Informed that the lines were made of blood and had been thumbed on, he fainted quite away and remained silent for a spell of twenty days. The bone conservators, as they insisted on being called, then began noticing how many pieces had been scrimshawed: on a thighbone, for instance, was etched a tricycle with wings, realistically rendered, and on one skull a fanciful map of the world had been indited, with Florida and Italy swapping their locations.

The laboratory reports of the specialists who took scrupulous samples of the murals (being careful not to damage the compositions, especially what came to be called the whiplash trees), and who also compared the chemical makeup of the outlines with that of jars of plum jam purchased at random from nearby markets (including a selection of local and national brands), would be, to the average interested scandalmonger, quite unreadable; so these results were simply announced one after another as they were reached: " 'The designs found on the walls of the shoe were not drawn in Knott's,' police experts said today, 'nor are they anybody else's jam or jelly.' "

It may be worth noticing that no real (that is, "theoretical," that is, "pure") scientists were called in, since their investigations, although they might have some distant bearing on the case, are regularly carried out at such remoteness from ordinary life as to be generally irrelevant to it, dealing, as they do, with protons and quarks and cosmic rays, which have no more been eyeballed by anybody than dragons, and whose descriptions and subsequent explanations are in a language so abstract and so difficult to master that they rival the abstruseness of economic indicators and slugging stats.

The elements of our mathematical languages are emotionally neutral (relatively speaking, since superstitions can attach themselves like webs to any bush), as are the concepts which the sciences develop, such as "black hole," "big bang," and "greenhouse effect." In these purified regions, monitored, calibrated, and systematic observations involving the detachment of the observer from personal passions equal to that of the machine (and the applications of a method held to be as evenhanded, regular, and unswerving as a divine judge) are expected to support conclusions free from moral smirch, political taint, or the influence of any ideology. Reasons given in such an ideal realm are supposed to be "free" reasons, reasons which represent no constituents who live outside the system, although it is worth noting that the arguments, descriptions, and general procedures of the sciences—so conceived—are not wholly separated from qualities which might be considered esthetic as well: elegance, economy, simplicity, and rigor, for instance, or coherence, inevitability, wholeness, and precision, for example, lucidity, completeness, even sublimity, and so forth.

Nevertheless, there would be a tendency, in the case under consideration, for most people to damn the scrimshaw and the finger painting out of hand and condemn as inhuman any objectivity of an esthetic sort, although such detachment would be permitted in, even demanded of, the pathologist.

Few felt satisfied when the children's deaths were ascribed to molecular dissolutions, even if these occurred. The question "Why did they die?" is not answered by describing the fire and pointing to the pot they were boiled in. At the "everyday level" of explanation, another set of aims is in play, aims that have elements which are quite different from the goals of ideal, or even practical, science.

A crime so tastelessly melodramatic as the old woman's was bound to draw much attention and many eyes, and consequently to encourage a proliferation of points of view, with the "point" in great part determining not only when an explanation was felt to have explained, but also what constituted relevant data, and the ways in which that data should be unified. There were those who wished to rearrange the bones to form individual skeletons, and those who cared only how many kids were killed; there were those who wished to write radio commercials which boasted about how their cleaning pads cut through the kettle grease, and those who were collecting life histories for articles and books. A moviemaker immediately copyrighted six different titles, including *There Was an Old Woman Who Killed in a Shoe.* Some psychiatrists have studied the mental state of the survivors, others the effects of such repeated cannibalism on society. More than fourteen lawyers have offered their services to likely clients for unlikely fees. The Shield of Shelter Insurance Company wonders whether a certain home owner's policy may still be in force. Politicians point out that this tragedy is a consequence of the administration's callousness toward orphans and the homeless. Social workers are screening applicants in search of appropriate foster parents. Literary agents have cooked up deals, and publishers are after Hanna's life story. The Auld Sod League is acting to lower the rising tide of anti-Irish feeling and to discourage the spread of blackly humorous dialect jokes. An old title, recently reissued—*The International Cannibal Conspiracy*—has besmirched some best-seller lists. People are beginning to wonder what they thought about before the Gruesome Discovery. Hollywood Preview Properties, a real estate sales and investment company, wants to buy the shoe with an eye to turning it into a Shrine of Crime.

Meanwhile, the thumb-line murals darken and decay, the leather walls of the house are being attacked by a fungus, bones have been stolen from a supposedly secure police storage area, flashbulbs will damage images otherwise safely obscured by a respectful darkness, and revisionists are doubting all the data.

Why are you so certain that Hanna did this ghoulish thing, I imagine I ask the chief of police. Because we have the evidence of grease, hair, and bones; because her fingerprints are everywhere on the dishes and utensils; because we can prove there are missing children; because we can show that the pile of bones belongs to them (well, not the pile, but the bones); because we have seven eyewitnesses (kids copping a plea); because of what we found in pumped stomachs; because we have reports of foul smells from the neighbors; because we have Hanna's signed confession; furthermore, because we know that Ireland is an old sow who eats her farrow; that Hanna O'Hare is Irish, every horrid syllable of her; and that she looks like an old sow too.

To a question such as "Why did you bake the fish?" reasons advance readily enough. It was too big to fry. I didn't want to dry out the flesh. It was the single recipe I had on hand. I know only one way to cook northern pike. Put a baby in the fish's place in the same query—why did you bake my straw hat? my left leather glove? that book of poems? his thought of you? our feel for the game?—and will these causes be excuses any longer?

Why are we so certain—the press, politicos, priests, vox populi—that what Hanna did was ghoulish? This question I had better ask the wind, for the facts are all the reasons we shall need. She cooked kids and served them to other kids for supper. For maybe tea. From the general description of the circumstances, to which both science and the law have put their signature, an odor of evil immediately emanates. Of course, in a corner, dim in the shadows, the sophist, from whom an odor of evil also arises, will wonder whether Hanna and the children were starving; will remind us that cannibalism is not an unknown human practice; that in Borneo, etcetera, or when marooned, or otherwise wholly up against it, *it* has happened; that one tribe of folks has been known to stick a fork into a tribe of another type—eating only enemies, to improve their potency and powers of perception—and slices of human flesh (to the weight of a pound) have been requested (our literature contains cases of hearts also being hors d'oeuvred and livers fried); that spiritually we feed on family and friends incessantly, and eat much other meat with relish, even raw, even the eyeballs of tender does, including the brains of monkeys and the intestines of rats, the fineline legs of sea spiders and the ink of squid; so that we'd better moderate our dudgeons, reduce our certainties, and quiet our conscience.

All very well, we can tell our sophist, but these possibly qualifying conditions are not in service here, in this description, *and it is from the description that the moral horror arises* (assuming we were not an eyewitness). Upon reading an account of the case, suppose someone said: "Gee, that wasn't a very nice thing to have done, do you think?" wouldn't we have to consider the comment oddly unnecessary, and the question peculiar? And if a few felt they had to justify their revulsion by citing the various moral laws which Hanna's behavior had broken, wouldn't we find this very strange too? because breaking the law is not the source of our upset; cooking kids is.

To God, the outrage lies elsewhere, namely in disobedience. If God says: Do not mail letters on Tuesday; or if God says: Do not fly off the ax handle with your brother; He will not care which command you fail to keep, because, to fathers, there is only one command: Do as I say. And it doesn't matter how obvious the breach or trivial the crime or horrific its character, there can be nothing worse than defying the deity. This is true, though often forgotten or ignored, regarding any law, because to break it is to challenge the authority of those who promulgated it and enforce its provisions.

Of course, few cases are as clear as I have tried to make this one. Had the shoe been a rowboat in the middle of an ocean, had Hanna been blind and under the impression she was roasting geese, had the kids driven her mad with their noise, their games, and their demands, then we might moderate our attitude. Differences of opinion would naturally arise, but if these differences did not spring from differences within us (that I was guilty of eating the ears of my companions while we were lost on the ice of McMurdo Sound, for instance, thus carrying a bias in the pocket of my past), they could generally be assigned to a lack of agreement on the facts: gaps in them, shifts in emphasis, additions or subtractions of details, irreconcilable conflicts of value such as lie at the heart of what we commonly call "tragic circumstances," for if some cases are relatively clear, others are sadly unresolvable.

It may be that explanations in the sciences are made through the mediation of models which bring together logic and experience like the slap of high fives; so that, while the data is supplied by eyes and instruments, the powerful inferences—their clarity, rigor, and degree of necessity—are provided by some suitably complete and coherent mathematical system. However these accounts and their conclusions are arrived at, it seems to me at least likely that we make ethical explanations by weaving appropriate physical facts together with historical, psychological, and social ones into a plausible narrative: how the shoe dropped out of the housing market, how it subsequently fell into disrepair, how Hanna came to squat in it, how the children were collected, the manner of their daily life and its exigencies, Hanna's income and outgo, perhaps a profile of the ogre herself, with family background and personal history.

If we come to the truth by comparing our descriptions of life with life itself, and by trying, then, to get our various versions to square, we arrive at our moral judgments through the narratives we fashion, during the composition of which various values simply make themselves manifest, with their positive and negative valences, their eventual weight and leverage. How these narratives were composed, of course, could be decisive, and very prejudicial too. Frequently, courts construct them. Many would insist that the relation between the scientifically determinate data and various moral principles or points of view would also be an essential element. But even in our own skeptical, plural, and relativistic era, few doubt the virtue of honesty, although they may doubt its value; it is, rather, the theories which claim to lend it friendly support, like those banks whose interest rates are usurious, which are the object of suspicion.

There is scarcely an excellence, an action deemed worthy, a

respectable end or aim, in the whole history of Western philoso-phy—whether instances of self-realization or cases of respect for law, moments of pleasure or acts of courage, the exercise of intel-lect or shows of self-restraint—which anyone strongly wishes to deny or reject out of hand. It is the preemptory place in which some values are put, the system which schemes to support them for other purposes, the ideological weapons which moral norms and notions band together to become, the hypocrisy and contra-dictions which are displayed and denied, which cause most of the quarreling. Even giving "reasons" why Hanna's actions were frightful is faintly offensive.

One can easily imagine partisans of one kind or other insisting that "this is what happens when you neglect the poor" or when you "teach home economics without a proper emphasis on family values." But it isn't what happens when you overlook the home or neglect the homeless; it's what happens when you have Hannas. Otherwise these kids might have died or come to grief in other ways.

In a scientific journal I could study a report and find that it made a convincing case for its conclusions; that is, from the report alone I might come to a modest and tentative belief in its truth. From a journalist's account (one which I might hope was made up solely of so-called neutral facts, calmly and grayly set forth), a story could unfold which would lead me to make—also modestly, most tentatively—some moral judgments concerning agents, their actions, or immediate consequences. But no rela-tion of facts, no presentation of data, no retelling (tiresome or not) of a novel's or a movie's tangled plot, no description of a painting, however detailed, no whistle even of someone's remem-bered music, could convey to me the least whiff or smidgen of esthetic value. I of course can, from reviews and catalogue copy and program notes, learn of the attitudes of others, and such descriptions can very often permit me to predict my own responses—given my previous knowledge of the artist, for example, or my acquaintance with other works of a similar sort, or my past agreement with the judgment of a particular critic, or simply from the general unlikelihood, at any time, of something being honestly outstanding; but I must see, hear, feel, read, think, dream, myself before the actual quality is realized and any judgments are verified.

Books are condemned without being read, movies are picketed before being seen, plays are hooted at on a whim, the music we immediately switch off is immediately mistrusted, yet these are moral judgments, not esthetic ones, and they are invariably directed toward content and meaning, not toward texture and form. When the moralist and the philistine ride the same horse, the naying is noisy and the manure is copious.

Next fall, from Skira, I believe, a volume reproducing the Hanna House Murals will appear. Peter Piaget has written the text, but it is the splendid quality of the plates which is most impressive, and the imagination and merit of the murals, now frequently compared to the best in the caves, which justifies its coffee-table price.

Art recalls us to our roots in the world, as science does too sometimes; and the theoretical study of art—aesthetics—is properly named, standing originally for sensation in itself and the refulgence of its forms. Both science and art are profoundly concerned with the same things: perception and perception's string of sensations, its yarn, with Nature's threatening irregularities and our inept attempts to provide law and order. For the scientist, however, sensuous quality is like the Great Man's first wife: a help through hard times, but one who is dumped as soon as the going gets good, and always for the sake of the Form Divine.

The moralist's case is in a state of constant nervous adjustment. Hanna's children were well fed. They attended parochial school, where they excelled in everything dutiful. They seemed, to their teachers, serene and untroubled. They loved handicrafts like carving and drawing. They remembered everybody's birthday and sang folk songs in a pure, untroubled voice, as true as the twitter of a bird.

With the passage of time, the world's attention turned away to other enormities. Now, having lost their tags as Hanna's children, the survivors have disappeared, and who knows what's become of them.

We never found out who the gifted ones were, or whether their skills declined as they grew older, or whether their art was the result of a peculiar atmosphere, or because they were all called Cora.

On account of the Hanna House Horrors, a great number of commodious and handsome homes for the wayward were built all over the country; family values were reaffirmed in the nation's schools; dietary laws were strengthened among many sects whose practices regarding pork and kale had grown negligent and slack over time; and politicians asserted the sacredness of human life itself on every occasion on which they spoke, at least during a period of several months following the first outbreak of the copy-cat crimes, especially the revengeful sacrifice of several elderly couples by rampaging kids in retirement towns in southern Florida.

Vegetarianism was given a big boost, and natural-foods stores began to open in L.A. and other coastal places. Several young women died, it was alleged, from too exclusively macrobiotic diets. Other women, who became obsessed with the Story of the Slaughter in the Shoe, were emotionally crippled in a number of symbolically appropriate ways, and an increase in barren wives was widely reported.

The moral character of any case can change with the addition of some fresh fact, since the case—its full, accurate, ideally unprejudiced description—is the moralist's demonstration. The esthetician, on the other hand, can offer no solace, no excuses, no pretty principles, no high-minded bludgeons. He can certainly suggest novel standpoints, fresh ways of looking at the world. He can work to create an informed eye. He can warn of bias, prejudice, hidden motives, greed, and cunning. He can chart the location of every obstacle the mind may put in the way of good sense. And he can honk like the geese of fable at every moralist's approach. He can try to sustain his interpretations, but these are just the cloak which embarrassment throws over the nakedness of its actual object.

Because, for the esthetician (on my view), the shoe doesn't matter, the history of the shoe, the old woman either, her knotted red hair, her smile as fixed above her teeth as the frame of a window. The fact that the wall has been adorned with blood, or that the scratches, so elegant and energetic at the same time, have been incised in human bones, or even that wagons and cycles and bouncing beach balls have been depicted there, or that the lines of blood were drawn with the blood still hot and steaming (as certain tests suggest): these things belong to other worlds and other interests. What counts is that the lines of blood swirl up to shape a space as much as they swirl themselves, granting to every unmarked blank a belief in a fresh life. As inhuman as the scientist is alleged to be, the lover of the beautiful bends to every surface the same welcoming panoply of sensuous receptors; he is interested in the quality of quality, in this or that specific, rather than generalized, relation. It is this particular pick in the paint that matters to him, and this distance to the next pock, and that pock's perky perimeter. So what he sees must always remain in the sky of its first appearance. The particularized universal entrances him. Every specific color is like cream to be spooned, every relation is like a violin's string, and the realm of Platonic Forms trembles when the bow passes over its face with the force of a former lover's remembered emotion.

You can point out to the youthful poet the cacophony of his confusing images, and he will change them to unbroken banalities. You can complain that his meters are monotonous, and he will sing by employing pratfalls and stumbling. These inept corrections will indeed change the poem, and for the moralist they could count in any revision of its ethical status, but what the young poet has not caught is the lack of sonorous tension in the vowel sounds, the precise thinness of his thought, the never-to-be-repeated ridiculousness of the ride of his mind—never mind monotony, cacophony, or mellowjello. So the young poet's depiction of Hanna as a heroine of history in the third stanza, and as an emblem of the enmity between generations in the seventh, may properly horrify the reader whose moral cap is presently pinned to his hair; but it will be the boring meters, the lame rhymes, the predictable images, which will affront him as a literary critic, should he put on that hat.

That the children drew with human blood and incised human bone is, first of all, a fact, determined by tests and observations. That this was, along with its causes and consequences, a morally reprehensible thing to do is evident and overriding to the moralist. However, the line which, etched over a shinbone, transcribes a tubular frame so skillfully as to suggest, through its almost imperceptible widening, the cycle's future wheel, while slight scratches like soft curls render the plush of the cycle's seat: well, these have to be seen to be believed, seen in a silence made of the silence of other voices, seen in serenity, seen . . . and seen again . . . and finally, simply . . . seen.

Is the historian a pure describer, as a naturalist might be, who puts the scientific facts coherently and correctly together and in that way simply presents us with the scene: throat-slit kids, their blood draining into tubs; the evening read, Hanna holding the youngest on her lap, doing first Granny and then the Wolf in "Little Red Riding Hood" so perfectly the children clap; the group's trips down alleys to gather goodies from garbage bins; the shoe's close quarters, which pinch the inhabitants as mercilessly as if they were toes; Hanna's ingenious uses for skin—book covers, bandages, drums; the infrequency of flu and other diseases, since the children didn't go to school; the preparation of pigments, models made of cardboard, lavatory jokes, and so on, laid out like sorted laundry? Here it is: how it was.

But wait. It was earlier alleged that the kids did go to school, where their progress was exemplary, their behavior perfect, their health at all times hale and hardy. Well, cracks show up in the smoothest, the most careful plaster.

Surely the historian is not an artist, contriving fictions from form and color, but perhaps he structures his paragraphs for rhetorical effect, or heightens this part, slights that, bringing out the inherent drama of some situations, the pathos of others, or perhaps he adds a likely conjecture to complete our understanding of a motive, or clears out a few causal paths to permit an untroubled and instructive flow of consequence.

Almost certainly the historian will be working from a religious, ethical, or political point of view. His selection of this or that period, within it of this or that event, if not a choice of newsy news, would be surely of the news of his chosen era, since life is full of occurrence—one might say, life is nothing else—but it will not be Lena's lemon pie he will select to describe or dwell on, or how the dog put his nose in the meringue while it was still hot so the poor beast howled for an hour and wagged his head as if to shake his nose off. He'll choose Horrible Hanna, perhaps, because, after all, the case became a cause célèbre; it made all the wire services; it went round the world and raised hackles in Zagreb as well as Bogotá. TASS reported that two of the children had Russian names; Hannas everywhere petitioned to have theirs changed. And jury selection took two years.

Hanna's incarceration in an Anaheim asylum satisfied nobody much. At least none of the jury wrote books, writing of any kind being quite beyond them. And public interest had moved on to the tragic events in Tasmania, which had the further attraction of being merely horrible, not morally and metaphysically disturbing, as Hanna's culinary habits were, especially since the defense maintained, during her trial, that she only cooked and served kids to the kids but never partook herself, saying that preparing so many meals always spoiled her appetite. What's done is done, the world said, turning round.

But wait. Didn't Hanna admit at one point that she had eaten her own offerings? Maybe she reserved her husbands for herself. Another crack in the plaster. Quite a long one.

It was nearly a generation later that the case came back to public consciousness and the Hanna O'Hare Rehabilitation Movement began, motivated neither by scientific truth nor by fictional freedom, of course, but by political and religious causes, those two great sources of human ignorance and grief.

☠ ☠

First of all, what would make the case of "the old woman who lived in a shoe" historical? Once the lurid light cannibalism was thought to throw upon society had dimmed and the crime had fallen out of favor with the scandalmongering press, what interest would it have for anyone? Who would remember Lizzie Borden if it weren't for the jingle?

> Lizzie Borden took an ax,
> And gave her mother forty whacks;
> And when she saw what she had done
> She gave her father forty-one.

The poets have not graced us with such a memorable ditty about the culinary triumphs of Hanna O'Hare, although one such effort, I remember, began

> Hanna O'Hare
> found her cupboard was bare—

to the tune of "Old Mother Hubbard," I guess. And fragments of an allegedly long poem of epic ambitions have occasionally turned up.

There Was an Old Woman Who

> Hanna O'Hare
> liked the forearm rare
> but kidneys raw
> stuck in her craw.

Is history the community's memory? Is it made of what we want to remember, what we ought to remember, or of what we want others to remember?

The interest of the law does help us organize, define, and unify a set of events into what it calls "the case against . . ." and "the trial of. . . ." But the law derives its description from partisan questioning and really has little interest in events as such, only in "breakage," only in transgression.

The liberal bromide that a person is innocent until proven guilty is repeated with pious smirks by every morals provider in the USA, but the phrase usually leaves out "in a court of law" and is always mistakenly understood. Hanna either did it or she did not do it—cannibalize kids, I mean. What the court must decide is whether she shall be punished or not. We know that not infrequently those who have done wrong are called innocent and go unpunished, and that sometimes those who have done no wrong whatever are seized and condemned and jailed. In short, courts decide punishments. They often become a part of history, but they do not determine it.

A historian, were he to take on the task, would compose his account from documents and written records, mostly, though there would be a few photos to worry about as well, and perhaps, if he were working near enough to the time of the affair, he might generate more data with his tape recorder by interviewing witnesses, tracking down now grown-up survivors. On the whole (the ruins of cities are an exception, as are the records of rocks and bones), the principal consequences of any event lie not in its immediate physical effects but in the amount of paper it generates, the degree of human attention which it stimulates. The Shoe House Tragedy, as a physical occurrence, soon loses all impact, the building is razed, its lot is turned into a corral for cars, and that, in turn, is occupied by a franchise of the Bugle Boy Breakfast chain: "Breakfasts Are Best at Any Time of Day." The spot does seem to have an affinity for food. That much we can say.

If the truth is to emerge from a comparison of a description with experience, then, to ensure accuracy, objectivity, and profitable use, the description should be set down in a formal language, and observations made by indifferently neutral instruments. Moreover, the data which confirm or deny hypotheses should be as repeatable as an A for an orchestra. History meets none of these conditions. Of Caesar's death we have some descriptions but nary a Geiger counter's groan. Nor can we murder him more than once, on capitol steps in Columbus, Ohio, as well as in Washington, D.C., just to check it out. And if we got our account right, assuming we were able, what use could we make of it, what good would our history do us, scientifically speaking, I mean? Very little, I suspect. We create historical descriptions for ethical and political reasons, and if our language, however detached and neutral it may appear to be, does not depict a war of the righteous against the unbelievers, the whites against the Apache, Yanks against Huns, rich versus poor; if it does not allow us to appeal to past injustices to excuse present crimes; if it does not help us to unify our group by fostering a solidifying hate; if it doesn't draw Destiny's line in our sacred ground; then we have no use for it. We remember the past to despoil the present. The honest historian's only hope is to tell a tale too true to be abused—an unlikely achievement.

The story of the Old Woman Who Killed in the Shoe comes down to us, as such stories usually do, in a confused state. Why should we regularize and clarify its lines, uncover the moral we may have planted there, or bother to realign its contours and prettify its face? Lizzie Borden did something worse than hatchet her parents; she cut filial piety to pieces. Children are not permitted to rise up against their parents, particularly if they are daughters. Violence is the prerogative of the male. Therefore, Lizzie could not have done what she did, just as O. J. Simpson could not have knifed his wife and her friend. No black male matinee idol can behave the way black males are perceived to behave. It too profoundly reinforces the stereotype. And no well-known black woman dare play Aunt Jemima and flip stacks of flaps wearing a kerchief and a wide motherly grin. And no mother must be found boiling her kids like pork for the beans. Hanna disgraced motherhood not only by demonstrating how mothers could be callously indifferent to their offspring (and affronting a major myth) but by doing so directly through Mom's nurturing function: feeding and care.

The lesson (for the let-us-remember faction) or the threat (for those who would rather revise or forget) might have had to do initially with the social ills of which the homeless are symptoms, but in time the crime may have been seen as damaging the institution of the family and the security of its values, in particular MOTHERHOOD, as sacred as godhead or the goodness of the motorcar. So our initial strategy, depending upon the ideological camp in which we find ourselves, may be to (a) admit to the horror while condemning only Irish mothers, thereby cutting our losses; or (b) admit to the horror but so widen the wickedness at issue that no one in particular, only an abstraction, gets blamed, arguing that such bestiality is customary with mankind, a species capable of anything; or (c) admit that it would have been horrible had it occurred but that (i) Hanna had never been a mother, so it wasn't her children she cooked; (ii) Hanna had been born a man, had an operation to alter her sex, suffered from the operation's failure, which left her a woman with a mean male's nature; (iii) it was actually two kids named Israel and Solomon who had cooked the meal-ticket tykes and not Hanna, who confessed to the crime only to cover for them, showing she was a real mother through and through; and by these maneuvers—through a verbal technicality, by redefining an essence, by leaving the deed alone but turning up new perpetrators—to alter the object's lesson and blunt its point.

If you are inclined to think these examples are too outrageous, I have real ones more outrageous still: that every female artist of any achievement is (a) unmarried (and not fully a woman), (b) frigid (and not fully a woman), or (c) a lesbian (and not fully a woman). These reasons will also suffice for tennis and swimming and skiing and golf. And ballet, if we are arguing the other way, and dress and stage and interior design.

Hitler wasn't to blame for the Holocaust, it was the German people; well, it shouldn't be the German people, actually, because look at the Jews in Palestine, the Serbs in Bosnia, the warlords in Somalia, the tribes in Rwanda: clearly there is something wrong with the human race. Which is certainly true but doesn't help us much with particular cases, since not every human being participates in genocide during their lifetime, or even murders a neighbor or two, or even considers it seriously.

Of course, we can always employ the typical liberal strategy of whining about environment, upbringing, background, and forces of society and nature. Hanna grew up in an Irish ghetto in Boston (and didn't have a chance); was poor and went weeks without food (and didn't have a chance); was beaten by a bunch of rough boys, raped too, with their little drumsticks, rap a rape rap (and didn't have a chance); was out of a job, down on her luck, left in the lurch, casting about, grabbing at straws (and didn't have a chance); had a serious hormonal imbalance, which prompt treatment might have relieved (and so didn't have a chance); lacked the wise guidance of a good man, suffered under seven Republican administrations and their heartless unworkable trickle-down economic policies (thus didn't have a chance); was of mixed parentage (orange and green Irish, Prot and mick) (and certainly never had a chance).

Went mad, but only temporarily (at mealtimes) (curious case);

was mentally defective (and couldn't tell Matthew from mutton); was led to believe Paul Valéry's remark that a good plot for a frightening tale would be the discovery that a cure for cancer was a regular diet of human flesh (the irony here is that Valéry actually specified living human flesh, so her cooking was not only needless but unhelpful).

For every guy who goes wrong, there are at least a couple who, under similar dreadful circumstances, play basketball and become as proud as pimps, join the clergy and molest choirboys, rob banks as members of the board of directors, take payoffs as police sergeants, enter politics and promise large results but deliver small change. However, the straights get no credit, and their nobler existence is ignored.

Drug dealers killed Nicole Brown; actually, it was that creep Kato Kaelin, racist cops, a band of marauding rich kids, a baseball player, an angry stalker, the Good Humor man. If the legitimacy, the accuracy, the truth, of any detail of the event can be questioned or any sloppiness or bias or malice can be encountered in the historian's methodology, then perhaps everything is inaccurate, false, doubtful. Red herrings are sent like black cats across the narrative path. Not as many blacks score above 100 on IQ tests as Orientals. Not as many five-foot-eight players succeed in the NBA as seven-foot-one players do. Not as many people eat fish on Tuesday as on Friday. So we should make Orientals go to college and keep blacks out? forbid shorties to enter the gym? close the fish markets Sunday through Tuesday?

Opportunities should never be narrowed simply because skill is rare and success is seldom. One rotten apple does not even imply that the barrel is bad. The character of a speaker cannot impugn his propositions. The fact that an alternative hypothesis can be formulated is not automatically evidence in its favor. The list of illogicalities is nearly as long as its instances. Yet we believe bad arguments, follow foolish leads, go up weedy garden paths, embrace nonsense as if it weren't always diseased, because we are too stupid to know any better; because we want to set a bad example, and hope others, to our profit, will follow; because we are eager for conclusions but bored and wearied by methods; because inherited belief is sometimes our only identifying mark; because we want to be as benighted as everybody else; because we will do anything, believe anything, to save ourselves from irrelevance, misery, and oblivion.

What is terrible about O.J.'s case is that a black man has been accused. What is awful about it is the attention being paid to it by the people and the exploitative media. What is harmful about it is the poor picture it draws of the jury system. What the case shows is the power of the rich. What is bad about it is the way it is being exploited for money. No. We should remember what is bad, bad about the crime—that two people were brutally murdered—and bad about the case—the way it was conducted. We should remember that the crime and the case aren't the same. Nor are any event and its accounts. And we must remember, and hold it hard against our hearts, that though O. J. Simpson clearly committed the crime, he will be innocent of it, since he has been found not guilty in a farcical yet properly authorized court of law . . . which leads me to formulate the following contrast between written history and the happenings which give rise to it:

If I say that we rewrite history for the same reasons it was written in the first place—to manage man, enjoy power, escape fate and other just deserts, and make oodles of money—does it follow that every history is a whore's tale, full of purchased movement, fake feeling, and meaningless relief?

Even if historical accounts supersede and replace the events they purport to describe; even if these chronicles favor one side over another, are composed in prejudice and appreciated by bias (reflect, as in some sense they must, their times and its tempers); this does not at all mean that there is no truth to what they've set down, that history has no foundation, that everything is relative and therefore equal as an object of choice; that thought is nothing but a dirty plot against the thoughtless. If every apple is flawed, only some are rotten; if every peach has a pit, each peach also yields its portion of nutrition.

Yet if I want to make the case of Hanna O'Hare more amenable to my aims, instead of redirecting its effect, or redefining its significance, or casting doubt on the details of the tale or the methods of its composition, or weakening the force of this or that point as if two or three bent nails would make a bed of mostly straights seem almost downy; I may instead try to float an ameliorating theory of history across the flood of human folly: one, for instance, which makes history the summation of every conceivable point of view, or one which reduces it to a collection of competing texts, or one so full of pious purpose that murder is no more than a messy method of achieving benign aims, or one, in addition, which makes it as forceful as a pistol at the head, compelling and exculpating. I can fill history with as many entities as there were heroes of the Soviet Union, so that it is what *they* do that matters—race, climate, temper of the time, economic conditions, human nature, destiny, design—not this or that iddybiddy Hanna O'Hare, about whom only who cares.

According to a presently popular view, history is not the representation of a reality; history is the reading of a set of carefully selected texts. The idea is to create an account that (1) is based on a theory of history which replaces the actual occurrences with grand themes, epic heroes, and irresistible forces; (2) serves certain ends and interests; and (3) uses language of such rhetorical persuasiveness that this account will be preferred to any other, the way Sean Bluster's revelations concerning Fiona O'Hare, Hanna's mother, so poignantly put, changed our entire understanding of that horrible affair which so stunned L.A. in its day—for when we learn how Fiona fed her children (too gruesome to recall) in passages of prose which practically put out the reading eyes of a nation, then we cannot but weep for poor Hanna and find the judge who wished her gassed as unfeeling as his gavel.

Or, human experience is what history is about, and it is therefore perspectival. There will be that history which takes the point of view of the children, or one of them, Cecil Maxwell III, for instance (an eater, not one eaten), and that which sees the shoe from its architect's standpoint (his career ruined for no reason), and that of the liberals, and that of *Household Management Magazine,* etcetera, just as a similarly misguided philosopher might insist that the penny on the table was the sum of all its possible angles of observation. Yet if each possible view were honestly and adequately rendered, one might be able to infer the "standpointless" position of the penny, for from only one place and condition could all the reported perspectives be correctly predicted.

But let us descend, for a moment, to bedrock and remember that however we describe Hanna O'Hare's shoegirt life, at the level of factual reality there are never any contradictions, ambiguities, patches of vagueness, loose ends; and that events fall out in only one way: a blue pot was chosen to cook Billyboy, or it was not; Cecil ate a piece of him, or he didn't; he liked what he ate, or he didn't; or if he felt several things at once, then he felt several things; because, of course, human feelings are a part of such scenes as much as anything else; nevertheless, if those emotions are mixed, then they are mixed in just one way, although getting at that mix, describing the stew and its stewy relations, may be immensely difficult, even impossible. *Die Welt ist alles, was der Fall ist.* No amount of relativism, no degree of deconstruction, no namby-pamby pluralism, despite debunking, the disclosure of bias, the so-called unreliability of observers and their cultural conditioning—their class and color blindness—or the oft-bewailed problems of representation, language's betrayal of the mind, should be allowed to shake the singleness, consistency, and wholeness of any happening.

The pot, if it was a pot, had a color, a complexion; if water, a pinch of salt, a few drops of olive oil, were boiled in it, they were not at the same time frozen; if a child cried out, the voice had a timbre, had, indeed, all the qualities it needed to exist at all, if, that is, a cry was cried. We know there weren't two pots in variant spaces waiting for some historian to decide which pot to dismiss, which to retain; there weren't partial entities, ankles without legs (unless after dinner), places without locations, sounds without durations. We know that once the pot boiled and the heat was reduced, it would not boil that particular boil again. That bit of boiling is over for all time and is no longer subject to change. Our attitudes and accounts may alter but not their ostensible object.

Moreover, as Aristotle observed, change takes place, even if by chance, in predetermined directions. The pot cannot become either kid or kettle, steam cannot become a scream, a footfall become a football; but what is white can turn blue, possibly, what is loud—the scream—can grow soft, what is steamy can condense. However much we might wish to alter nature, we are stuck with its basically obdurate character, as the alchemists should have known. C. S. Peirce called this Firstness.

Above all, events cannot be redone after they are over; the dead will not rise to be rearranged. The Over is over, and it is over in its own way. "Just *once,*" Rilke wrote, in the "Ninth Elegy," "Everything. Only *once. Once* and no more. And we as well: *once.* Then never again. But this having *been* once, although *only* once, having been earthed—can it ever be cancelled?"

Ah, but in the realm of quantum mechanics . . . ah, but we are not in the realm of quantum mechanics; we are in the realm of human life.

We can deny that O. J. Simpson murdered his ex; we can write the Holocaust away in a few words; we can pretend that Hanna O'Hare lived in a shoe and boiled boys; but our denial will not alter the facts, our lies will not remove the millions whose lives were erased, our imagination cannot lift Hanna O'Hare from these pages and clap her in any actual jail, even if her hair is blond and long, her cooking accomplished, her bosom lovely, however hard we wish. Even if a thousand words make her feel real. A fiction is forever a fiction, and everything that was will remain as it was eternally.

But we can certainly rewrite what we've written. Nothing is easier. I can say that a child's cry rose from the kettle in the guise of steam. I can claim the meals were made mainly of pigs and goats changed by a perverse Circe into children. And if I can get people to disbelieve the Holocaust, or have faith in magic, in Hanna's plan to keep goats and pigs in town in defiance of the local laws by disguising kids as kids and piglets as plumpish little persons, then they will indeed act on these beliefs, so that falsehoods will have more historical efficacy than the truth. There is nothing new or remarkable about that: the virgin birth is a translator's error. And Hanna's transubstantiation of goats into girls is no more remarkable than water to wine or wine and crackers into blood and body.

The historical record, distorted to suit some cause, is then captured by the organizations whose interests the cause serves. This record is protected, its language becomes sacrosanct, otherwise corrections and rewrites might be made which would undermine the values the text promotes. These accounts are never merely descriptive—this happened this way, that then happened that way—they are explanatory. "Let me tell you what history teaches," Gertrude Stein once wrote, "history teaches." It teaches, it admonishes, it warns, because historical events are supposed to be capable of repetition. If X led to Y once upon a time, then when X comes round again, so will Y and all its tragic consequences. Given a certain constellation of conditions, one can expect Inflation, followed by Depression, followed by Civil Disorder, followed by the appearance of Tyrannical Regimes.

Beliefs based on protected texts—for example, that Germany lost the First World War because it was betrayed, or that the Japanese attacked Pearl Harbor solely for wicked reasons—become centers around which pseudo-thought turns like a dog on a leash, and the slogans which emerge are handy weapons in the word wars. Groups formed, as they think, by beliefs they hold in common (instead of the grievances, fears, and interests which the belief text serves) begin to regard themselves as leviathans (in Hobbes' lingo) or as corporations (in contemporary terms) and give themselves qualities like shame (when we lost the war in Vietnam) and honor (which we regained in the Gulf War) and glory (the name we gave the Stars and Stripes in the old days) and superiority (selected by history to be the richest, most powerful, and of course most moral of people). The way we eat walk talk dress drive worship make love raise kids become shibboleths, setting us apart; but nothing defines a group more securely than its acceptance of a common history—common and special and, perversely, unique.

To speak bluntly: all this is garbage. God is garbage. National honor is garbage. So are peculiar histories, goals, destinies—garbage. Most of the ideas which motivate the actions of people and nations are false. More than that: stupid, incomprehensibly silly, so severely baseless as to humiliate the human mind. Stephen Dedalus' "shout in the street." Which gives some observers the idea that history is wholly relative and subjective and governed by power and rhetoric. Indeed, most of it is. Any honest historian must realize that what is being chronicled is largely human folly. The geological record is one of weather, rocks, and time. The continents do not drift because they are tired of sitting still. But in Hanna's case, her hunger, her outcast condition, had to pass through her consciousness in order to come out as a menu. Then the news of her behavior had to pass through still other sewers of awareness in order to appear in the papers. Then more minds mess with it before someone tries to get a bill banning copper kettles passed by Congress.

Minorities who feel they have been left out or mistreated by the conventional chronicles will embrace both error and paradox in order to get into the game. Propositions which may be true—that nature has its genetic favorites, for instance, although who the favored are will certainly change over time—may be vigorously denied, because such beliefs are seen to be exploitative (which may also be correct). It is true that basketball favors the taller athlete, but it would be wrong, on that account, to prohibit short people from playing. It would also be a mistake, in order to right that wrong, to deny the truth the wrongdoers misuse. The disadvantaged also tend to see customary history as a calculated lie while remaining happily blind to the falsifications which make up their own—a story that's pure true honest educational and elevating. Not just more humbug.

But in spite of all their sophistical enemies, the facts do remain. O.J. slew the pair. The kids were eaten. Jews were gassed in the bath. Lizzie Borden got in her whacks, although the latest scholarship has lessened their number. Bias, decay of data, misleading details, cover-ups, confusions, stupidity, connivance, poor judgment, lousy scholarship, hidden agendas: these obstacles to objective assessment can be largely removed, and patiently, over time, some progress can be made in getting a proper picture of the past.

Recent attacks on the Philosophical Enlightenment, which slur reason, science, and careful observation by miring its results so deeply in the anxieties and needs of a particular time as to render them as local as hometown news, are nothing but parochial themselves, and squarely in the pay of society's new masters: commercial interests which are so busy selling to the First Second Third Fourth Fifth Worlds they require both relativism and pluralism, and a skepticism about all absolutes except money, to support the sale of lifestyles to the masses around the world. Everyone is a customer, and the customer is always right, just as our goods are universally super in every price range, although you may wish to bump your belief system up a grade along with your new house, car, and dinner jacket. Each new cultural or political movement means money in a fresh market, one which can be precisely targeted. Whether major, minor, or Little League, their members will need uniforms, logos, bats, balls, gloves, dark glasses, Walkmen, drugs, and guns.

The events most in danger of being distorted are those which occur in all innocence of their impact upon theory, and not just upon a theory of history but upon popular positions in ethics and theology, economics and politics, as well. In science, data which supports or contravenes a hypothesis is collected daily, reality is really evidence; but elsewhere a fog sets in, doctrine snoozes happily on the hearth, the catechism sits on its mat. Belief systems are round-the-clock employers, always in need of protection; consequently, the standard techniques of defense—rationalization, hypothecation *ad hoc,* and various applications of what C. S. Peirce called "the method of tenacity," as well as *tuo quoque*s, *ad hominem*s, and red herrings—are always at work.

The Holocaust is just such a challenging item, one reason there are those who would prefer to remove it from the course of history altogether; because if it remains inside the causal stream, it becomes just another pogrom, the largest so far, to be sure, but merely big, not otherwise special. Its name, "the Holocaust," will flutter about, lighting not only on past persecutions—of the Armenians by the Turks, for instance, or the Soviet extermination of the Kulaks, or even the Nazi murder campaign against the Poles, robbing holocausts of their Jewishness—but on contemporary conflicts too—such as tribal genocide, Serb aggression—casting doubt on the Holocaust's uniqueness, lessening its horror, shifting guilt from the Germans as a national group to man as a species, in any case making mass murder almost a semi-annual outing.

On the other hand, if the Holocaust is treated, paradoxically if not perversely, as a sacred occurrence, like a miracle made by Satan, it has no conditions or causes, and certainly no historical consequences. As a sacred occurrence, gentiles, pagans, Moslems, others, can be denied it as an object of comment or study, just as the subject of feminism is reserved for feminists by some of its priesthood, or questions of Color for whoever has the right hue. What does this honky think he's doing, writing a biography of Malcolm X or Martin Luther King?

Or we might strengthen our remembrance of less vast crimes

by transferring some horror and outrage from the Murder of the Jews to them on the ground that they are more approachable. You remember the Holocaust, I'll remember the *Maine*. Martin Jay warns:

> Historicizing the Holocaust need not mean reducing it to the level of the "normal" massacres of the innocents that punctuate all of recorded history, but rather remembering those quickly forgotten and implicitly forgiven events with the same intransigent refusal to normalize that is the only justifiable response to the Holocaust itself. (in *Salmagundi,* spring/summer 1995, p. 21)

In or out of history, there the Holocaust is, all the same: unless we can rewrite it away. And the old explanation of Jewish persecution, namely that God was using the Philistines as a lash to punish violations of the Covenant, takes on a rather hollow sound when the Holocaust is alleged to be a warning against assimilation. Or was necessary to establish Israel. We might ask the same question of Hanna O'Hare's deity: what kind of god works in such mean, merciless, and wasteful ways? The answer arrives without strain: the god who kindly took these beautiful children home to heaven early.

It is not simply the criminals who wish to rewrite history, justifying their actions or getting themselves let off with only a warning; it is the victims too, who find their faith in ruins, their ontological protection gone, their explanations empty.

If the Holocaust is unique, it cannot recur. Is this consequence comforting? If there could be a Second Coming of this catastrophe, we could never predict or prepare for it. Let us bow our heads, for nothing can be done or said.

If the Holocaust was a terrible blow to Semites, it was not exactly a pat on the back for the anti-Semites. It really did put this ancient prejudice in the dock, and, one might think, banished it, like smallpox, from human society. But the Holocaust, horrible as it was, horrible as it is to remember, couldn't even do that; for the anti-Semites are back, practicing their persecutions, spreading their lies, inventing excuses, finding Jews to blame. And every other sort of murderous discrimination is flourishing, as though the six million hadn't died. So the Holocaust was not the massacre to end all massacres. It didn't end anything. "Let me tell you what history teaches, history teaches."

History continues to think of itself as a narrative; it has been overcome by story (after all, "story" is a considerable part of its name); it has been enticed into error by the pleasures of anecdote, by the cogency lent events when agent and action are joined, just as fiction became entranced by character and plot as it followed history's lead. "After this, therefore because of this" was a fallacy history made saintly. History actually thought history had an aim (like someone with a plan for the future); that history, like anecdote, had a point, a meaning even, and wore a value like a badge of honor through every happenstance. History thought it had culminations as well as beginnings, like scenes on the stage; ripe roundings-off as well as inevitable developments, chapters made of verse. So there could be periods, and movements, and eras and tempers and spirits and destinies. And lessons, surely, many lessons. History teaches.

I would rewrite history by denying the general application of this kind of determining linearity to human events. Only the word "life" has meaning; life itself hasn't even four letters. There is nothing beyond. And the things which happen to us are the results of a complex interrelation of differently weighted factors the way the ingredients of a stew mingle to make its range and play of flavors. That we shall end up somewhere seems to me certain, but the way a river arrives at the sea, through the fall of the terrain, not the way the tour boat does—tooting at towns as it steams to New Orleans.

I have always felt that historians spent far too much time on wars and revolutions, the rise and fall of kingdoms, the pontificating of congresses and diets, councils and assemblies, the appearance and actions of villains and heroes, for they say or change remarkably little about us in the long run, one set of bureaucrats simply replaces another; whereas whatever alters the nature of the human mind, such as the creation of abstract ideas, the discovery of logic, the invention of musical notation, Arabic numerals, or the alphabet, the adoption and abandonment of perspective, the operation of the printing press, the menace of the motorcar, the three alleged burnings of the library of Alexandria, the critique of narrative and other modes of linear thinking, the development of non-Euclidean geometries, the continued triumph of scientific procedures in the face of repeated Luddite attacks, the tendency of technology to destroy civility, the eventual disappearance of baseball . . . these events and others like them belong in the center of the stage, since it is human consciousness that counts, it is its presence that determines whether we are alive, it is its quality which figures our value, and it is its discoveries, its decisions, which will save us and every living other from destruction or, worse, mediocrity if there is to be any salvation at all. It is not death that is to be feared but, rather— and something history should be devoted to demonstrating—the loss of excellence. What else that's positive have we contributed to this world?

Transformations

Many centuries before computers made writing a mental matter, writing was not merely a mechanical and external activity pursuant to the composition of letters, the creating of poems, or the invention of plays; it was the scrivener's profession, the calligrapher's craft. The Word had only recently begun to slide from a sacred condition where its very making—since its origins, its character, and its intentions were holy—required devotion, contemplation, skill, illustrative enrichment, and unceasing elaboration. What one wrote might pretend to art, but writing itself was a craft, a discipline for the hand, as manual as carpentry or painting.

The facilities of both earth and sky were called upon, as well as the products of human industry. One would require a desk placed near a window, a candle to illumine night or alleviate shade, a basin of ink, some sand to hurry its setting, a sharp edge which would later be called a penknife after its specialty, and of course the quill which the blade would refine. Then upon a parchment, vellum very often, the writer—who might still be able to feel on the underside of the sheet the remaining hairs of the beast's pelt—on that surprisingly inviting surface the writer would indite his lines: sentences very plainly put together out of words, words assembled letter by letter, carefully because materials were costly, because mistakes were not easily or neatly remedied, and because care in composition would have been a well-schooled habit of the mind.

Here what was in one's heart, what had occupied one's mind, what had, in times before, required lodging in one's memory—the sight of greening hillsides, skies islanded with clouds, a gloomy castle on a distant bluff, even the bitter cleanliness of ale on the tongue or of watercress that had been harvested to unclog a stream—would find lodging in language; possibly some notion, suddenly conceived or unwittingly borrowed—perhaps the scarcely original thought that the world was another of God's pronouncements, was a book made of His words, or perhaps was a play instead, a war of opposites, the dream of a giant whose head was the Hill of Howth—could be set down and saved somewhere other than in one's consciousness, fragile and fleeting as it was. Imagine such a transformation. Actually, not one such change but many would be required if the work of writing was to proceed—more metamorphs than most imaginations were ready for.

Look at the whitebud's leaves in a summer morning's sunlight, and how the dew has slowly settled to their drooping tips, so that a single drop glistens everywhere; from every twig, branch, bough, a bit of brilliance clings. Of course, they might be compared to the ends of runny noses, these dewdrops, or made a sign of unhealthy humidity. Thales may have been right: this moisture has been condensed from the atmosphere, a circumambience to which, warmed by the sun, it will return again, unless the dew is heavy enough to gather and swell like fruit, to drip free of the leaf, only to drop silently down upon the earth, seep into it, and disappear. Eventually, these drops will water a rootling, and some treeseed will send, just as the poets have said, when April comes again, a water-engendered shoot.

Let's say this is something I have seen, something I have thought. To say I have seen it is to imply that my nervous system has translated (out of all that's been sent in its direction) frequencies relayed from the tree, its leaves, their moist surfaces—beams, in short, of encoded light—into conditions and qualities of consciousness, into the very green and glisten I say I have observed. Quantities, best noted down and expressed in number, have been transformed into qualities. Rude substance has been sublimed. Now this energy shapes a scene on a screen of the Soul. The poet Rainer Maria Rilke preferred to think that the world was waiting to be realized in just this way, to become invisible—just as, to others, each of our realms of awareness is—invisible—although nothing is more vivid, solid, substantial, now, than even the most melancholy of our experiences, for instance, the loneliness of a room rented by the week.

> Silent friend of many distances, feel
> how your breath still enlarges space.
> From the dark tower let your bell peal.
> Whatever feeds upon your face
>
> grows strong from this offering.
> Transform matter into mind.
> What is the source of your deepest suffering?
> If drinking is bitter, become wine.
>
> In this limitless night, be the magical force
> at the intersection of your senses,
> the meaning of their intercourse.
>
> And if what's earthly no longer knows you,
> say to the unmoving earth: I flow.
>
> To the rushing water speak: I stay.
>
> *(Sonnets to Orpheus,* part 2, 29)

This is the transformation which is the model for all transformations. It is ontological to a point of completeness: physical relations are retained but only as relations; that is, the points from which transmissions have been sent are faithfully recorded, the differences between frequencies are precisely noted; the several kinds of transmission (flower odor, leaf rustle, dew dazzle) have been received by their appropriate receptor; however, the little dancing globe that to a cruder poet might have been seen as snot belongs to Rilke's innerworld space and is nowhere else to be found. So much of importance rests on this absence, this immateriality, because not only has a frequency of light been read as green; it has been given the shape of a leaf, a leaf against the sky, a leaf on a tree, a green as extended in its own interior realm as a bundle of photons in its. That is: space itself has been transformed. As Plato's formula, set out in the *Timaeus,* puts it: the realm of Becoming, our empirical world of sensation and change, is the qualitative expression of quantitative law.

Thousands of years of thinking have rarely raised the question, let alone answered it: when the brain transforms a signal, why does the mind receive the signal from the leaf as green? the filling of the candy as sweet, the bite of the bee as stinging? I mean: why is such and such a frequency rendered as color at all, let alone khaki?

I could have thought, about what I'd seen, that the whitebud is weeping; but I am not a sentimental sort. I could have thought (actually, in the guise of another I did think) of the tree as suffering from a sort of sinus condition. Instead, I chose to see glitter, be impressed, and conclude jewels. But by the time I have picked one possible thought to develop, the dew has dried, the leaves are dull despite the brighter light, their natural droop seems a bit worn, a trifle weary. If I don't make a note of my thought, it will soon be gone too. Another moment of life lost. So what? Most of them are.

What did I do when I thought: these leaves have been bedizened . . . ? When I lose my keys, I may envision their likely locations; when I entertain myself with an erotic dream, I may imagine a slope of perfect skin; when I try to remember what side of Italy Macerata is on, I may outline Italy's booted leg in the mental atlas most of us keep; but when I think, when I judge, when I describe, when I recall, I cannot return the dew to its drop at the leaf's lip; I can only summon the words "leaf" and "lip" and gather them together into a phrase, "drop at the leaf's lip," or ought I to think "drop at the leaf's tip" instead?

What is the nature of these words? for they are not uttered, they are not shouted or sung, although the shadow of their sound—for example, that of "leaf"—is retained, and perhaps a certain vestigial muscle movement can be felt, local to the larynx. Having subvocalized much of my sentence, I begin to write it down, but cautiously, since I know mistakes cannot be erased. The pencil hasn't been invented yet. There it is, orthographed: "leaf." Amazing. Now I can look at it: not at dew but "dew," not at leaf but "leaf."

How will my eventual sentences sound to the sweet ear to whom I am sending them? "Life is like a dew-stained leaf . . ." I intend to begin. Consequently, we've but little time to enjoy the pleasures that ought to be ours, I'm going to suggest. Dust has closed Helen's eye. Melted are the snows of yesteryear. That's my main message. So dance the orange, girls; gather ye rosebuds while ye may. Hey—you know why?—dew dries. Already I have found a community of phrases, lines, even rhymes, made with words as different as can be, which I nevertheless believe express one and the same idea: life is fleeting; and indicate the presence of one and the same intention: dear lady, let's go to bed.

Of course, poets cannot be counted on to be consistent, and Rilke uses the same ideas in a context that suggests that love is as quickly over as a cough. This ruins my argument with the lady, for how can I recommend, because life passes so swiftly, that we indulge in a passion as fleeting as any?

> But we, when we feel, evaporate; oh, we
> breathe ourselves away; from coal to coal
> we cool as perfume fades. Though someone may tell us:
> "You've got into my blood, into this room, the springtime
> is rich with you . . ." What good is that? He can't keep us;
> we disappear within, on either side, of him. And those who
>   are
> beautiful, who can capture them? Expressions go forth
>   from their faces

only to be reabsorbed. Like dew from morning grass
we relinquish what is ours as easily as steam from a
    warm dish.

(Duino Elegies, 2)

Something else should now be noted. It is less interesting but more important: in no time, without effort, I have put to work three versions of my word, for every word has three modes of existence: as written, as spoken, and as subvocalized. Which one is the real word, and which are merely substitutes for the original one? It would appear that some words like "tintinnabulation" ought to be sounded; some, like "nociceptor," are meant to be scripted; while most are comfortably acey-deucy, and can go both ways. That is: while all words reside in these three realms and therefore in ontologically different climates, some seem more at home in one than in the other. "Nociceptor" can be subvocalized, but don't hold your breath. Other words need to be spoken by a performing reader in order to sustain any hope they might have for an auditory life. Such are Chaucer's lines now:

> Whan that Aprille with his shoures sote
> The droghte of Marche hath perced to the rote,
> And bathed every veyne in swich licour
> Of which vertu engendred is the flour . . .

The serious writer, whom I shall assume I am inventing, and setting back in quill time, will not be writing for a mute inglorious scanhappy reader, nor, of course, for one whose experience of words, when it comes to their composition, is mainly of the shadowshapes which appear upon his computer screen when he types. He will know, this possible Elizabethan, that the primary word must be heard. I shall not rehearse all the reasons why the claim by the written (or, rather, the printed or, rather, the pixilated) word to be first and foremost should be ridiculed, but pause only to excuse technical terms from this debate, since, of course, "nociceptor," like "proprioceptor," though it can be pronounced: *no-see-sep-tor,* wasn't meant to be noised about but was designed, like the names of racehorses, to display its lineage visually. I won't forbear pointing out that the words which are the heart of all the humanistic arts were the earliest learned, and learned in an emotional setting of extraordinary significance: in Mama's arms, where the words were cooed; in Father's rules, where they were shouted; to form Brother's threats, where they were hissed in private; in the family quarrel, where they were bandied about and laid on forlorn ears like blows. Such words, in every vital sense, "go back," even when, with "masquerade," it's only to the Norman Conquest and, through the invading French then, to the Arabs, who no doubt used their version, "maskharah," often and with relish, inasmuch as it meant "buffoon" to them. I note in addition that the syllables of no-see-septor have their own individual charge, each of them having been used in words from every part of the language map and throughout the length of language time.

Speech is a richer medium than writing. It exploits stress, pitch, pause, speed, accent, and timbre and is often enough employed face-to-face that it can enjoy gesture and smile and grimace as well. Speech can take place in a context of exchange, contribute to a babble, form one corner of a quartet.

If we look up "leaf" in German, we receive *Blatt* like a pie in the face. We'd better count on French. Yes, *feuille* is ever so much better. As for "dew," well, there's *rosée* to set against *Tau*—no contest—however, it's hard to beat "dewdrop" in German: *Tautropfen.* That drop bounces a bit when it hits: *trop-fen.* If the dew of morning grass is *Tau* in the *Morgen,* it is possible for me to translate the English into the German and vice versa. In addition, then, to the inscribed, oral, and subvocal types, there must be the word that refers to what is common to "dew.Tau.rosée" and which exists somewhere like one of the Platonic Forms: the word as pure meaning, standing for "leaf" or "dew" as they may occur in any/every language. Corresponding to the Form, which will, of course, be clean of embarrassing homonyms (such as: "just do it," "I'd just as lief leave you as look at you," "the Tao is the only true way," "I just hate rosé, don't you? it's to wine what a smirk is to a smile"), is its equally purified denotation: just leaf, just tree, just dew, damn it, and not a thing or condition or quality more. Since no leaf is merely a leaf but carries always a load of individuating properties, the referent of the word is as artificial as its meaning.

Any instance of a written or a spoken word is called its token. Every token is an exemplification of the pure or Platonic type expressed in some particular language according to the rules each language has for writing or speaking the word. It is these language types, as they are called—indifferent to fonts and heedless of accents—which function in the language and which consequently gather to themselves all the strange associations such juxtapositions achieve. When I take up my quill to write to my darling the words "dew" and "leaf" and "life," I am invoking, first of all, ideas common to people everywhere, hence the immaterial Form, the Pure Type with its purified referent. But I indite, when my quill moves, the English version, spelled according to the rules L E A F not L I E F. This is the Language Type. But I will also reveal my education, for I was taught to form my letters according to directions in writing manuals favored by my teachers and my school. In these books there are plates depicting how, ideally, the letter *l,* say, should be formed, how large its loop should be, how thin or fat the line, and so on. These are Token Types. By imitating my parents' speech and the speech of others around me, I do the same thing with my vocalizations. Raised in hoity-toity circumstances, I may diphthong every vowel I can: deu come in and meet mater. As if these distinctions weren't enough, my own nature will particularize every scrawl, so that there will be my characteristic way of doing my lowercase *d*'s, enabling handwriting experts to identify the kidnap note—"Drop the dough in a Dumpster on Davidson Drive"—as in my extorting hand; and voiceprints of my threats anonymously left on the answering machines of the louts who reviewed my last book will implicate me through my plangent tenor or reedy baritone as well. These are Personalized Token Types.

All I have said about spelling goes double for syntax. Beneath German grammar, under French, hidden in Hebrew, Chomsky surmised, must be another syntax, the syntax essential to the very idea of language itself, otherwise the varied grammars of the world could not be rerepresented and, what is worse, there would be syntactically different versions of the world to which the users of a language might be grammatically inclined.

As if this weren't enough: "Wither, midst falling DEW . . ." I can shout or wheeze or whisper. "DO AS I SAY IF YOU VALUE YOUR LAWN MOWER'S LIFE," I can write in commanding caps. And in red ink. I can dot my *i*'s with quill holes; I can fiercely x-out compliments, as if I had thought better of making them; I can misspell words on purpose, as Ezra Pound preferred, so he'd read like Uncle Remus. Yet, use as many conventions as I like, write as carefully as I can, every letter dee or el or ef will be slightly different from every other ef or el or dee I scribble. If you have ever had to write your name a good many times in a short while, you will remember weariness, carelessness, boredom, but also embarrassment, and how you slovenized your already slovenly signature. There will be your proud Declaration of Independence hand, your memo scrawl, your hesitant signature on the motel register. What matter does is particularize, as Aristotle argued; it individuates.

In short, my speech, my handwriting, will refer to the world, invoke universal ideas, reveal the region in which I was raised, as well as my education and social status and a lot of my personal character besides. In addition, what I say or write will often expose my state of mind at the moment. Unless I've gone to a scrivener and hired his pen, what principally my writing will testify to is the fact that I can read and write—a significant thing in

Elizabeth's reign. And what will it say of me if, in addition, I have a *style*? a late style, an early style, a middle style?

It was Rilke's conviction that the true poem, the poem *he* had written, was alive in the hand he had used to write it. Printed versions, with their standardized fonts and customary layouts, were merely impersonal copies. Even so, those handwritten originals were transcriptions of that chanting, shouting voice that repeatedly unnerved the servants who had to attend to his needs when, otherwise alone, in winter, castle-sitting, he composed. The elegant calligraphy in which Rilke's later poems first made their appearance, to be posted, then, to this patron, that lover or friend, was nevertheless another disguise, since, years before, Lou Andreas-Salomé had pronounced his handwriting insufficiently "poetic" and strongly suggested that he change it, which Rilke, happy for another mask, obediently did.

How material the personal letter used to be, how particular, how specifically registered! Let us walk a moment behind the march of time. We once indented clay, scratched stone, smeared slate, made use of palm leaves and shells, bark and wood and wax. A stick, a thorn, a pointed piece of metal or ivory, was preferred for inditing. In the following fashion, an old scribe dedicated his implements to Hermes, now that they were of use to him no longer:

> Philodemus, now that his wrinkled brows owing to old age come to hang over his eyes, dedicates to Hermes the round lead that draws dark lines, the pumice, rough whet-stone of hard pens, the knife, flat sharpener of the split-reed pens, the ruler that takes charge of the straightness of lines, the ink long kept in hollow caverns, and the notched pen blackened at the point. (*Aucilla to Classical Reading* by Moses Hadas. New York: Columbia University Press, 1954, p. 12, quoting Paul the Silentiary)

Rolls of papyrus coated with cedar oil were gradually replaced by tablets made of wood and containing wax-filled depressions that the pen then indented. Wires sewn like thread helped hinge stacks of tablets together, and the form of the book was approached. Now parchment and vellum sheets replaced papyrus, and what was called a codex was accomplished, one column of writing to a page, twelve pages to a quire, twelve quires more than sufficient for a volume.

Thus a book was built, and the sense of it as a building was profoundly felt. In medieval times, covers were got up like massive doors, with boltlike bumps and heavy straps. Illuminations were treated like windows. In the eighteenth century it was customary to use an architectural motif as a frontispiece. The terms that began to describe a book's parts were drawn from both the building and the body: spine and cover, column and head (*tête* and title), chapter and volume, verse (or vertebra), stanza (or room).

"Verse" is a word particularly rich. It meant a turning, basically of the body, hence a measure of distance (like a verst), a whirlpool too, a vortex, and a furrow in the earth, as well as a turning of it, which finally became a line. This runnel controlled the growth of a crop, the course of the eye. But before the space of the book/body/building could be inhabited, words which represented both the world and the mind had to be written in it.

Ink was made of the residue from burning pitch, or sometimes black paint derived from the pine's resin was prepared, then softened with soot from the furnaces which warmed the baths. Sometimes wine lees were used. Those of good wine were said to be as inherently dark as India ink. The skins of grapes yielded a deep stain, as did burned ivory, but such was human ingenuity at work on behalf of writing that the blackening that adhered to the bottom of bronze pans was scraped free. Charcoal was collected from charred logs, and from the cuttlefish was drawn its secretions of attack and fright. Inks were darkened by exposing their fluids to the sun, while walls were prepared with washes of gum and glue. Vinegar, it was learned, made black pigments indelible.

Once one who wrote prepared his pigments like a painter and respected his tools as much as any Japanese craftsman did, having the good sense to revere his material and his implements as gods and to seek their assistance. Obstacles made for meditation, determined form.

In Plato's day, boys learned to write as they learned to read. Much attention was given to the disciplining of both hand and eye. Students copied over and over the sample their master's own efforts provided. Quintilian even suggests that

> as soon as the child has begun to know the shapes of the various letters, it will be no bad thing to have them cut as accurately as possible upon a board, so that the pen may be guided along the grooves. Thus mistakes such as occur with wax tablets will be rendered impossible; for the pen will be confined between the edges of the letters and will be prevented from going astray. Further by increasing the frequency and speed with which they follow these fixed outlines we shall give steadiness to the fingers, and there will be no need to guide the child's hand with our own.
>
> (*Ancilla to Classical Reading,* p. 15, quoting Quintilian)

Erasmus advised that the first time a pupil recognized the shape of a letter, and sounded it, he should be given a cookie baked in the same form as his success to reinforce the connection.

Many persons of quality, disdaining all things manual, continued the practice of dictating to a scribe. A scrivener rode by Caesar's side in his carriage, and Pliny's servant might have had to make shorthand notes while peering through the steam of his master's bath or, in winter, wear gloves against the cold that came like an enemy from every corner. In this way the gentry remained firmly in the oral tradition. Since writing was so manual, so muscular, the sounds of words grew muscles too.

The quill gives way to metal nibs; the paper is soon made of rags and wood; the writing handbooks try to achieve, for their students, a solemn simple clear and useful hand. Which will not call attention to itself. Which will be easy to read and understand. Critics were eager to extol the simple straightforward no-nonsense style of businessmen and scientists. It was said that the English language ought best to imitate Defoe, be Swift. Like one's tea, one's dinner, one's making of love—in this sad puritanical time—one's writing ought to be short-ordered, unceremoniously served, and unconcernedly gulped.

That is, for the sake of efficiency, the reader was to ignore the forming or sounding of words in order instead to see and to hear through them scenes and ideas directly: words were as forgettable as windows once the stained glass had been removed and the outside had been let in, like jugglers, players, ladies of the evening, to titillate the soul. How could the word be the Word of God now? It was in everyone's mouth; it was written everywhere; blasphemous and pornographic books were made of it. The word had but a Use, and all the elegance of dirty drawers and the beauty of a bum wipe. There was no place for Edmund Spenser's "daffydowndillies" now.

Wordsworth could pander to the people, but it was only a poetic ploy. Ordinariness was okay. He extraordinarily said.

The typewriter arrives, and now typefaces fall from one's fingers like loose change. Still, the typewriter was for offices, for business, for impersonal affairs; you certainly wouldn't send a typewritten letter to a friend. But how it eased the effort of writing: no more weary ink-stained fingers, no more increasingly sloppy sentences and signatures, impossible to make out. You could still hit x a few times, or run a dash through a line you wanted someone to think you'd thought better of; though the line remained there to be deciphered, its meaning suffered. And keys could be hammered in rage, ribbons could make faint sentiments fainter, fonts would wear like cathedral steps, and papers smear and yellow and tear at their folds. A detective could trace the ransom note, with your demand for dough to be deposited in a Dumpster, to your battered old Remington.

Ah, but now great firms like IBM come to our rescue. The

electric arrives, our work grows light, our thought even lighter. Every letter has the same distinctness, there are no emotional indentations, typing has been made even easier, errors are more quickly correctable, fonts can be interchanged, the page can be gussied up like a harlot, as the writer himself recedes into word choice and almost out of view. A quirky grammar is all that is left of the soul. Finally, the computer completes our journey. Efficiency in almost every physical realm of the writing activity has been immensely improved. It allows novelists of any age to be garrulous as grandpas and to run on like an Ancient of Days. Meanwhile, grammar decays like week-old fruit. No longer do you need to eye the page and calculate the price of a mistake. There is nothing to impede a first thought, alas, from becoming your last. When the machine informs you that you have spelled "catafalque" correctly, you feel a glow of achievement. Writing loses weight, becomes thin, becomes internal, self-absorbed. The communication of blats is instantaneous. Language no longer has the materiality which made it great. Words are rarely heard in the head and never felt in the fingers. Utility is triumphant. Poetry is written as if it never knew music, and readers forget to chew its lines but *zooop* them up like noodles.

Words on a disk have absolutely no permanence, and unless my delete key is disarmed I can invade Thomas Hobbes, without a trace of my intrusion, to replace his lines with mine: and the life of man in a state of nature suddenly becomes solemn, rich, pleasant, generous, and long. Words on a disk have visual qualities, to be sure, and these darkly limn their shape (I can see them appearing right now as I type), but they have no materiality, they are only shadows, and when the light shifts, they'll be gone. Off the screen they do not exist as words. They do not wait to be reseen, reread; they only wait to be remade, relit. I cannot carry them beneath a tree or onto a side porch; I cannot argue in *their* margins; I cannot enjoy the memory of my dismay when, perhaps after years, I return to my treasured copy of *Treasure Island* to find the jam I inadvertently smeared there still spotting a page precisely at the place where Billy Bones chases Black Dog out of the Admiral Benbow with a volley of oaths, and where his cutlass misses its mark to notch the inn's wide sign instead.

The popular description of the Internet is misguided. No one should be surprised about that. "Misinformation Alley" is an apter designation, although it is lined with billboards called Web sites obscuring whatever might be seen from the road. Moreover, "highway" has the advantage of reminding us of another technological marvel, the motorcar, and of all its accomplishments: the death of millions around the world, the destruction of the landscape, the greedy irresponsible consumption of natural resources, the choking of cities and the poisoning of the atmosphere, the ruination of the railroads, the distribution of noise into every sort of solitude, the creation of suburbs and urban sprawl, of malls and motor homes, of consumerist attitudes and the dangerous delusions that afflict drivers, the tyranny of highways and tollways in particular, the creation of the road-borne tourist, who drives, who looks, who does not see, but nevertheless clearly remembers "having been there." In short, blessings are invariably mixed.

Socrates would not have seen the dewdrop whose formation on the leaf of the whitebud I began this essay by invoking, because he was uninterested in nature and looked mainly at the soul, something he alone seemed able to catch sight of. Plato might have observed the dew, but he would have regarded his word for the drop as more important than the drop itself, since the word directed him to the Idea, which had the advantage of being universal, unoval, unwet, undryable, undroppable. In short, not like a dewdrop at all.

So when I replace the fact (which I can never see, which is a construction) with my perception, and my perception with a series of words—"dewdrops formed at the tips of the whitebud leaves"—two series of transformations will have intersected: that of Nature becoming Experience, and that of the thought-sounded sentence sliding down an arm into its written form and thence, having been greeted by sufficient applause, into its printed one. In that way an easily overlooked event in the world became a perception for which was soon substituted a verbal thought, only gradually formulated (ah . . . dew, gee, glistening at the tips, those leaves, yes, dewpoint higher than I thought, St. Louis weather, like a laundry, all right, my whatjamacallit, okay, dewdrops, what about them? formed at the tips of the . . . nose . . . no, like a sexual lubricant . . . no . . . the whitebud leaves . . . the innocent tip of the whitebud leaves), to be finally written down on the back of an envelope, then inserted into my great ode titled "Weeping," which was included a year later in a collection I called *Pure and Simple;* only a year after that "Weeping" was set to music by Armand Passacaglia, but only after having been translated into Italian (northern Italian, I should reassuringly add) by Gian Gianfreddy. Armand's version, after being orchestrated by Ivan Osver, was recorded in performance by Liam O'Hara and the Sapporo Symphony Orchestra at the Graz Autumn Music Festival. In Italian my poem is twice as long as it is in English, and Passacaglia's song is twice longer than that, there are so many refrains and repetitions, but Osver's bloody "Weeping Turtle Suite" lasts an interminable half hour because of the overuse of trombones, tubas, and other fat brass.

Suppose I had written a little anxious note to my arborist: "Dewdrops are forming at the tips of my whitebud's leaves. Is this normal? Please look into it." I should be quite shocked if my arborist (Passacaglia, one and the same) had responded with a note of his own: "Bellissimo, chéri, such phrasing is found only in Dante." After looking for the joke and not finding any, I'd have to conclude that the maestro had a mistaken understanding of the language. Why? because he had treated it as if it were not a piece of disposable utilitarian exchange but a line, perhaps, from my great poem "Weeping" itself.

In order to understand the extent of Passacaglia's error, let's look at some other types of ontological transformation. There is, of course, that of Gregor Samsa, who wakes from an uneasy sleep to find himself a bedbug . . . well, a bug in a bed, at any rate. His transformation is incomplete because, at least for a time, he still feels and thinks like a human being. But Gregor can no longer live like one. Egg, caterpillar, chrysalis, the butterfly, not only are—to a degree—different in terms of physical quality; they must sustain themselves and function in different ways as well, and this is why their changes can be called ontological. Yet, ontological or not, throughout all their stages, they remain members of the same species, something poor Gregor Samsa cannot manage.

Though if some of us began to make a habit of it . . .

When the soul, according to theories of transmigration, is reborn, time after time, in a different body and into another life, obedient to the rules of karma or poetic justice, it remains the same soul; only its fleshly clothing has been changed. Sometimes the soul is permitted to remember its sojourn in the body of a dog the way we may recall a vacation spent in Venice, but Platonic transmigration insists that the soul sheds its past each reincarnation, since one's memories are memories of this or that body and are buried with the body, to rot at the body's pace. Apollo, on the other hand, can inadvertently cause Daphne to be changed into a tree by chasing her; and Zeus is able to disguise himself as a bull, the better to carry off Europa, as easily as we costume ourselves for a masquerade. (There is that Arab word again.) The high jinks of the gods became a serious philosophical model, however, because the early Greek philosophers could not imagine a state of affairs altering into another without some bit of the initial condition's continuing unchanged. How else would one recognize the difference? State-of-affairs A can be replaced by state-of-affairs B, of course, but that only means someone new is renting the room. The roomers haven't segued into one another. Music can become loud or soft, Aristotle argued, but it cannot become white, for were it by some miracle to do that, we would never grasp the alteration unless within the whiteness we could hear, even distantly, the sound of singing.

Though change itself must continue to change if it is to stay the same (for how protean would Proteus be if he took the form of the Sphinx for a thousand years?), the unchanging—the underlying substance of all things, the convictions of a Southern Baptist, or one of the eternal Forms—simple as each has to be to resist subdivision and decay, must nevertheless possess more arms than Siva, more glints than a gem or a dewdrop poised upon the tip of a leaf, more faces than Bill Clinton in front of the press, otherwise it will prove . . . it will be . . . uninteresting to any prolonged contemplation . . . because the eternal, in every case I know of, likes being admired, loves, like the hawk or the evening star, being above and beyond all things, lives in the light of that adoration.

God is father, son, holy ghost, the good earth, all the saints, but not Satan and his sons, or . . . wait . . . perhaps, deep in the bowels of even Lucifer's fire-filled being . . . yes, there is a touch of Our Lord's self-serving feudal love, as in every one of us, for we . . . what are we but transformations: images of His refulgent, infinitely faceted Being? The Absolute is One, but it has so many many predicates. The Form of the Good, no less than Jehovah, contains all the lesser Forms, which therefore may be deduced from It, from Him, the way conclusions, or golden calves, are born.

A line is a furrow, etymology tells us; a field of furrows is a verse, the line turning back upon itself; but look again and see the vertebrae of the backbone and its neat page of ribs, or rows of pews in a church filled with parishioners who, like words to a hymn, have come here to worship; and then there are the aisles or margins where the boundaries lie, those spaces between plantings, paragraphs of corn, which gather each plant into a higher meaning, stanza after stanza, room after room, column after column, page after page, acre after acre, floor after floor, story after story, until all of the bones of the back are there, and the spine . . . the spine and its volume are complete. "Will transformation," Rilke writes:

> Be inspired by the flame
> where a thing made of Change conceals itself;
> this informing spirit, master of all that's earthly,
> loves nothing more than the moment of turning.
>
> (*Sonnets to Orpheus*, part 2, 12)

Alexander Calder draws the outline of a rooster in one of his notebooks. Later he takes thin wire and gives that wire a similar shape. He has made two lines, one of charcoal, one of wire. The rooster, poised in space, well lit, turning in an imaginary wind, casts its shadow into a corner where two exhibition walls have been instructed to join, and suddenly there are lines once again, clearly made by the wire rooster, a crowing cock, but distorted by the cant of the partitions, the position of the light, the movement of the mobile, multiplying itself in addition, for there is a shadow for each reflective surface, as well as one on the ceiling, if we look there, and, blurrier, another in flight upon the floor. Amid this dance of drawings the cock turns, expressing its dominion through the echoes of its outline, crowing in a kind of semipermanent dawn.

Why do we insist that the one real Calder is the cock depicted by the twisted wire? The drawing becomes merely preparatory, and, after all, we can't sell the shadows.

What about the real rooster? He belabored many a hen before he was retired to a meager stew with some chunks of carrot, shreds of cabbage, a few slices of onion and hunks of potato, in whose company he was boiled for a long time to loosen his tough skin and soften his mean disposition, before he was eaten with several rather doughy dumplings. Hunger made the meal memorable, for the guns of an encircling force could be heard the entire time, and the teeth of the diners wondered, as they chewed, if this would be their last mastication. When the siege of Leningrad was lifted, an account of the repast was found folded though never mailed, as a letter often isn't, in the breast pocket of one of the last to perish. Of the cock and its crow, the meal and its participants, only lines remain—lines quoted in a notable history of the siege, lines in a roil of shadows on the National Gallery's East Wing walls.

Facts exist not only in many modes (heard by Ilya, seen by Anatole, smelled by Ivan, tasted, felt, by Sophia [who survived]) but described in various sorts of words, depicted in several kinds of lines (photo'd, painted, who knows?), and among these some will be acknowledged to have more reality than others. Why? In some cases because they are stages, say, of growth; because of the consequences that follow them; because of their lasting, repetitive powers; because of the contexts in which they may find themselves—cultivated, hated, prized; because our simply hearing the bird elevates the air he's made shudder to the status of a signal. The caterpillar crawls, chews, excretes, destroys, while the pupa simply clings stubbornly to a stick, sleeps inside itself, enduring winter winds and sleet, until at last, warmed into action, a butterfly is formed and released into the world as a wad of wet scales. Then, like Gregor's sister Grete, it opens out, unfolds its wings, takes its first flight, and on its way to a rose, before it can suck up its first syrup, before it can mate or pollinate, catches a collector's eye. Pinned, it is its own sarcophagus: in a kid's collection (the parsnip swallowtail, for instance) it is nothing remarkable; netted by Nabokov on a visit to Turkistan (the magnificent Blue Mormon wouldn't be hard to find) it is intriguing; exhibited in a museum in Jamaica (like the frequently collected Homerus swallowtail) it represents a seriously endangered species.

Ah . . . I hear the critic complain . . . these latter examples are but corpses, bitter ends, no longer what they were. Yet, the label says: GRAPHIUM WEISKEI, PURPLE SPOTTED SWALLOWTAIL, NEW GUINEA, LIFE CYCLE PRESENTLY UNKNOWN. After all, which, in this world, is more important: long-dead King Tut, his memories, his military might, his used-up days, or his swaddled mummy, his jugs and precious platters, a somewhat threadbare sofa in his present tomb?

Ah . . . another cry comes canoodling to my ear . . . important to whom? To mankind, of course, or to several hundred of them, Egyptologists all. To the rest King Tut is nothing but a spread of photographs in back issues of *Life*. Which is not to discount the image. The World Cup was not seen by the world. Only its screen self, only its hoopla, the smiles and signatures of its stars, were seen, and cheered, and spent upon. The game is mere occasion, a distant cause. Yet soon the great parade will pass; every happy glow caused by the rare and estimable victory will vanish, leaving French unemployment quite the same, the future every bit as glum.

I have, in a previous essay, used the activity of making a snowman as an example of several ontological transformations: first, of the snow, whose shape and place are altered to make the body of the sculpture; second, of the carrot and two chips of coal which are pressed into the smallest ball to serve as eyes and nose; third, of the broom, muffler, and stovepipe hat which make of the snowman a chimney sweep and complete the change.

When the snow is scooped up and packed, or a ball is formed by rolling a starter over the ground, the snow remains snow, as it will throughout these activities, though its context, form, and significance will change. At the end, we shall have made a snowman, not a man. The carrot and the coal have merely been removed from their place in kitchen or scuttle to be placed in the snowman's face; however, they are now eyes and nose—not coal eyes or carrot nose, but features of our creature. The broom the snowman appears to hold, the hat on his head, are broom and hat still, as the snow is snow while a body as well, though the hat signifies a sweep's garb and the broom one of his tools; that is, their ontological change is partial and symbolic; whereas the muffler, which the snowman wears around its neck, remains a muffler, busy about its business, unaware of any futility.

That is: the snow stays snow while the piled-up rolls shape an iconic sign for a man; the hat and broom become a sweep's, and bring the snowman along with them into that irony. Their suggestion is that the snowman will be doing a sweep's work and won't stay clean for long. Have you ever seen a snowman covered with coal dust? It will give the mind a happy turn. The coals and the carrot are eyes and nose and no longer coals or carrot at all, though we can recognize their former nature, and we must admit that, in addition, the coal continues the snowman's symbolic move into the sweep's role.

I don't see a snowman, though, do you? Here, he is only an example, so were I able to make one for you, the snowman that might stand in the wind outside, freezing his balls together, wouldn't be a snowman, ultimately, but an instance of the many transformations of being that take place during such an innocent and ordinary activity. Snow. Snowballs. Snowbody. Snowman. Snowsweep. Snowsign of commonplace changes of being. Snowart.

Snowart? Where we've been heading. Polyander Calder has sculpted a traditional chimneysweepsnowman, constructed a glass icebox for it, and stood the snowman inside the container, which will now stand in the Museum of Modern Art, perhaps in the lobby to greet you as you enter, and maybe only during the Christmas season, when it's taken from its basement storeroom and, after a ceremony, placed in its traditional spot, where it has signified the cheery commercial season to art-loving New Yorkers (and a few German tourists) for already a dozen years. Postcards and Styrofoam reproductions of the festive snowsweep, as well as tee shirts bearing its image and the inscription CLEAN UP CHRIST-MAS, are for sale in the museum's bookstore, where it is a perennially popular item. The museum board is contemplating putting an image of the Calder on one of the flags which flies over the museum's marquee to add to the holiday jollity.

If you were to take a most ordinary word—if you were to take "paint" from a householder's order: "I want you to paint the living room walls the peach you see on this paint chip"—or if you were to remove from a geology text a technical term, "anfractuous," for instance, and place it with the right sort of skill in the right sort of sentence, a sentence shaped like a stanza to give the reader the right signal, you could expect the same sea change to occur that the carrot suffered when thrust into that famous Calder-contrived snowpack—you know, the one in MOMA's lobby.

> Paint me a cavernous waste shore
> Cast in the unstilled Cyclades,
> Paint me the bold anfractuous rocks
> Faced by the snarled and yelping seas.
>
> (T. S. Eliot, "Sweeney Erect")

"Into" is the operative word: into a shower of gold, into a laurel tree, into a gleaming swan, into a bedbug or a shadow play. Into a book, an artificial head, a constructed awareness. If we were to compose a poem about the dew that had gathered at the tips of all those whitebud leaves, we should be in the business of transforming what our receptors already had: frequencies of light into actions of the rods and cones of the eye, into stimulations of the sensory nerves, into an excitation of cells in an appropriate section of the brain, into, presumably, perception itself, now in the realm of the publicly Invisible, followed by fragments of thoughts in fragmented phrases, and finally into considered words, but words, in this case, artistically altered from their common employment in daily life and put, as composition proceeds, into a different world—that of poetry—where their focus is on one another; where conveying commands, expressing attitudes, uttering truths, cursing fate, comforting the proletariat, are only gestures, forms, and reenactments; where words can be lords and masters, not the servants of what they relate; where not the object but the quality of consciousness counts.

The poem is such a thing. It is the Invisible made audible, hung out in public once again like washed wash, where it can be worn by everyone, as if it had always belonged to them; consequently, it represents a penultimate kind of transformation, because all that has been lost through the progressive rarefication and mechanization of the mind over centuries of time, as well as all that has been gained in complexity, depth, and range as a result of the same astonishing developments, must be rescued, explored if not exploited, recombined, and freshly realized through the materiality of verbal music and the memorial strategies of the oral tradition, along with the particularities of print, where the word is visualized, where it burns brighter than the burning bush (or Southwell's "Burning Babe"), a bushword far more enduring than its flame, because when the bush has been burnt out of being, when the Lord's voice has disappeared like a pebble pitched over a cliff, when the dew has dried and the leaf loosened, its symbolism will survive, the line will abide, will find its page, live on in a book, so that some idle afternoon a reading eye may chance upon it—see/hear/respond—

> Sweet day, so cool, so calm, so bright,
> The bridal of the earth and sky:
> The dew shall weep thy fall tonight;
>   For thou must die.
>
> Sweet rose, whose hue angry and brave
> Bids the rash gazer wipe his eye;
> Thy root is ever in its grave,
>   And thou must die.
>
> Sweet spring, full of sweet days and roses,
> A box where sweets compacted lie;

Transformations

My music shows ye have your closes,
          And all must die.

Only a sweet and virtuous soul,
Like seasoned timber, never gives;
But though the whole world turn to coal,
          Then chiefly lives.

                    (George Herbert, "Virtue")

whereupon the ultimate transformation takes place, in another Invisibility—in another awareness—in a soul—if not now more virtuous, at least made, for a moment, finer than it was.

A NOTE ON THE TYPE

This book was set in Fairfield, the first typeface from the hand of the distinguished American artist and engraver Rudolph Ruzicka (1883–1978). In its structure Fairfield displays the sober and sane qualities of the master craftsman whose talent has long been dedicated to clarity. It is the trait that accounts for the trim grace and virility, the spirited design and sensitive balance, of this original typeface.

Rudolph Ruzicka was born in Bohemia and came to American in 1894. He set up his own shop, devoted to wood engraving and printing, in New York in 1913 after a varied career working as a wood engraver, in photoengraving and bank-note printing plants, and as an art director and freelance artist. He designed and illustrated many books, and was the creator of a considerable list of individual prints—wood engravings, line engravings on copper, and aquatints.

Composed by Digital Composition, Berryville, Virginia
Printed and bound by Berryville Graphics,
Berryville, Virginia
Designed by Peter A. Andersen